Art Therapy with Young Survivors of Sexual Abuse

D1500711

Dealing with the aftermath of childhood sexual abuse remains one of the major issues in child and adolescent mental health. Yet, until now, little has been written for art therapists and related professionals involved in this sensitive field.

Art Therapy with Young Survivors of Sexual Abuse is a guide to practice with this group. Containing a range of illustrative case material from both individual and group therapy, the book addresses the important issues faced by professionals, including:

Male therapist countertransferance

The therapist's relationship with the client's family and wider networks

Assessment using art therapy

Art materials and sensory experience

The value of art therapy in groups

Art Therapy with Young Survivors of Sexual Abuse will provide not only art therapists, but other professionals working with sexually abused children and adolescents, with a stimulating discussion of the current issues in this area.

Jenny Murphy is a senior art therapist in a child and family consultation service where she has been involved in developing a programme of group work for sexually abused children.

Art Therapy with Young Survivors of Sexual Abuse

Lost for Words

Edited by
Jenny Murphy

Routledge
Taylor & Francis Group

LONDON AND NEW YORK

First published 2001
by Routledge
27 Church Road, Hove, East Sussex, BN3 2FA

Simultaneously published in the USA and Canada
by Taylor & Francis Inc
270 Madison Avenue, New York NY 10016

Transferred to Digital Printing 2011

Routledge is an imprint of the Taylor & Francis Group, an informa business

Typeset in Times by
M Rules

British Library Cataloguing in Publication Data
A catalogue record for this book is available from the British
Library

Library of Congress Cataloguing in Publication Data
  Art therapy with young survivors of sexual abuse:
  lost for words/edited by Jenny Murphy.
    p. cm.
  Includes bibliographical references and index.
  1. Sexually abused children – Mental health.
  2. Sexually abused children – Rehabilitation.
  3. Art therapy for children. 4. Child psychotherapy.
  I. Title: Lost for words. II. Murphy, Jenny.
  RJ507.S49 A78 2000
  618.92'85836–dc21   00-042498

ISBN 13: 978-0-415-20571-9 (pbk)
ISBN 13: 978-0-415-20570-2 (hbk)

Publisher's Note
The publisher has gone to great lengths to ensure the quality of this reprint
but points out that some imperfections in the original may be apparent.

This book is dedicated to the many children with whom I have been privileged to work, and to my colleagues; also to my family: to my husband David, for keeping the onion patch weeded while this book was cooking, to my mother Belle for her encouragement, to my beautiful daughters Carla and Kate, and to the memory of my father John.

Contents

Illustrations

FIGURES

Contributors

Felicity Aldridge has a degree in textiles and fashion and trained as an art therapist at Goldsmiths College, London University, where she also undertook her advanced diploma and MA in art therapy. She trained as a post adoption counsellor with the Post Adoption Centre in London. Having worked for many years as an art therapist with children for Social Services and the National Health Service, she now specialises in working with attachment and loss.

Maggie Ambridge is an art therapist who has experience of working with children and with adult survivors of childhood sexual abuse over a period of some 15 years. She has previously worked for both Social Services and the NSPCC, and practises currently within a specialist child protection project as part of an NHS Trust Child and Adolescent Mental Health team.

Jo Bissonnet MA, BA(Hons), Dip SW, ATC, RATH graduated in Fine Art before training as an art therapist at Goldsmiths College. At present she works as an art therapist for children with chronic illness, within the health authority at a child and family centre run by social services, and in private practice. Her recent writings include a contribution to *Development and diversity* edited by Doug Sandle, 1998, for The Free Associated Press.

Ani M. Brown MA [Art Psychotherapy] is a state registered art therapist working in an NHS Adolescent Mental Health Clinic in the south-west of England. She is involved in individual and group assessment and treatment of young people with a range of emotional and psychological difficulties. Her research and clinical interests include sexual abuse victims and perpetrators, psychotic and borderline states, eating disorders, and depression and self-harm. As a member of the British Association of Art Therapists her areas of professional interest include clinical effectiveness and the training of art therapists.

Richard Buckland. After 10 years in varied careers including the merchant navy, and a physics degree, Richard Buckland trained in child psychotherapy at the Tavistock Clinic. On qualifying, he became part of a developing child and adolescent mental health service team. He has a particular interest in working closely with foster parents and fostered children, and in individual work with severely disturbed children. Over the last 10 years he has been involved in developing group work for sexually abused boys and girls and their parents – work currently being extended to include perpetrating young people.

Lyn Douglass began studying fine art at Hornsey College of Art at 16, moving on to Ruskin College, Oxford. Economics forced aside aspirations of becoming a painter, and she began work within the NHS and the community as an unqualified art therapist. Work with schizophrenia and autism led her to seek further qualifications and in the 1980s she graduated with a psychology degree and as an art therapist. After several years in Social Services she joined the voluntary sector and is currently working with abused children and adults.

Karen Lee. Drucker grew up in New York City where she completed a BA in sociology and psychology, followed later by a Masters in Art Therapy and Creativity Development. She came to Britain in 1978 and for the past 20 years has worked as an art therapist in a variety of settings. Currently she works in a department of child and family psychiatry, freelance with children with cancer and life-threatening illness, and privately with adults and children. She has been involved in the establishment of a Diploma in Art Therapy course.

Ann Gillespie originally trained at the Royal College of Art and worked as a designer for many years. She qualified as an art therapist in 1979, and gained an Advanced Diploma and MA in Art Therapy in 1990, all at Hertfordshire College of Art and Design. She has worked with both adults and children, including 10 years as art therapist at the Catholic Children's Society's *Family Makers* project in Gravesend, Kent. She has lectured on her work there and written several articles for *Adoption & Fostering*. She is now concentrating on her own creative work, combining visual art with movement, voice and performance.

Simon Hastilow has a degree in fine art and trained as an art therapist at Hertfordshire College of Art and Design, St Albans, going on to get the diploma in advanced training in art psychotherapy at Goldsmiths College, London University. He works predominantly with adults with mental illness and with personality disorders in an NHS Secure Unit. He also runs groups for young offenders in a prison.

Marianne Latimir MA [Clin Psych] is a clinical psychologist working in an NHS Adolescent Mental Health Unit in the south-west of England, involved in the assessment and treatment of young people with a range of emotional and behavioural difficulties. She is a graduate member of the

British Psychological Society. Her research and clinical interests include sexual abuse victims and perpetrators, adolescent depression and self-harm, and burns and plastic surgery with children and adolescents.

Jenny Murphy, Dip AD, Dip ATh, Dip Adv ATh, MA, SRATh, trained in art therapy in the early 1970s and at first worked in adult psychiatry. For the past 15 years, she has been part of the multi-disciplinary team in a child and family consultation service, where she has been particularly involved in providing a programme of group work that includes groups for sexually abused children. MA studies led her to research the contribution that British art therapists are making to the recovery of sexually abused children and young people. A shortened version of this research was published in 1998 in *Inscape*.

Becky Smith is a clinical psychologist with nine years' experience in child and adolescent mental health services. She has a particular interest in work with children who have experienced sexual abuse, and in facilitating carers who support such children. Becky also works with attachment issues and these interests often converge when working in the field of fostering and adoption. Becky Smith also practises family therapy with a 'reflecting supervision team' within a clinic.

Louis Thomas is a trainee child psychotherapist employed by United Bristol Healthcare NHS Trust. He is also a qualified art therapist having worked with children and families for many years. He is a co-author of *Development and Diversity: New Applications in Art Therapy*.

Mark Wheeler is an art therapist working for eight years in NHS child and family therapy after a similar number of years working with adolescents in a therapeutic community. He is particularly interested in the use of photographs in art therapy and family therapy. Mark Wheeler was knocked off his motorcycle and seriously head-injured while writing this chapter, which is now partly compiled from material that was already in preparation. Mark hopes to be able to return to work in the future.

Foreword

This book is much needed. It makes a contribution to the literature in a field of art therapy in which much excellent, innovative work is being done. It is, of course, very sad that this work has to be done at all, as it means that children continue to be maltreated, that families continue to be destroyed, and that societies are shamed: in our affluent, market-led culture, children are perceived as objects to be used, abused and often disregarded. Their rights to a secure base from which they can develop as creative and humanistic adults have been entirely ignored. Instead they learn not to trust, are traumatised and live in fear.

As the art therapists who have presented their work here have shown, art therapy can give a chance for an abused child to share overwhelming anxiety, rage, shame and terror that may have been carried for many years, usually in secret. The authors point out that engaging in art therapy may give an opportunity to open a window onto the child's world and their experience of internal damage, and enable them to form a relationship with someone who will be able to cope with their communication, however painful and messy, without retaliation. It is worth stressing that it is very hard for an abused child to trust, when in the past trust has been betrayed. The work often proceeds slowly, the art therapist may receive a torrent of anger, the art materials may be attacked and the room and its objects threatened with damage. Or the child may withdraw into a passive, non-cooperative state, leaving the therapist feeling helpless and useless, unable to see a way forward.

The material of the sessions is deeply distressing and can produce profound discomfort in the therapist. Supervision is essential. As someone who has supervised art therapists working in this field, I can vouch for the powerful, upsetting feelings that arise in both the therapist and myself when contemplating the tragic network in which abusive relationships are trapped.

My reaction to reading these moving stories is to applaud the art therapists and their colleagues for being able to tolerate 'being there' for their young clients, and in providing a place where words are not necessary and where a child can take its time to begin the process of healing. The book began its existence as a result of Jenny Murphy's research in 1998 and I feel certain that as well as providing a valuable source for others working with abused children, it will provide a sound base for further research. I wish the book every success and thank the authors for the chance to write this foreword.

Dr Diane Waller
Reader in Art Therapy, Goldsmiths College, London
Visiting Professor, Queen's University Belfast

Introduction

Jenny Murphy

A 6-year-old girl draws and paints a story in a sequence of 14 pictures:

> *A little girl pig is attacked by a man who whacks her with a big stick and hits her in the face with a stone, although she had done nothing wrong to him. So the police come and take the man away in their car, under a blanket, and the little pig is taken to hospital by ambulance, 'real bad hurt'. It's a very long way. In hospital, she is put onto a stretcher, also under a blanket, and taken for an x-ray. She's 'real worried' about it and her mother doesn't know she's been hurt. In the x-ray picture, sticks and big lumps of stone can be seen inside the pig, where the man has wounded her. The little pig is so ill, she looks sick and her face is still damaged, she might die . . . is she going to get better? She's a little bit better . . . just a bad eye . . . now she's really better, wearing a pretty dress, decorated with a red heart. The End.*

Not all children who have experienced sexual abuse can tell such symbolic or complete stories; in fact as this book will confirm repeatedly, what many choose to do with art materials is to make a tremendous mess. This story contains many important themes for the abused child: the experience of physical damage, the sense of injustice, feelings of isolation, the absence of the mother, the fear of dying, the longing to feel whole and healthy again. A feature of the story is the implication that the piglet's recovery from the assault begins when the x-ray is taken, the child showing symbolically how important it is for a window to be opened onto her internal world and specifically to her experience of internal damage. Once this damage has been acknowledged, further steps on the road towards recovery, though shaky and uncertain as in this story, become possible to visualise and to achieve. It is my conviction that art therapy and the art therapist are particularly well placed to offer sexually abused children and young people the opportunity to look at and contemplate the views through such inner windows.

SEXUAL ABUSE IN CHILDHOOD AND ITS EFFECTS

What is meant by child sexual abuse? Whether an isolated incident or continuing for months or years, sexual abuse can encompass a continuum of sexual behaviours from exposure of the genitals through to invasive physical contact such as penetration of the anus or vagina (Kilgore 1988: 225). Sexual abuse

> . . .usually involves an adult, almost always someone known or related to the child, using his or her authority to coerce the child into sexual activity. The offender will generally continue to attempt molestation as long as he or she has access to the child, the child does not talk, or the offender does not get caught. Abuse may be an ongoing situation involving one child or it might be a group situation involving many children.
>
> (Malchiodi 1990: 135)

The perpetrator of sexual abuse uses their position of trust to manipulate the child into sexual behaviours, often by a process of 'grooming' which may involve the giving of gifts and rewards. The secrecy of the relationship may be maintained by bribes or by threats to harm the child or those whom the child loves most. This results in such fearfulness that it often becomes an insurmountable problem for the young person to disclose the abuse at all. In addition, very young children are not in a position to question the validity of what is happening to them, nor do they have the vocabulary to describe it, and when abuse starts at a very early age, the child's normal development can be profoundly affected. There is evidence that when sexual abuse is violent, prolonged, intrusive, when the perpetrator is a primary caretaker and with onset in early childhood, it is most likely to produce a long-lasting traumatic syndrome which will require psychiatric help at some time (Herman et al. 1986).

Initial effects of sexual abuse may result in children suffering from any or several of the following: anxiety, depression, a poor self-image, isolation, outbursts of anger and hostility, an awareness of sexuality inappropriate to their chronological age and anxious or overfamiliar behaviour with others. Longer-term effects seen in adult survivors are '. . . depression, self-destructive behaviour, anxiety, feelings of isolation and stigma, poor self-esteem, a tendency to revictimization, and substance abuse' (Browne and Finkelhor 1986: 72). Memories of the abuse are stored in the body, which may come to feel contaminated, spoilt, anaesthetised or repulsive, and it is not surprising that survivors may become involved in self-harming behaviours or develop recurring somatic symptoms or life-threatening disorders such as anorexia or bulimia (Bannister 1989). Successful intimate relationships may be difficult to establish, sometimes resulting in involvement in prostitution or in promiscuous behaviour; survivors of abuse may seek out relationships that re-enact the abuse, either becoming perpetrators or continuing as victims. Chapter 10 describes the possible impact on adolescent sexuality.

Sexual abuse can result in a cluster of psychological symptoms typical of post-traumatic stress (Finkelhor 1979, Russell 1986, Johnson 1987, Kilgore 1988, Young 1992) and non-verbal signs of this in younger children are described in Chapter 6. Dissociation, a disowning of the body's experiences, may start initially during the traumatic event, but become a continuing mechanism for survival at the cost of experiencing pleasurable sensuous and proprioceptive experiences. (Young 1992) The splitting-off of any parts of the self connected with the trauma reduces the victim's ability to attach words to feelings, to symbolise or fantasise (Johnson 1987).

By offering help to children near to the time of abuse, it is hoped that the long-term effects can be avoided. It is important that such help is age-appropriate and takes into account the difficulties encountered by youngsters in verbalising their sexual experience either through lack of vocabulary or fear of the consequences of talking. Such difficulties have led to the growth of research by art therapists and other clinicians in USA who attempt to identify 'graphic indicators' of sexual abuse in children's drawings (Cohen and Phelps 1985, Kelley 1985, Sidun and Rosenthal 1987, Hibbard and Hartman 1990, Riordan and Verdel 1991). By discovering a set of signs universally used by sexually abused children in their art-making, researchers have hoped to identify the child who has yet to disclose abuse verbally, and even to provide evidence that might prove effective in the courtroom. It has not been possible to establish a set of signs to give a definitive diagnosis of sexual abuse; nevertheless, some graphic features were found to have clinical significance and to necessitate the clinician, or the teacher (Briggs and Lehmann 1989, Riordan and Verdel 1991), being alert to the possibility of sexual abuse.

ART THERAPY LITERATURE REVIEW

Studies of art *products* are quite different from those that explore the value of the creative *process* within a psychotherapeutic framework (Stember 1978, Peake 1987, Malchiodi 1990, Sagar 1990, Thomas 1998). Both Stember (1980) who brought art materials to children and families in their own homes in her 'artmobile' and Malchiodi (1990) who worked in a battered women's shelter doing brief art therapy assessments, stress the need to develop a therapeutic alliance that has clear boundaries so that trust can develop and the child can experience a close relationship with an adult which is not sexual (Malchiodi 1990: 138). Art therapy can be seen to offer a transitional space which is experienced as safer and less intense than a verbal therapy relationship, and transference onto the materials as well as the therapist can take place (Johnson 1987, Sagar 1990). Within such a relationship, the art materials or images provide a means of expressing, holding and recognising the feelings resulting from traumatic experience and so the beginning of separating from it. Involvement in the creative process itself has the potential to rebuild damaged self-esteem, strengthen the ego and to make good any developmental delay (Naitove 1982) and a sense of achievement can be experienced in a non-sexual area (Carozza and Heirsteiner 1982: 167).

The tactile qualities of art materials relate directly to sensations and emotions that may otherwise be denied and can make art therapy particularly helpful to sexually abused children for whom dissociation is a coping strategy: such materials as clay and finger-paint allow for a re-awakening of physical sensations in an acceptable form (Carozza and Heirsteiner 1982, Sagar 1990). In the UK, Sagar (1990) provides vivid descriptions of messy mixtures which may be spread on a surface, put into containers or made into packages passed to the therapist for safe keeping, seeing such mixtures as also representing the child's 'internal chaotic feelings where "good" and "bad" are indistinguishable' (Sagar 1990: 92). A tangible search for boundaries and for differentiated feelings can be identified in this play with mixing, spilling, pouring and containing materials. It has also been observed that children in the general hospital managing feelings about invasive surgery and concerned with the passing of liquids into and out of their bodies seem to reflect concepts of *inside* and *outside* in the images they make. This is facilitated at least in part by the 'physicality, fluidity and plasticity' of art materials (Cody 1987: 43). Boundary issues also arise in working within the framework of the edge of the paper (Levens 1995: 67). As well as the sensuous use of art materials, Sagar sees their potential to be used in rituals of the youngster's own devising, often relating to repair, cleansing and purification (Sagar 1990: 110). Such rituals may produce an art object or image holding projected feelings, which can become a 'scapegoat' to be disposed of or preserved in a meaningful way by the young person (Schaverien 1987, Sagar 1990).

Anger felt by the survivor of abuse towards both the perpetrator and the non-protecting parent can be expressed physically with art materials, but in safety (Malchiodi 1990: 138). Recognising and dealing with anger, the desire to punish and for revenge are important parts of recovery, before they either become re-enacted in a continuing cycle of abuse towards others (Levinson 1986, Naitove 1988, Sagar 1990) or threaten the individual's long-term health as they are turned against the self. The potential for the safe disposal of anger and of abusive feelings aroused in the survivor can be seen as one of the distinctive aspects of the art therapy process. However, when the young survivor of abuse has not yet developed, or has lost, the capacity to use materials symbolically, Thomas (1998) has observed how the terrifying trauma may be re-presented to the art therapist, who must expect to bear witness to painful experience as the child becomes both abused and abuser. The re-presentation of the trauma in its raw emotional state can be a precursor to its symbolic representation and over time, the act of image-making facilitates the process of

. . . the differentiation of the self from the internalised bad objects/people and their ways. The image is an object that comes from the self, yet gradually becomes separate. The child can take from it what she needs, and with the help of a thinking other, leave the rest behind.

(Thomas 1998: 38)

As we have seen, children's response to art materials can often be closer to play than to purposeful image-making; play may often be preferred by children when they need to relive a profound experience in order to gain control over its influence (Case 1987: 61). Unlike adults, children have a less developed capacity to use words for inner thinking, so '. . . to a large extent the child is compelled to play in order to think things out' (Dalley 1987: 21). Art and play have in common the spontaneous externalisation of images that enable children to face anxiety-provoking situations metaphorically. In art therapy, youngsters may move seamlessly from one medium to the other and clear examples of this will be found in Chapters 6 and 8.

It is important to acknowledge the contribution of dedicated group work for survivors of abuse. It is often described as the treatment of choice in this field (Knittle and Tuana 1980, Steward et al. 1986, Howard 1993, Kerslake 1995) for three main reasons: first, the sense of isolation and stigma can be addressed in a peer group who have shared similar experiences. Second, group therapy avoids the emotional intensity and balance of power of the individual relationship which may be felt to replicate the abusive relationship (deYoung and Corbin 1994: 143). Group therapy can also be intimate, but at different times for different children as they become willing to be the focus of the group's attention. For adolescents, distrust of adults and authority figures can also contra-indicate individual therapy, whereas interaction with a peer group is acceptable (Knittle and Tuana 1980). Third, many children who have been sexually abused come from dysfunctional and abusive families. For these children, the interaction with other youngsters in the company of two thoughtful and nurturing co-therapists creates an experience of the group as a surrogate, healthy family (Steward et al. 1986, deYoung and Corbin 1994). Some art therapy groups appear to be highly structured and task-oriented (Powell and Faherty 1990) towards verbalisation of feelings and experiences. However, Carozza and Heirsteiner (1982) suggest that because sexual exploitation is a private experience, verbalisation is not necessary, although involvement in the art project is. In their groups, art images are expected to be the primary vehicle for the sharing of experience (Carozza and Heirsteiner 1982: 169). Parallel group therapy may be offered to mothers or carers of sexually abused children (Hildebrand and Forbes 1987, Dover et al. 1997) and such an art therapy group is described by Hagood (1991).

While a good deal of attention has been given to the effects of sexual abuse in childhood, appropriate ways of helping children and adolescents to recover have been slower to evolve. For me, reading Hagood's (1992) article

raised many questions about what therapeutic approaches British art therapists might be developing to facilitate the recovery of this client group, and
led to my own research in this area (Murphy 1998). I was aware that many
mental health practitioners consider that drawing might provide a non-
threatening medium which could lead a child gently towards a verbalisation
of his or her experience, and this would be their main therapeutic goal. I was
also aware of the body of literature that reflects a fascination with detecting
children's abuse in their imagery (see earlier) and that some attention has
been given to the use of play in helping children to express their experiences
(Doyle 1987, McMahon 1992, Bray 1991) However, my own clinical experience suggested that art materials in themselves seemed to provide youngsters
with the opportunities for processing abuse. Liquids seemed important:
paints, water, drinks, glues. It was not uncommon to see an attractive painting suddenly swamped with the whole contents of the upturned palette,
transformed into a dark mess and, uncontained by the boundary of the
paper, drip off the table's edge; or to see a child making a package with
layers and layers of paper, sellotape, string and glue, or mixing a potion of
clay, paint, sand, tea-bags, milk, glue and sawdust in a bowl to be kept. Was
it the qualities of the materials themselves that other art therapists found
central to their work with sexually abused young people, or did they usually
see image making as a non-threatening precursor to talking about the abuse
experience, or indeed were there other features of art therapy regarded as
more important? These questions initiated my research and linked me with
many art therapists working in this field, some of whom have been willing to
expand on the themes emerging from the research as being particularly significant. It is out of their experience and enthusiasm that this book has
been born.

RESEARCH THEMES

Before introducing the chapters, I would like to indicate briefly some of the
ideas that emerged as significant in my initial research and therefore began to
shape the book. The theme that therapists returned to again and again was
that of the significance of therapeutic boundaries, not only those of space,
time, calendar, agenda, confidentiality and trust, but also managing destructive, or seductive, behaviours and the youngster's frequent wish to maintain
control over the therapist. Therapists expected boundaries to be vigorously
tested and for young people to demonstrate uncertainty about the safety of
the therapy environment. Most art therapists believed that it was the establishment of the therapeutic alliance above all that made the most significant
contribution to recovery from the experience of sexual abuse. The negotiation
of boundaries was seen as an important aspect of this, as was the recognition
of transference and countertransference issues and the non-judgemental atti-

tude of the therapist. Remembering that survivors of sexual abuse have experienced the invasion of so many boundaries – physical, emotional and social – almost always violated by someone who had been entrusted with keeping them safe, the building of an alliance with the therapist can be anticipated as being fraught with difficulties.

The art processes that were explored in the context of the relationship were also seen as significant and confirmed my own clinical experiences: art materials were seen to facilitate further exploration of boundaries in a tangible, physical way, partly through pouring, spilling and mixing liquids or other materials, which might have been contained and kept, or might have messed and flooded the therapy room. The child's desire to clean up, or to abandon the mess, might also have been an issue. Youngsters had a sensuous awareness of materials and might use them in unusual ways and combinations and even use the environment of the room itself as material.

Indications were that the inevitable feeling of anger about being sexually abused and the subsequent abusive feelings aroused in the youngster could be recognised and directed safely through art materials. Certainly they often provided an opportunity for symbolic punishment and disposal rituals. Some art therapists expressed the view that if abusive feelings could be recognised and directed safely through art materials, it would be less likely that either a cycle of abuse would be perpetuated, or that a pattern of self-harming behaviours would become established; longer-term studies will be needed to ascertain this.

Images could also carry ambivalence and conflict which needed to find a means of expression when the perpetrator of the abuse was a person whom the child also loved and was sometimes the only person who had ever shown affection to him or her. The creative process itself was acknowledged as empowering and allowing the young person to experience control; it was also seen as promoting the development of self-esteem through meeting the challenges and risks of creativity.

Finally, in connection with art images and disclosure, British art therapists demonstrated their reluctance to use images made in a therapeutic context as evidence in court, partly because of the ambiguity of images, but also in the belief that the therapeutic relationship would be damaged and that both child and therapist were likely to be left feeling discredited.

Three further themes emerged from the research: first the importance of the social context of the therapeutic relationship and of establishing and maintaining links with those around the child: i.e. their parents or carers, who themselves might also be offered art therapy or concurrent family therapy. Second, maintaining good communication with those other professionals involved within the immediate team or the wider network. Third, art therapists repeatedly and emphatically commented on the importance of support from their working colleagues and appropriate supervision in order to manage the stressful nature of the work.

This book brings together the writings of experienced art therapy practitioners who have been working with sexually abused children and young people for some years and who want to convey the particular qualities of this work, not necessarily their successes, but some of the struggles through which learning for both the client and therapist takes place. Because the writing has grown out of practical experience, there is a great deal of illustrative case material which plays a vivid and central role; there is also a variety of writing styles. The book is divided into three parts: the first explores how the therapeutic relationship relates to the context of the family, the team and to outside agencies; the second part features aspects of individual case work, with reference to play as well as to image making; and the third part describes three experiences of working with groups of children and adolescents.

PART I. THE THERAPEUTIC RELATIONSHIP IN CONTEXT

This section of the book explores some of the issues that arise for art therapists who, as emerged in my research, emphasised the importance of relating not only to the child in therapy but also to the family and wider professional networks. Mark Wheeler's diagram on page 40 shows one way of describing the interrelation of these systems, with the child's image at the centre. Understanding and communicating to others what the child is expressing in therapy is often a significant part of the work and the way that profession-appropriate supervision is essential to this process is also discussed in this section.

These issues are explored in the first chapter by Louis Thomas in his case study 'Containing the bad object', seen in the context of his immediate team and the national organisation of which it was a part. He describes with frankness how anxieties at all levels of the organisation threatened to affect the course of the therapy in an unhelpful way because of the team's relative incapacity to reflect on the work. The therapist is the subject of the child's fantasies and powerfully affected by countertransference feelings; in this particular case, the seductiveness of the child and her pushing of therapeutic boundaries created anxieties that his immediate team found hard to manage and this was in danger of undermining the therapy. Thomas believes that the ability to think and speak about all aspects of sexual material must be nurtured within a team designated to work with sexually abused youngsters and he emphasises the need for this to be complemented by profession-appropriate supervision. His candid case study demonstrates the demanding nature of the work.

By contrast Mark Wheeler and Becky Smith, in 'Male therapist countertransference and the importance of the family context', describe how parallel therapy with a 9-year-old girl and with her adoptive parents was well held within a reflecting team over a period of 14 months. We are invited to consider the difficulties inherent in the individual therapy relationship when the therapist is male, as was the perpetrator. Despite the potential difficulties, these authors suggest that a relationship with a non-abusing male may be therapeutic in itself for the child, but the therapist must also be aware of the countertransference feelings to which he is subject: guilt at being male like the abuser, fear of possible further disclosures, or feelings of revulsion or anger towards the perpetrator and how these could have a negative effect on the therapy. How to be appropriately masculine becomes an issue for the non-abusing males around the child whose perpetrator was also male. Supervision is an integral part of the therapeutic work, allowing for the recognition of themes common to the parallel therapeutic relationships and for the identification of the countertransference feelings of both therapists.

For the most part, this book is concerned with the provision of appropriate therapeutic interventions for children who are known to have been abused, but art therapists are sometimes required to help establish whether abuse has taken place or not, and the third chapter represents this area of work. Lyn Douglass works for an agency part of whose function is to provide assessments for Social Services and in 'Nobody hears', she presents two very different cases: a brief intervention with three brothers in care who had been showing behavioural problems and a risk assessment of a 3-year-old girl. The urgency of the first case demanded a different response from that of working over a longer period with a very young child and Douglass contrasts a systemic and a psychodynamic approach. Because the assessments have been requested by other professionals, the art therapist necessarily has to feed back to them following the assessment and they may, or may not, be felt to respond adequately or appropriately, even when, as in these two case studies, the assessments led to grave concerns for the safety of the children. One of the difficulties Douglass identifies, when the system sees only verbal disclosures as valid, is how to convey the non-verbal communications, especially of very young children, with equal authority.

PART II. WORKING WITH INDIVIDUALS

The first account in this section explores the theme of supporting therapy for the child by working with her carer. As in chapter 2 we are invited to consider the significance of parallel working, this time in the way in which a mother is offered help alongside her sexually abused daughter. In 'Using the reflective image within the mother–child relationship', Maggie Ambridge reminds us that a substantial proportion of mothers of young clients reveal that they too were sexually abused as children. The extent to which they have been able to face up to and work through their own abuse affects their ability to hear what their child is saying, so work with the mother may need to take place before the child is able to benefit from therapy or to begin to communicate with his or her mother. Ambridge's study is informed by elements of attachment theory and an understanding of the dissociative states that are adopted as a defence against the abuse. When these states persist into adulthood, the mother's sensitivity to what may be going on is reduced, causing her to miss the very thing she believes she is being vigilant about. Ambridge presents a series of vignettes in which children's images communicate to mothers the reality of hidden experience which can then become visible, no longer secret and unspeakable, and can move their relationship forward. The capacity of images to hold significant emotional material relating to both mother and daughter is evident. In also describing the artwork of adolescents and of an adult survivor of childhood abuse, Ambridge conveys the complex generational issues involved.

One of the features often commented on in research was the potential that art materials held for the re-awakening of youngsters' sensory experiences blunted by disassociation in order to cope with intolerable situations and relationships. In 'Into the body', Ann Gillespie focuses on how the sensuous qualities of sand and water provide both a tactile experience and a way for those children who anticipate inevitable failure when trying to make an intact image to be involved in a non-product, non-achieving activity. She sees this activity as providing a multitude of skin sensations which can lead to experimentation with memories stored in the body and many issues too complex for the deprived and abused child to understand at a conscious level. Along with the child's increasing awareness of his or her own body, joint exploratory play with the sand as an intermediary permits the child to make a safe relationship with the other body of the therapist/mother. Gillespie illustrates her ideas by describing work with a girl who had suffered early deprivation and was verbally limited, and a boy who at first attempted to make intimate physical contact with the therapist, but became able to use the sand to explore his needs symbolically.

In 'Why can't she control herself?' Karen Drucker presents an illustrated case study of a 10-year-old girl who was coping with separation from her birth family and being in foster care as well as with her history of incest. Her client Ann, who was presenting with very difficult behaviour both at home and school, used art materials to express images of inner feeling states interspersed with dramatic images created through role play with the therapist. In the role playing, a multitude of characters represented different facets of Ann and explored issues of trust, closeness and distance, victimisation and control. Eventually Ann was able to be more openly thoughtful about her feelings and to begin to take responsibility for her behaviour. Ambivalent feelings towards her mother who could not protect her, yet whom she loved, were often present in the therapy; outside therapy, she was strong enough to face her father and demand an apology from him. When a child such as Ann has been abused during her earliest, preverbal years, it interferes with the normal developmental processes and an offer of a long-term therapy relationship may be necessary to repair this early damage.

When working with abused youngsters, a recognition of what is possible and appropriate at different stages of a child's development is considered by Jo Bissonnet in 'Tell me your story so far'. Her work is informed by Erickson's model of psychosocial development, which is fundamentally optimistic concerning the resolution of conflicts if not as they arise, then at later stages in the individual's life. In her case description, we are introduced to Hannah, a 7-year-old who was aware that her own mother had also been sexually abused as a child. Hannah had many unspoken questions about whether her mother knew she was being abused, or might have colluded in it or whether the badness of abuse is passed on from mother to daughter. At her stage of development she was unable to formulate such philosophical questions verbally, but could pose them through art and play activities. Both her fragility and her resourcefulness were evident in these. Hannah liked to paint on the therapist's skin at times and Bissonnet points out that if the boundaries are clearly negotiated, this can provide a child with a model of a healthy intimate contact with an adult. Adolescence will inevitably bring issues both of sexuality and of separation from mother to the fore again and further therapeutic help may be appropriate at that next stage of development.

PART III. EXPERIENCES WITH GROUPS

Group work is often recommended as the most appropriate therapeutic intervention for survivors of sexual abuse and offers the opportunity to share experiences with those who can most understand. What happens when art materials and a therapeutic couple are added to the mixture is explored in the three contributions to this section. All the groups described allowed issues to emerge gradually from the group process, permitting the group members an experience of control; the longer the group, the more possible this was. This contrasts with much of the literature which describes brief, focused groups that work through a series of theme-based sessions (e.g. Powell and Faherty 1990).

A therapeutic group for young girls aged 6 to 9 is discussed by colleagues who approach it from their professional backgrounds as child psychotherapist and art therapist. In 'Jumping over it', Richard Buckland and Jenny Murphy describe how the girls move in and out of art and play activities, and in the process explore family relationships, express anger towards the perpetrators of their abuse and find ways to symbolically cleanse themselves of their sense of being filled up with bad stuff by the abuse experience. In particular, the girls play stories of rebirth over and over again, sometimes starting in the womb, eventually recognising their shared wish that they could go back and relive their lives without the abuse having taken place. The therapists find that in groups where creative processes form the core, children are jointly able to demonstrate great resourcefulness in the service of their own and each other's recovery. Children still unable to verbalise their difficulties benefit from those who are already more able to do this and, because many of them are likely to come from fragmented or chaotic family backgrounds, they also benefit from their experience of being with two thoughtful parental adults, who can stay with and reflect on the children's feelings of disempowerment, anger and confusion.

Work with a fragmented family of four boys living in separate foster homes is the focus for the next group experience. In this case, the children are blood relations and have a shared history of which the therapists are not a part, although they are inevitably caught up in the children's transference to their natural parents and consistently subjected to testing behaviours. In 'Is it safe to keep a secret?', Felicity Aldridge and Simon Hastilow suggest that a male and female therapeutic couple would make it possible for the children to fully explore parental and sibling issues, and they provided an environment where this was possible through the use of copious amounts of clay and water along with other art materials and games. Often involvement with the art activities brought up issues that were then explored through playing, dramas, acting out or fighting. Some of the important issues that concerned the boys were: the safety of the environment and the capacity of the therapists to keep them safe; secrecy and information sharing; rivalry and the negotiation of hierarchies; breaks in therapy and the fear of abandonment. The description of the setting up of this group highlights the great investment in time and energy of the large number of professionals needed to support the work; where sexual abuse is concerned, group therapy is offered not because it is a more economical option, but because it is the most appropriate and effective intervention. Therapists have to be prepared for the intensity of such groups and when inevitably the children show signs of increased disturbance during the period of therapy, need to be able to withstand any demands for therapy to finish prematurely due to the raised levels of anxiety of those in the network.

The book concludes with a group for adolescent girls, 'Between images and thoughts', described by Ani Brown and Marianne Latimir who, over the last 10 years have developed a joint approach which combines art therapy with cognitive therapy. They see the art-making process as central in bringing unconscious thoughts and feelings into awareness, where a cognitive approach can begin to address the distorted beliefs that the sexual abuse survivor comes to hold about herself: for example, concerning issues of responsibility, shame, guilt or depression. A picture of the group is presented from its early stages as the peer group established links and showed their distrust of the adults, partly by their resistance to the use of art materials offered. The girls denigrated their artwork to start with, but were gradually able to invest it with meaning as the interplay between image making, talking and thinking developed, based on the establishment of trust within the group. Individuals became able to recognise distorted thinking in each other and from that perspective, each could begin to reassess her own beliefs with more objectivity. The therapists emphasise the importance of their communications as co-therapists both in processing material in the here and now of each group, and also following the sessions, when they would use their countertransference feelings to process the group and to formulate interpretations.

As Bissonnet points out in her chapter, it is still rare to meet sexually abused women who have experienced therapy as children. Two women do offer insights into the experience of the abused child from a mature perspective through their artwork (Miller 1986, Mariette 1997). As adults, both had to break free of the conventional ideas they held regarding an approach to painting before rediscovering the hurt child within through the creation of imagery. Their struggles as adults to access feelings is a further indication, if one were needed, of the importance of helping children while they are more in touch with the traumatic experience of abuse, before it becomes split off or too deeply buried. They demonstrate the capacity of images to hold meaning when the image-maker is lost for words. I hope this book may demonstrate that wordless feelings, however confused, painful or intense, can find expression when art materials are freely available to children and young people within a containing psychotherapeutic relationship.

REFERENCES

Bannister, A. (1989) The effects of child sexual abuse on body and image, *Journal of British Association for Dramatherapists*, 12(1): 37–43.

Bray, M. (1991) *Poppies on the rubbish heap*, Edinburgh: Canongate.

Briggs, F. and Lehmann, K. (1989) Significance of children's drawings in cases of sexual abuse, *Early Child Development and Care*, 47: 131–47.

Browne, A. and Finkelhor, D. (1986) Impact of child sexual abuse: A review of the research, *Psychological Bulletin*, 99(1): 66–77.

Carozza, P.M. and Heirsteiner, C.L. (1982) Young female incest victims in treatment: Stages of growth seen with a group art therapy model, *Clinical Social Work Journal*, 10(3): 165–75.

Case, C. (1987) 'A search for meaning: Loss and transition in art therapy with children, in T. Dalley, C. Case, J. Schaverien, F. Weir, D. Halliday, P. Nowell Hall and D. Waller *Images of art therapy*, London/New York: Tavistock.

Cody, M. (1987) 'Art therapy within a general hospital paediatric unit', in *Image and enactment in childhood* (Conference proceedings), Hertfordshire College of Art and Design, UK (pp. 40–3).

Cohen, F.W. and Phelps, R.E. (1985) Incest markers in children's artwork, *The Arts in Psychotherapy*, 12: 265–83.

Dalley, T. (1987) 'Art as therapy: some new perspectives', in T. Dalley, C. Case, J. Schaverien, F. Weir, D. Halliday, P. Nowell Hall and D. Waller *Images of art therapy*, London/New York: Tavistock.

deYoung, M. and Corbin, B.A. (1994) Helping early adolescents tell: A guided exercise for trauma-focused sexual abuse treatment groups, *Child Welfare*, LXXIII(2): 141–53.

Dover, S., Hunt, C. and Fitzmaurice, M. (1997) A support group for carers of sexually abused girls, *Young Minds*, 25: 9–10.

Doyle, C. (1987) Helping the child victims of sexual abuse through play, *Practice*, 1: 27–38.

Finkelhor, D. (1979) *Sexually victimised children*, New York: Macmillan.

Hagood, M.M. (1991) Group art therapy with mothers of victims of child sexual abuse, *The Arts in Psychotherapy*, 18: 17–27.

Hagood, M.M. (1992) The status of child sexual abuse in the United Kingdom and implications for art therapists, *Inscape*, Spring issue: 27–33.

Herman, J., Russell, D. and Trocki, K. (1986) Long-term effects of incestuous abuse in childhood, *American Journal of Psychiatry*, 143(10): 1293–6.

Hibbard, R.A. & Hartman, G. (1990) Genitalia in human figure drawings: Childrearing practices and child sexual abuse, *Paediatrics*, 116(5): 822–8.

Hildebrand, J. and Forbes, C. (1987) Group work with mothers whose children have been sexually abused, *British Journal of Social Work*, 17: 285–304.

Howard, A. (1993) 'Victims and perpetrators of sexual abuse', in K.N. Dwividi (ed.) *Groupwork with children and adolescents: A handbook*, London and Bristol, PA: Jessica Kingsley Publishers.

Johnson, D.R. (1987) The role of the creative arts therapies in the diagnosis and treatment of psychological trauma, *The Arts in Psychotherapy*, 14: 7–13.

Kelley, S.J. (1985) Drawings: Critical communications for sexually abused children, *Paediatric Nursing*, 11(Nov/Dec): 421–6.

Kerslake, A. (1995) *Readings on groupwork intervention in child sexual abuse*, London: Whiting & Birch.

Kilgore, L.C. (1988) Effect of early childhood sexual abuse on self and ego development, *Social Casework: The Journal of Contemporary Social Work*, April, 224–30.

Knittle, B.J. and Tuana, S.J. (1980) Group therapy as primary treatment for adolescent victims of intrafamilial sexual abuse, *Clinical Social Work Journal*, 8: 236–42.

Levens, M. (1995) *Eating disorders and magical control of the body*, London/New York: Routledge.

Levinson, P. (1986) Identification of child abuse in the art and play products of paediatric burn patients, *Art Therapy*, July: 61–6.

Malchiodi, C. (1990) *Breaking the silence*, New York: Brunner/Mazel.

Mariette, N. (1997) *Painting myself in*, Otago, NZ: University of Otago Press.

McMahon, L. (1992) *The handbook of play therapy*, London and New York: Tavistock/Routledge.

Miller, A. (1986) *Pictures of a childhood*, New York: Farrar, Strauss & Giroux.

Murphy, J. (1998) Art therapy with sexually abused children and young people, *Inscape*, 3(1): 10–16.

Naitove, C.E. (1982) 'Arts therapy with sexually abused children', in S.M. Sgroi (ed.) *Handbook of clinical intervention in child sexual abuse*, Lexington, MA/Toronto: Lexington Books.

Naitove, C.E. (1988) 'Arts therapy with child molesters: An historical perspective on the act and an approach to treatment', *The Arts in Psychotherapy*, 15: 151–60.

Peake, B. (1987) A child's odyssey toward wholeness through art therapy, *The Arts in Psychotherapy*, 14: 41–58.

Powell, L. and Faherty, S.L. (1990) Treating sexually abused latency age girls, *The Arts in Psychotherapy*, 17: 35–47.

Riordan, R.J. and Verdel, A.C. (1991) Evidence of sexual abuse in children's art products, *The School Counsellor*, 39: 116–21.

Russell, D.E.H. (1986) *The secret trauma*, New York: Basic Books.

Sagar, C. (1990) 'Working with cases of child sexual abuse', in C. Case and T. Dalley (eds) *Working with children in art therapy*, London/New York: Routledge.

Schaverien, J. (1987) 'The scapegoat and the talisman: Transference in art therapy', in T. Dalley, C. Case, J. Schaverien, F. Weir, D. Halliday, P. Nowell Hall and D. Waller *Images of art therapy*, London/New York: Tavistock.

Sidun, N.M. and Rosenthal, R.H. (1987) Graphic indicators of sexual abuse in draw-a-person tests of psychiatrically-hospitalised adolescents, *The Arts in Psychotherapy*, 14: 25–33.

Stember, C., (1978) Change in maladaptive growth of abused girl through art therapy, *Art Psychotherapy*, 5: 99–109.

Stember, C. (1980) 'Art therapy: A new use in the diagnosis and treatment of sexually abused children', in *Sexual abuse of children: Selected readings*, Washington, DC: US Department of Health and Human Services.

Steward, M.S., Farquar, L.C., Dicharry, D.C., Glick, D.R. and Martin, P.W. (1986) Group therapy: A treatment of choice for young victims of child abuse, *International Journal of Group Psychotherapy*, 36(2): 261–75.

Thomas, L. (1998) 'From re-presentations to representations of sexual abuse', in D. Sandle (ed.) *Development and diversity*, London/New York: Free Association Books.

Young, L. (1992) Sexual abuse and the problem of embodiment, *Child Abuse and Neglect*, 16: 89–100.

Part I

The therapeutic relationship in context

Chapter 1

Containing the bad object

Observations and thoughts on the generation of bad feelings between people in an organisation, a professional network, a therapist, and a child attending individual art therapy

Louis Thomas

INTRODUCTION

In this chapter I shall attempt to describe some of the key issues experienced through the conducting of one-to-one art therapy with a pubescent girl ('Joany') who had accused her grandfather of sexual abuse.

As part of Joany's testimony in court she had been found to be clearly lying about one aspect of her account of events leading up to her abuse. She had admitted in court that she had lied, but said she had only done so to try and make sure her grandfather was imprisoned for his crime against her. As a consequence, her other evidence was then treated with suspicion by the jury and her particular attempt to secure safety for herself influenced the direction of the case. As a compromise in what became a very convoluted enquiry, the court forbade Joany's grandfather any contact and he was subject to a restricted movement order.

It was at this point that Joany came to my attention, carrying all the ambiguity that her family and professional network were unable to bear. They had become resolutely split into those who believed her and those who did not. Grandfather was seen as either an evil man who deserved an unpleasant death, or someone incapable of any wrong-doing. Joany was seen as either a crazy liar or a child giving an accurate account of an abusive experience that she had suffered. There was little space for anything in between. The anxiety created in Joany by the splitting of her family and professional network only served to compound her already fragile mental state. In a stark and transparent way the case of Joany mirrored many of the difficulties inherent in this work ever since Freud (1905) began uncovering and attempting to unmesh the reality of both actual abuse and childhood sexual fantasy. But perhaps most ironic of all was the way that this case highlighted for me how very susceptible we can all be today to employing splitting as a defence against unbearable uncertainty.

This chapter concerns itself with the generation and dynamic movement of bad feelings between the one-to-one therapy relationship, the professional network and the organisation. It will therefore be useful first to provide selected information on the organisation and the context within which the following casework transpired. (The example organisation is no longer in operation.)

PART ONE

The organisation

With current political and ideological concerns moving towards caring for vulnerable children in a family setting wherever possible, the organisation (hereafter referred to as t.o.) took steps to develop a much needed service which would begin to address topical child protection needs. A special project was created which aimed to provide therapy for children who had experienced sexual abuse, or where it was deemed 'highly likely' that they had experienced such abuse.

Several months into the life of the project an emergency meeting was called because of increasing unrest over difficulties being experienced in working with this client group. In response to this disquiet, in-house training was provided for the worker/therapists. A feeling expressed at this training was how ill-equipped people felt themselves to be for the job of therapy. Also, increasing concern was voiced as to what forms of support worker/therapists would receive in the event of a false accusation or 'honest lie' (Ironside 1995) being levelled at a therapist 'specifically in the therapy situation'.

It is interesting to note that the two main ways of dealing with these particular anxieties were: (a) seek further training and clinical supervision, or (b) do not undertake therapy work, but instead attempt to deal with the emotions raised by teaching the children how to 'say no to paedophiles'. The latter option was considered but eventually rejected. There are likely to be many reasons why this second option even got as far as it did. However, I think one partial reason is because it is a serviceable way of unconsciously converting the emotionally disturbing material brought by the child into anxiety-relieving action, which in turn, by processes of projective re-introjection, pulls the primary anxiety now embellished with guilt and shame back into the child. This is a quite ordinary defence against experiencing overwhelming emotional pain, but a form of splitting that, if not promptly addressed, creates additional problems for the child and sows the seeds of divisive defences to become underwritten as part of team culture.

The therapeutic setting and my theoretical orientation

The Centre was based in the community. My manager, colleague therapists and I each had our own dedicated therapy rooms and there was also a comfortable waiting area.

My own practice is informed by a range of psychoanalytic theories and recorded modern practice with children by child development researchers, for example: Stern (1985) and Piontelli (1992), baby observation and personal psychotherapy. I employed a variety of public or shared toys and art materials together with private art folders. I saw children on an individual basis once weekly for up to three years. I also offered discussion time to parents on a less intensive basis. Frequently, my manager, co-therapists and I would work jointly with a family, usually with one of us providing work for the parents while the other/s worked with the child or children, Here, we found an 'open systems' approach (Skynner 1987:307) invaluable.

The network

The professional network consisted of the usual public-sector children's services including the more well known voluntary childcare agencies.

The therapy team

Good case management supervision was provided by my manager. However, it was part of t.o. policy that external clinical supervisors should not be used for reasons of security of sensitive information. I was very fortunate in being able to retain essential external clinical support in the form of a 'discussion group' which was accepted as an extension of the further training I had embarked on before taking up the post.

Although it was difficult for t.o. to appreciate the therapist's needs for external profession-appropriate supervision, t.o.'s training committee rapidly responded to requests for clinical support by recommending a private consultant who specialised in the use of auto-suggestive techniques. To give an example of the person's style: when attempting to explore awful feelings of adversity (splitting) causing acting-out within the team, we were advised to visualise (in difficult moments) a child's potty in the middle of the floor in which we were to imagine defaecating.

Even after consultative experiences of this nature, the pursuance of profession-appropriate supervision was still discouraged, as it was felt by t.o.'s training committee to be more important to continue to seek support from what was described as more open-minded, 'eclectic' therapists rather than from people familiar with what was felt to be more medically sympathetic practices. Of course, this view led to tensions developing, which were all the more difficult to digest because, ironically, different ideas from outside t.o. could not penetrate to help circulate and process the many feelings that were coming to light during the unfolding of much disquieting work. The individuals that combined to make up t.o. had by now become pierced by a quite paralysing and indiscriminate fear of intercourse. There seemed little difference between the fear of abuse and the feelings raised when suggestions were made to involve an external supervisor. Although this defence is primarily one driven to protect, it does so by incestuous means.

The concept of 'difference' and the quality of the emotions this idea raises in people working specifically in this field does seem to be a key issue to try and understand. The lack of acceptance of profession-appropriate clinical supervision, coupled with the tendency to idealise eclecticism, points (in this instance) to a confusion developing between accommodating to unsatisfactory working relationships and relating by having different needs and qualities recognised, nurtured and built upon. Particularly noxious tensions develop around forces that pull towards skills mixing or forces that push for individual recognition and the complementation of unique strengths and skills. Perhaps one way of beginning to understand the conflicting anxiety and resistance surrounding these concepts is by observing the tendency of many of the referred families to have difficulty with the range of emotions that help demarcate the needs of the adults from what is healthy for the children in their care. Often it is deeply disturbing for families operating on this enmeshed level to allow their children an ordinary level of separate functioning. The need to project inappropriate personal qualities into the child, and subsequent unsuccessful attempts to control these in the 'object' of their fantasies, is indeed massive. Absorbing such disturbing material in large quantities and without access to clinical supervision greatly increases the chances of such dynamics needing to find an outlet in t.o. and team. It became a struggle at times to disentangle identifications made with the abused and deprived parts of the children in therapy from the more ordinary management and worker agitations stirred up, for instance, by time restrictions necessary due to a growing waiting list.

What did become clearer was how overwork with sexually abused children, together with deprivation of training, personal therapy and profession-appropriate supervision, can eventually be translated into power conflicts and controlling actions instead of emotion-attuning thought. Without the basic supports in place, sharing thoughts about the patients' emotional lives raised too much pain and conflict to deal with effectively. For example, it really was difficult for the team to hear about Joany's inner world and my closeness to it without becoming caught up in the fantasies stimulated by such intimate case material. Getting close to an abused child on an emotional level became a dreadfully frightening proposition for everyone concerned.

Through processes of projective identification the children are putting into the therapists the fundamental fear that closeness leads to loss of sexual control – after all, this is often part of their experience. What appears to be happening is that the revelation that sexually abused children need to use their therapy time to test out their own, the internalised abuser's and their therapist's sexuality, provokes yet further alarm within the system.

Preparatory work in the form of pre-therapy case conferences with all involved professionals, to look specifically at the complications involved in working with transference issues with children with damaged or limited symbolising capacities, becomes an important part of the work before any kind of therapy begins. It may be that where it is known that a sexually abused child's capacity to symbolise is impaired in any way, therapists should take the necessary precautions in securing at the very least an understanding and supportive professional network before commencing therapy.

Here it would be useful to move into the very material that instinctively raises such anxiety, as one's own sense of intimacy meets with the child's and the abuser's by proxy.

PART TWO

The clinical work and commentary

Joany, Session 28, Aged 10

Joany paints a picture of herself drowning in an ocean with a lightning storm raging above her. She cries out to her mother and, drawing a speech bubble coming from the mouth of herself, writes: 'Mam you weren't there.' The painting depicts a prone and spread-eagled Joany being engulfed in a 'messy and polluted-sea'. Above, in the sky, there are two clouds, a lightning bolt and much rain. The juxtaposition of the elements in the sky gave the impression of a bristled face bearing down. As Joany painted this picture she told me that her mother and father can't hear her when she asks for help, but that I can. (I was wary here of not wishing to collude with any possible idealisation of me, while also bearing in mind that she seemed to be expressing a need to experience me as someone who can listen to her.)

Joany told me that her mother doesn't realise that she (Joany) needs help when she communicates this to her by '. . . not eating my food or being grumpy with other people'. I said that perhaps a lot of adults find it difficult to catch on to children's hints. Joany replied: 'But you do' (meaning I do catch on). I told Joany that I knew she was unhappy and calling for help because she had both told me so and had shown me with her painting, and so in this way perhaps I had an unfair advantage over her parents. I thought aloud: 'I wonder how your parents might hear that there are times when you need a cuddle?' (Joany had also mentioned her needs for cuddles). I tried various other ways of attempting to lead Joany to the discovery that maybe she would benefit by telling her parents, to no effect. Eventually I just suggested that maybe she could tell her parents too? As I spoke Joany leaned on me with her elbow. I allowed her to do this as I felt she was in touch with a part of herself that had felt deprived of emotional nurture, and that she was perhaps needing to experience a benign non-sexual touch. However Joany then tried to kiss me on the cheek and I backed away, telling Joany that I could not allow kissing. Joany took a step back and slapped me across the head as she left the art therapy room to use the toilet.

When Joany returned, I asked her if she had felt rejected by my refusal to let her kiss me on the cheek. Joany confirmed this and added that she thought I was cruel and 'even worse than cruel. You're childish! I only wanted to kiss you on the cheek.' (I wondered if Joany experienced my recoiling from her as a form of sexualisation, in that what she had regarded as a benign action was taken by me to be one that was malignant or perverse.) I tried to overcome what I experienced as a dilemma between maintaining the appropriate boundaries while also conveying (in a sense) that she is lovable, by recapping on the preceding interactions and feelings, giving them a benign or nurture-seeking interpretation. I said that I thought Joany had wanted to kiss me on the cheek at a time when she had felt very needy for her mother. I explained as best I could how experiencing this emptiness for her mother may in some way help her to understand something about her wish to kiss me. It was as if my listening to Joany had awakened a deprived part of her in a way that was at first experienced as persecutory. Joany said, 'My mother has somebody. My father has somebody. You have somebody' (with anger). It seemed that Joany had tried to fill her sense of emptiness by trying to seduce me. When this failed, she said that she wanted me to know what this felt like: she used the sand tray to mould effigies of my wife and new baby (Joany had overheard this news in the waiting room) who were ceremoniously killed in a pseudo-religious ritual before being buried.

There is both relief and outrage in Joany when she cannot seduce me and in many ways her therapy is an important testing ground to help her work with a confusion between emotional needs and sexuality. It might have been useful in this session for me to have encouraged Joany to spell out the meaning of specific words. For example, what did Joany mean when she said 'You take hints'? Is it possible that she was talking about sexual hints and therefore experiencing me like her grandfather in the transference?

Session 29

In the art therapy room Joany slumped into a high-backed chair next to the main table where I was sitting.

J: I'm zonked. I went to a sleep-over last night; didn't get back 'till half past one in the morning. It was really, really embarrassing; my mother walked in on me! . . . we were playing spin the bottle.
L: Something about your mother walking in on you at 1.30 in the morning made you feel really embarrassed?
J: Yes. My friend Jed was just about to give me a big kiss. It was bad.

Wouldn't you feel bad if your mother walked in and caught you and your wife?

L: Yes. It could be embarrassing.

Joany collected herself a piece of paper and her set of paints. Using brushes that were too large to fit into her paints she said: 'These are too big.' Gathering larger paints Joany adds: 'This is going to be an announcement poster.'

L: Like a poster that tells us of something that's coming?

J: No. It's going to tell us about something that is.

For most of the following session Joany seemed to explore our relationship and that of her new-found boyfriend, while painting.

J: How's your baby?

L: She's doing very well.

J: I wonder if your children go to my school? If they did you'd be in real trouble then. Because I wouldn't be allowed to talk to them. You said that I'm not allowed to talk to you if I see you in town. [I hadn't.]

L: Maybe some of the rules that I have for myself here, feel like I'm pushing you away altogether?

J: I'm not allowed to talk to you outside. You're not allowed to pick me up not even if I was dead?

L: If you see me in town Joany, you are welcome to come and talk to me, and I would pick you up if you were dead. [In an earlier session Joany pretended to be dead, just as it was time to leave. I didn't pick her up.]

J: I have Jed now anyway, he doesn't have the same stupid rules as you.

L: I am not like a boyfriend?

J: No, and I don't want you to be either. You're an old fogey with your rules. You're old enough to be my grandfather you fogey. No offence.

L: I'm not offended. Maybe there's a part of you that wants me to be *like* a boyfriend, and another part of you which is happy that I am not?

J: No, I don't want you as a boyfriend, and don't you try anything because my boyfriend will beat you up.

L: I am quite clear on my own rules about myself.

J: Louis, do you have sex with your wife?

L: That's a very personal question Joany. Why do you ask?

J: You must have. You've got children. Did you have permission or did it just happen all of a sudden like?

L: We both planned to have children.

J: I bet you did it all the time, like about twice a day for about two days?

L: Perhaps it can be exciting to wonder about my wife and I?

J: Yuk. I can't imagine you doing that, its disgusting.

L: It's a part of my life that I share with another adult person and that must be very hard to bear at times.

Joany continued with her painting. As I observed she gave me a concerned-looking sideways glance.

L: What's the matter?
J: Oh nothing, just something that I've seen before. It's just that I thought you were Jack [grandfather].

In the recalling and sharing of this session it is important to understand what Joany is doing. It is useful here to think of Joany in terms of action. In this session I am forced into action by giving Joany information that is not appropriate, and giving reassurance rather than understanding, almost as a way of surviving the perversion being employed. Joany attempts to get me out of role, like an abuse experience, by provoking and inducing my concern, making me feel sorry, which could be seen as the displacement of an emotion attached to her own feelings of envy. The penis/paintbrushes are too big for Joany and she searches for bigger paints, wishing it would seem that she herself was bigger. The reality of her not being an adult/woman able to make babies is extremely hard for her to cope with, she is excluded from the relationship between me and my wife. It is important to try and acknowledge Joany's seductive urges in a way that does not feed into her erotic fantasies. It is not easy to know when Joany is using me to help her contain her envious feelings or when she is putting her envy into me while in a mood of mania in which she can feel triumphant and omnipotent.

Session 31

At the beginning of this session and with no manifest context Joany made a comment about angry feelings being 'dim'. Elaborating on her choice of word, Joany added that angry feelings were 'stupid'. I said that I thought her angry feelings were very important and that her anger was, at times, a useful feeling to have.

J: She is always where we go and I don't like it. Sharron [father's new girl-friend] is always there whenever I see my father.
L: That must be very difficult Joany? [with appropriate feeling].
J: Yes, when I go to see my dad, he should be seeing me, but instead *she* is *always* there! I find it so hard to cope with, but I have to. I have to learn to accept that Sharron is there.

Joany also spoke about how difficult it felt to have to share her mother with her new boyfriend. I spoke to Joany about how the jealousy she had just shown towards Sharron felt similar to that brought up the previous week, where the subject had been that of my own marital relationship.

L: Maybe it's important for you to bring those kinds of feelings here first?
J: Yes. I bring them here first so I can get to know them.

Session 34

J: We all have to have aids tests in the school. I've already had an aids test so I don't need one. But my boyfriend has told me that if he has got aids he's going to finish with me because I would have given it to him. But that's stupid. You can't get aids from French kissing, from saliva, it has to be from someone's blood or if they have sex with their organs or orgasms or something. As if we are going to be doing that, having sex in the school yard. If only Mrs Williams could think back to when she was a child then she wouldn't stop it.
L: If Mrs Williams could think back and remember her childhood she might remember something like?
J: Well, like when she used to kiss or something. She's being so childish banning kissing; you can't catch aids from kissing you have to have an organ – organs – orgasm. You know what I mean don't you? You know what an orgasm is. Tell me what an orgasm is and I'll tell you if it's what I know it is?

Joany's requests for this new information was met by a refusal on my part to give it. This raised such anger in Joany that she left the room for approximately five minutes. When she returned I tried my best to empathise:

L: I know it must hurt Joany when it feels like I've got something that I won't share.

Joany left the room again for several minutes and returned crying, saying how much she hates her parents having new partners and neglecting her.

J: I feel torn apart.
L: It hurts to see your parents choosing new partners and to experience them leaving you out of much of their relationships. And to have me refuse to talk about sex with you. Perhaps Joany, kissing your boyfriend or trying to talk to me about exciting things helps to cover these terrible feelings of being left out?

In this session, for me to have talked about orgasm would clearly have supported Joany's fantasy that I am her partner. It is extremely difficult for me to pitch things in such a way that they are not experienced by Joany as either a

come-on or a persecuting rejection. Joany's boundaries between fantasy and
reality are seen here to be very loose, and her communications with me can be
viewed as her struggle to try to make sense of, or piece together, what has
happened to her and what she fears may happen again. A central question for
Joany seems to be: how can she think with me about these things – express the
curiosity and confusions – when the anxiety raised in her by doing so makes
her both want and fear physical comforting? My interpretations also make me
separate, reminding Joany quite painfully of my difference.

Session 39

Joany's therapy review is due and in this session some of her concerns surrounding this are expressed:

J: . . . what if I say that *everything* that I have said since I have been here is
     a lie, what then?

I asked Joany if she could give me more of an idea on the kind of lie she was
meaning.

J: Have any of the children who come here told lies about what people
     have done to them. Like taking them to court, or putting them in jail
     when they haven't done something. [With anxiety] Not that that's a clue
     mind you.

Joany told me that she had a secret which she was afraid to tell me in case I
gave her 'hell', adding: 'But what would you think Louis if someone did
that?'
    Joany then wished to know about private therapy. What it was and could I
offer it.
    From previous experience of reviews Joany understands that a main con-
cern will be: how much longer will therapy need to last? Joany seems to feel
very vulnerable about the future of her therapy. She is aware that if her therapy appears to be doing well, this can be viewed prematurely as 'successful'
and tends to be followed by discussion on endings, as does also therapy that
doesn't appear to be doing well.
    Another concept that we advertised at the Centre was that therapy was
only available for children who have been sexually abused (or where it seems
highly likely). The Centre (under the guidance of t.o.) also advertised its
commitment to the idea that children never tell lies about abuse. It would
appear from the latter extract that Joany has found a valid problem with this:
Here she is wondering where I stand within the advertised organisational
philosophy. Do I have space for thinking with and tolerating children who lie
or are confused about abuse? Within the context of her recent explorations,

would her therapy have to stop? Indeed, does she feel compelled to have to maintain certain confusions in order to protect her therapy under the present philosophy?

Session 49

Joany tells me how her grandfather used to be a bus driver and how recently she 'saw some bus drivers the other day when I was in town, I asked them about Jack and they said that they knew him. Then one of them said: "He used to work here but there was a young lady who made him lose his job."'

I wondered aloud over how the young lady did this, then said: 'Perhaps there is a part of you which blames yourself about your grandfather losing his job?'

J: No. Get a life.

With the issue of false accusation being raised by Joany in her recent sessions, her struggles between fact and fantasy, today's part exploration of a young girl's potential to make a man lose his job, and my less than satisfactory securing of a supportive professional network, my reflections and interpretations understandably become fuelled by a concern to protect myself rather than seek understanding. Had I had the presence of mind in this session, it could perhaps have been useful to have viewed my counter-transference feelings as a means to understand something of Joany's anxiety over feeling 'ruined' or defamed by her abuse or account of it, or both. In this session I revert to action in the sense that my communications seek further validation of Joany's capacity to be 'false', so that should the worst happen, this aspect of her personality is recorded.

Around this time I thought it essential to seek the views of the other team leaders and worker/therapists regarding the very specific problem of the potential for some children to level a false accusation or 'honest lie' (Ironside 1995) against their therapists. By bearing such possibilities in mind it makes sense that we can become better equipped to protect such children, their therapy and ourselves. Soon after these discussions took place, video cameras were supplied for each therapist to use as they felt appropriate.

Notwithstanding the advantages that the video can bring, this concept could be viewed here as perhaps our concrete expression of the need to have an understanding and supportive 'third other' involved. The defining, developing and maintaining of a professional and personed 'framework' could also, of course, be productive in terms of managing and helping contain such anxieties, so that therapists are less burdened by the potential for the destructive forces in therapy to bring it to a premature and possibly disastrous end. One question that could usefully be borne in mind when attempting to develop a more effective professional framework is: 'What people do we need around us in order to do our work when part of it involves us setting our-selves up to be frightened by children?'

In Joany's case, it was vital to find another professional to trust with the real concern about the possibility of a false accusation, as was a role for him or her when and if this seemed to be on the horizon. If I could view part of my work as perhaps helping Joany to define certain questions, while not nec-essarily being the best person to help her answer them, this might be a useful way of introducing the third other: at the 'potential' times when an accusation *may* be made. Interestingly, these potential times often arose when I was shortly due to take a holiday, and were preceded by well defined questions asked by Joany. I made arrangements to meet an allied professional whom I shall call S. I told S how, in the not-so-distant past, my holidays had brought the feelings of loss and abuse together in therapy in a way that had been con-fusing for Joany and anxiety-provoking for me. I explained that as well as the accused abusive grandfather being hated by Joany, there was also a part of her that loved the other aspects of him, feeling at times greatly saddened by his loss as he was the only person who played with her. I also explained that these fused concepts of loss and abuse seem to get especially stirred up just before I took a break. I told S the two specific questions that can arise from Joany around these times, and should they arise again, I would be grateful for S's assistance and close working partnership. The questions were: 'What hap-pens if a girl tells a lie about a man and gets him sacked?' and 'What would happen if a girl told a lie about what a man had done and took him to court?'

I told S that I thought it would be very beneficial for Joany if she knew she could ask her (S), someone outside the immediate therapy relationship, these questions, adding that in Joany's case it would also be of benefit if Joany could also experience us (S and myself) as a sort of working couple. There are several benefits of striking up this kind of professional relationship in such 'dangerous' cases. First, it helps the child to have an experience of a man and woman who can bear and survive the various seductions in a more tangible way. S and I are not divorced or split, as it were, by Joany's troubles. Second, it helps to slow Joany's fantasies of coupling with me down to a more man-ageable tempo. Third, it may provide the therapist with an actual safety net and the child with a greater sense of safety during the more equative (Thomas 1998: 29–40) and therefore dangerous moments, where the child's memory and fantasy struggle to make sense of the present and its unknown potential.

Ending

As reports from Joany's parents, teachers, and myself were favourable, it was formally suggested at her review (which Joany attended) that art therapy be ended by the coming school summer holidays in five months' time. Planning the ending before her long school holidays gave Joany a usefully extended period in which to assimilate her experience of therapy without having the extra demands of school work. Joany understood and agreed somewhat reluctantly with the proposal to finish her therapy in the given time span. Consideration was also given to the potential levels of public service support Joany's family may need during the period immediately following the end of her therapy. At the review, Joany had one proviso, which was agreed, and this was that her art therapy continue until at least one session after her father's new partner had given birth to the child that was due around the same time as the suggested ending of therapy. (Joany had expressed how ambivalent she felt about the coming child and needed to know that should she react adversely to the new arrival, her feelings had somewhere to be held.)

Over the following months, Joany was absent on some three occasions, and even though I was contacted by either Joany or her mother and given reasonable explanation, I came under a good deal of external pressure on each occasion to terminate therapy immediately and to write to Joany saying that art therapy (I) was no longer available. It took much effort on my part to retrieve the therapy on these occasions and to justify continuing to work with Joany towards the more reasonably considered ending agreed at her review.

One of the greatest obstacles the therapy team found itself having to deal with during this time was a growing potent fear that spending so much time in the company of such children would lead to irreconcilable dependency situations developing – either the child with the therapist or, more worrying for some, the therapist with the child. Perhaps because Joany was the longest-treated child at the Centre, her case seemed to raise so many demanding questions about sexual abuse work. Considering such dependency fears, I feel that within the given context they are another aspect of the fear of losing control – that the child's needs for nurture, attention and love coupled with her capacity for perversion will breach the therapist's ego defence with disastrous consequences. Unconscious defences that began to emerge in the face of having no clinical 'thinking space' to air and clarify such fears and fantasies included the team's wish to withdraw from conducting what was felt to be the more 'dangerous' longer-term work, and the projection of demoralising loss-of-control fantasies on to people who were attempting it. It is sad to say that during the Centre's relatively short lifespan it required the scapegoating of two people whom I greatly respect in order to survive the emotional gravity of the perverse psychodynamics that were rapidly unfolding in the work and rebounding on the team. We found ourselves in a work situation where one of the central tenets of psychotherapy, *to allow transference affects to be noticed but not even symbolically re-enacted*, carries considerable risk to the professional. One has to be exhaustingly vigilant in noticing where and when the child's play may be drawing one into an unconscious symbolic re-enactment. The costs of falling into symbolic re-enactment with this client group are greater than with any other clientele. It is easy to see why practices that reduced time alone with these children became increasingly desirable within t.o. Unless these issues are subjected to some hard thinking, the future of one-to-one therapy with this client group is endangered.

Session 70

Joany sang me a series of songs with similar themes, i.e. songs that seemed designed to raise or strengthen hope, when a loss was imminent, for example Vera Lynn's *We'll meet again*. This was followed by a song describing her sense of love and being loved. Joany said that she saw her therapy as 'A kind of love.' Joany then sculpted me three different pieces of plasticine to show me the changes she felt she had been through over the years. Starting with 'In pieces', then 'Going cold', and finally having a sense of 'A hole in my heart, which somehow makes me feel warm. I'll always have a hole where Wednesdays were' (Joany).

It would seem from Joany's comments that the extended bearing of the space, the separation (the difference) between people experienced in therapy, is what enabled her to experience the warmth of the relationship. The hole is the space between us where feelings can be thought about without being acted upon.

Joany attended for another two sessions, within which her stepmother to be gave birth to a baby boy. Although there was a mixture of feelings for Joany about her father's perceived favouring of his 'long-awaited' son, Joany on the whole seemed to feel reasonably secure about her future prospects with a new brother.

Much of the last session (following) had been communicated (at Joany's request) non-verbally through the medium of a glockenspiel. Here is a brief extract taken from my notes:

Session 72

Joany asked if I could watch how she played the instrument and then copy this myself. She stressed how important it was that I remain silent during the musical play by putting her fingers to her lips in a 'hush' gesture. The rhythms and movements that Joany made became increasingly sophisticated and tested my memory. Once Joany was satisfied with my observation and reflection of the tunes (they did not have to be exactly the same, she did allow me to have some creative leeway), she altered the emphasis of the play into that of wanting me to support certain parts of her composition. It took four or five attempts for this to be communicated non-verbally (including mouthing) by Joany and for me to pick it up in a way that brought a series of 'OK' signs made by raising her hand and displaying a circular shape formed by her thumb and forefinger). Eventually, Joany felt that my understanding was good enough for our sessions to be brought to an end; this was communicated by giving a 'cut' gesture as performed by orchestral conductors.

J: What if you leave now?
L: If I do leave here I would leave my next work address with the secretary.
J: No, I mean if you finish being a therapist now?
L: Oh, I'm not going to finish being a therapist. I'm going to be working for a long time to come.
J: It's not as if I'm never going to see you again. I could always come back if I needed to have a session at sometime?
L: Yes, it could be arranged if it was needed.
J: Can I take my folder now?
     [I had always told Joany that I could keep her folder of artwork safe until she felt she needed to take it home.]
L: Yes, of course.
J: Can I take my time sheets as well? [Time sheets are child-specific calendars which show at a glance a three-monthly term of therapy dates.]
L: Yes, but I will need to dig them out of my files. Do you mind if I send them on to you?
J: No, that will be fine.

There are two very important messages that I learned from Joany in this last session: One, how there are ways of carrying thinking forward via the fantasy, without having to talk directly about it. And two, how important it is for Joany to try and find a way of making duets with people, for creating moments of subjective attunement that bring her towards experiencing different realms of emotional closeness.

(I didn't feel it appropriate in this last session to attempt to take up issues that may have been linked to magical control or thinking. That she wondered if I might stop being a therapist at the same time as she stopped being a client suggests the likelihood of some unresolved fantasies of being merged with me at some level.)

CONCLUSION

One of the aims of this chapter has been to raise a healthy questioning of some of the more difficult areas of treating children who have been sexually abused. I hope that as well as making people more aware of the difficulties of this work, it will also help managers and therapists to plan more thoroughly together before embarking on such specialised clinical work with deeply disturbed children. One of the most important things I have learned about working with sexually abused children concerns the relationship between thought and action in this most demanding area of practice. How one way of attempting to defend against the emotional pain and self-disturbance stimulated by 'getting close' is to convert the accompanying thoughts and or fantasies aroused by so doing into action rather than thinking. This can be observed, for example, in my more defensive interpretations where my first concern needs to be self-protection rather than furthering the understanding of the anxieties raised in the relationship. Joany's struggles against 'doing-to' when fearing she may be 'done to' were evidenced by her needs to persistently control me in the sessions and in my manager's wish to find a technological answer (videoing) to the problem of false accusations. This particular genre of action points to moments when thinking about things that threaten our lives quite humanly needs to give way to defending ourselves against thinking about them – paradoxically making us more vulnerable.

So that therapists can increase their capacity first to have thoughts, and further, to link these in the creative act of thinking about such difficult emotions, several steps need to be considered in order to support the work, including:

1   Ensure that profession-appropriate supervision is available and is an integral part of a therapy project's culture.
2   Enlist the support and consultation of a variety of qualified and experienced child protection workers and, most essentially, child mental health practitioners at the planning stage.
3   Ensure that each therapist has access to personal psychotherapy from a UKCP or state-registered psycho/therapist.

Even with these supports in place it is still, I feel, inadvisable to work exclusively with this client group. Some of my reasons for this are as follows: it becomes more and more difficult to grasp how non-perverted childhood sexuality and relationship-forming presents itself in the therapy situation, as one's experience is limited to sexual perversions. Also, specialising with this client group tends to magnify associated anxieties and the subsequent defences required to manage them, making workers, therapists and managers more vulnerable towards adopting the same coping mechanisms as their client group. In the worst cases I feel that unsupported teams could eventually fall prey to creating the conditions in which stress-related illnesses and professional bullying can thrive.

Perhaps the crux of beginning to thoughtfully contain the bad sexual object is to try and identify both its emotional tone and the quality of the resistance experienced when attempting to do this. One of the difficulties I have drawn attention to in this study is the fact that to begin to emotionally contain the child's bad sexual object the therapist needs to become a receptacle for the abused child's projections and transference material. This involves tolerating being thought of and fantasised about like the abuser at least until the child has had ample opportunities for testing you out, discovering otherwise and gaining a common sense of how such fantasies can influence the development of the new relationships he or she is forming with you and others. This can only be achieved in a culture where thinking and speaking about sexual matters, both healthy and perverse, is nurtured. Of course one has to constantly weigh up whether or not talking in the therapy situation about sexual matters is part of a seduction or defensive process, but generally speaking, in the work force it has to be expected and encouraged among the professionals.

The psychodynamically orientated therapist who encourages transference material needs to feel reasonably safe and supported in the knowledge that transferences are not only seen for what they are, but that charges also understand that this is the very material that psychodynamically orientated therapists welcome. For without it revealing itself, it is not possible to process it with one's shared thinking. Managers and employees need to think together about the rather frightening implications of allowing people to make themselves available on a full-time basis to receive the projections of child-internalised paedophilic qualities and anxieties, by children whose symbolising capacities may well have been damaged by the abuse. I do not think there are any recipes or short cuts to resolving this most demanding problem as, for the sake of protecting each child, each situation needs to be assessed on its own merits. This is important, as any prescriptive thought-cutting system will become vulnerable to misuse.

ACKNOWLEDGEMENTS

I am grateful to Hilary, Elizabeth and also to the members of the Bristol and Cardiff Work Discussion Groups for their support and their contributions which are present in the more thoughtful aspects of this study.

REFERENCES

Freud, S. (1905) *Fragment of an analysis of a case of hysteria ('Dora')*, Harmondsworth, UK: Penguin Freud Library.

Ironside, L. (1995) Beyond the boundaries: A therapist and an allegation of sexual abuse, *Journal of Child Psychotherapy*, 21(2), London: Routledge.

Piontelli, A. (1992) *From fetus to child: An observational and psychoanalytic study*, London: Routledge.

Skynner, R. (1987) In J. Schlapobersky (ed.) *Explorations with families, group analysis and family therapy*, London: Routledge.

Stern, D. (1985) *The interpersonal world of the infant: A view from psychoanalysis and developmental psychology*, New York: Basic Books.

Thomas, L. (1998) From re-presentations to representations of sexual abuse, in D. Sandle (ed.) *Development and diversity, new applications in art therapy*, London: Free Association Books Limited.

Chapter 2

Male therapist countertransference and the importance of the family context

Mark Wheeler and Becky Smith

This chapter is of special interest to male therapists and to those who supervise male therapists who may have similar, if vicarious, experience of these issues. It may also be useful to those who work alongside male therapists and even those who share coffee breaks with male therapists who may have just experienced some of the issues discussed.

This chapter will examine the role of individual art therapy and its relationship with the family system, and concurrent family therapy in particular. We will explore some of the countertransference issues that arose, particularly for the male therapist, and their management. We will use a 'milepost' session to exemplify some of the 'stuff' that crops up. By analysing particular moments in the history of one client's therapeutic episode, within the overall context of their therapeutic history, this chapter addresses certain points that arose for two therapists in a particular therapeutic encounter:

*   with the child who had experienced sexual abuse;
*   with her adoptive family;
*   with the wider professional systems.

ART THERAPY REFERRAL

GPs and other agencies refer clients to our clinic as a whole. They are seen as a whole family or carer system and may also, if appropriate, undergo individual therapies. Family therapy usually continues concurrently. Clinicians are very aware of the particular therapeutic strengths of colleagues, which makes us a particularly effective multi-disciplinary team. Clients are not directly referred to the art therapy service from other agencies unless it is from another art therapy service perhaps in another locality.

SESSION STRUCTURE

- Art therapy sessions last one hour with a thirty-minute gap in between clients to clear up and write notes.
- Each session begins promptly when the therapist collects the young person from the waiting room, exchanging no more than pleasantries with parents, carers, or social workers who have brought the child.
- Any attempts by adults to discuss a child's recent behaviour or some aspect of the therapy are forestalled at this point, and deferred to a review meeting if appropriate.
- Once in the art therapy room, an age-appropriate reminder of the boundaries of confidentiality and child protection is often given.
- An appropriate invitation to make use of the space, the materials and the therapy may sometimes be needed, although most young people launch straight in after a couple of sessions.
- Messy play with materials is OK and children can see the evidence of this around the room itself.
- Other people's work is treated with respect and off limits to comment or touch, demonstrating value.
- Half time is noted by the therapist and there is a five-minute warning of the finish time.
- Young people help with some clearing up, particularly of tools like brushes, for a couple of minutes at the end to punctuate the close of therapy until next time.
- Flat work is either put straight into the young person's drawer, or onto a drying rack.
- 3D work is stored in a cupboard.
- Young people's work remains at the clinic until they finish attending, unless they specifically ask beforehand for a different arrangement with a particular piece.

Other than this basic framework and boundaries, sessions are usually non-directive, often very materially messy and yet safely contained by these simple boundary markers.

HOLDING AND CONTAINING

To hold such work safely and thus enable it to proceed effectively there are profound implications for the therapist and for the other systems in which the client exists, which include:

1   The issues may be too big and complicated and too threatening in nature to be held onto and contained completely within a one-hour session per week.

2   Some kind of appropriate supportive structure needs to exist around the people living/caring for the individual, e.g. for material that may arise between sessions.
3   This depends on the nature of the support for the carers, including where relevant: adoptive parents; biological parents; foster parents; residential unit staff or similar system.
4   Appropriate support needs to be tailored to enable the carers to provide a secure enough base from which/within which the young person can explore/make use of individual therapy.
5   However, the individual therapist must have a capacity to hold onto the material, within the supervisory context.

Some therapists might argue that the individual therapy's capacity to hold entirely onto such magnitude of damage would equally be a reason for seeing the young person three or more times per week. However, this is not without potentially harmful side-effects in the context of a child's psychosocial development, for example posing obvious limitations on the child's availability to live a 'child's life' which is one of the things already damaged by the abuse experience.

It also might be particularly counterproductive to see the child very frequently for individual therapy, especially when working with a child whose experiences impede the development of new attachments. A particularly high frequency of individual therapy might effectively block any opportunity for developing attachments between adoptive family members.

MALE COUNTERTRANSFERENCE ISSUES

There exists a mythology that a male therapist should not see people who have been abused by male abusers – but there may be advantages in such a therapeutic encounter:

- The positive experience of a non-abusing male with the capacity to hold onto the potentially annihilating emotional material that arises from an abuse experience may be healing in itself.
- Transference is commonly gender non-specific, for example the male therapist will often be the object of 'mother' transference.

Therapists often have to work with their own revulsion and anger at the acts that may have been committed on their patient. They may also have to overcome their own fear at the nature of the unknown further disclosures that may arise during the therapy. This fear, if uncontained, may lead to a state of unbelief through the therapist's unconscious need to self-protect. This has parallels with children's self-protective withdrawal of allegations when the cumbersome machinery of the law intervenes. To avert one's gaze from the issues that arise from working with children who have been abused is to mirror the denial and gaze aversion, perhaps in the victim's own family system, that has allowed abuse to continue to take place.

In addition to the range of emotional responses that sexual abuse engenders in therapists, Male therapists may experience, in the countertransference, the guilt that should have been felt by the abuser. This countertransference guilt may be so overwhelming as to disable the therapist, perhaps as the abuser should have been disabled by guilt and thus prevented from actually abusing. The overwhelming magnitude of the guilt is therefore not useful in the context of the therapy. Such guilt should have been sufficient to prevent an adult from sexually abusing a child, even if they were so motivated, and hence may be strongly experienced by the therapist. This is perhaps especially the case given a presumption of the absence of such feeling being experienced by the abuser.

Female therapists may also experience this countertransference guilt, but this should be more readily identifiable to the female therapist, perhaps in supervision. The male therapist's countertransference guilt is compounded by being male himself, like the perpetrator. At the present time, the vast majority of convicted sexual abusers are male, and the idea that abusers are male is therefore our culturally received wisdom.

The guilt of maleness is a covert guilt because the admission of feelings of guilt might, in an almost inevitable pathological concretising of thought, be interpreted as guilt by fantasy, intention or association. Thus, the countertransference guilt experienced by male therapists becomes self-reinforcing, and must be recognised and worked with in supervision if the unconscious content of the therapy is to be constructive rather than destructive or negatively ruminative.

It would be alarmingly possible for the male therapist to be the unwitting reinforcer of destructive unconscious process in the therapy, by experiencing the guilt that belongs to the abuser. This could allow the burden of guilt to interfere with useful processing of those feelings in the therapy. Supervision is the proper context for such processing, where these loaded states may be safely contained and processed, and it is the duty of the therapist to be able to hold these feelings until the supervision session.

Where two therapists are working separately with one family system with different modalities, there are many potential systems and subsystems of relationships both conscious and unconscious. Some of this complexity is represented in the diagram of systems and metasystem in Figure 3.1, which also illustrates the container of supervision.

There are other issues specific to the male therapist working with this client group. One such is the fear that the therapist might also be accused of abusing the client, perhaps as a consequence of the transference itself. This demands good clinical supervision, good management supervision and clear unambiguous practice from the therapist himself. If such fear is not appropriately

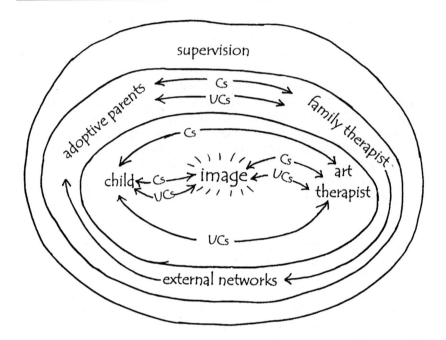

Figure 2.1   Systems in the metasystem (Cs = conscious, UCs = unconscious)
Source   Drawing by Mark Wheeler

managed and contained by the therapist, its presence will be experienced by the client, perhaps unconsciously, and may result in a therapeutic encounter that is more destructive than beneficial. Among the risks would be the possibility of reinforcing the post-traumatic elements of the client's experience.

Therapists working with children who have experienced sexual abuse may also experience very protective countertransference. This may be aggressively protective and include violent hostility towards the child's abuser. This hostility may also become generalised towards all abusers, which has particular implications for those therapists who also work with perpetrators. In male therapists there may be an unconscious attempt to drive out the countertransference guilt of maleness through the formation or expression of extreme opinions regarding society's treatment of convicted abusers.

THERAPEUTIC EPISODE

Identifying nomenclature

The terms 'biological mother', 'stepfather' and 'adoptive parents' have been used throughout this chapter to distinguish between the various parental adults in Amy's life, although at the time of referral their legal status was 'fostering with a view to adoption'. There were two therapists involved who will be referred to in the third person for clarity. The child's name has been altered for anonymity.

Amy always referred to her biological mother by her first name; she always referred to her adoptive parents as 'Mum' and 'Dad'.

Initial therapy at C&FT

An adoption worker made the referral to the child and family therapy (C&FT) team, after Amy had disclosed a history of sexual abuse by her step-father.

Therapeutic work was prioritised based on concerns about the placement breaking down in association with:

1 The level and nature of Amy's acting out distress following disclosure.
2 The nature and intensity of feelings evoked in the adoptive parents in response to the disclosure of sexual abuse, six weeks into the placement.
3 The feelings evoked by 'experiencing' Amy's emotional distress as, in part, expressed through her behaviour.
4 The feelings evoked in Amy's adoptive parents centred around themes of helplessness and powerlessness in being able to provide a secure base, and containment of Amy's feelings and their own feelings.
5 The adoptive mother's ambivalence in continuing to invest in the process of attachment.

The clinical psychologist carried out initial assessment, and some family therapy work was undertaken with both adoptive parents. From this it arose that there were particular issues for the adoptive mother, which indicated that individual support sessions for the adoptive mother would be the most appropriate intervention at that stage.

Initial art therapy sessions and development of transference

Amy was 9 years old when she was referred for art therapy. Prior to the first individual session the art therapist was introduced into a family session. In this forum explanations were made to her adoptive parents and to Amy together of the therapeutic and confidentiality boundaries. Amy clearly understood them and the explanation was repeated to Amy at the beginning of the first few sessions and sporadically thereafter.

The confidentiality boundary is a particularly difficult and emotionally loaded issue to explain in therapeutic work with child survivors of sexual abuse. Sexual abuse is often presented by the abuser as 'a special secret' between victim and perpetrator. The last man who used the word 'secret' to the child may have been the abuse perpetrator. The last person to use the word 'confidential' may have been a policewoman or social worker whose interview may have immediately preceded the break-up of the child's family. An explanation of privacy without catastrophe becomes a potential minefield at the outset of the therapeutic episode.

The art therapist began by exploring Amy's understanding of the reasons she had come to therapy. Children's understanding of why they have been referred is often very different from that expressed by parents, schools, or referring agencies. Amy's understanding was that she had been referred in order to help her settle in with her adoptive family, but she understood that she could make the broadest use of the sessions.

Amy explored the physical and metaphorical boundaries of the space during the early sessions. In the first session, once the formalities were over, she checked in the cupboards she had been shown, checked whether other clients' work really was kept private, and then quickly, but carefully, painted an idealised house image. The idealised house and home emerged as a theme that recurred throughout her therapy. At the close of her first session Amy used the wipeable white-board to write 'I love Mum' before inviting her adoptive mother, who she calls 'Mum', into the room to collect her.

Amy never talked directly about the abuse to the art therapist. She appeared to be concentrating her efforts in the individual therapy on constructing an alternative past and future. Amy had already been through a lengthy legal process during which she had to relive and describe repeatedly the specific and most unbearable details of her abuse experiences. Amy tested the therapist with guessing games and, as she began to trust the safety of the art therapy room, she developed a playful approach to the materials, to the therapist, and to the space.

In the therapy she was playing with the innocence of a 5-year-old – she wasn't merely rewriting history but creating and constructing alternative experiences she should have had at an earlier age. The first anniversary of her adoptive placement occurred during this period, which the family celebrated like a birthday.

Although Amy never spoke of the abuse overtly, the therapist's countertransference experience is evidence for her unconscious processing of these experiences. This will have arisen through the image making or through the play, in structure, content and inarticulate form. This countertransference response should remain separated from the therapist's own pathology in the countertransference. The therapist's own pathology may arise from previous work with clients who have suffered sexual abuse, and work with clients who may be perpetrators, and a priori emotional contexts including culture. The therapist in supervision needs to check that countertransference is indeed due to what is happening in the sessions, rather than being based on his emotional countertransference response to the a priori information that he will have gleaned from the case notes which contained details of the abuse.

The countertransference that is useful to the therapist in the session is that which arises from the session and from previous sessions. That countertransference which arises from any a priori knowledge of the case history may actually interfere with useful countertransference processing if it arises from material that is not actually that which the client is unconsciously attempting to process in the sessions. There are therapists who choose not to read the case notes in an attempt to avoid such issues, or to avoid responding to the perceived prejudices of other professionals which they believe may not be useful to them. They might, however, also inadvertently become prey to the countertransference responses of other professional colleagues with whom they inevitably liaise, which may be harder to identify if they are in ignorance of the case notes.

Milepost session

For this one session the processes were superficially unique to that session, but in the continuum of the therapy it allowed the therapeutic process to take off in a different direction.

A milestone is a traditional roadside marker that indicates how far the traveller has progressed but does not usually indicate any new directions. A signpost indicates potential directions of travel. This session indicated how far the therapy had come and was a signpost indicating which direction the therapy may now be about to take. It thus represents a milestone and a signpost, hence a 'Milepost' session.

The venue of the session was altered from the usual art therapy room to a family therapy room in another part of the building. This set up a potential for pathology in the therapist that he is a bad therapist. The session was a particularly wet, messy, painty session, and towards its close Amy asked for an item that she knew to be in the art therapy room elsewhere. The therapist went to fetch this material. The therapist was somewhat reluctant, as it is not normally his practice to exit the room on any pretext at all during any session. However he was perhaps overly anxious to please due to his own concerns about the room change. This errand took about five minutes. On the therapist's return, Amy was standing looking at her reflection in the large one-way mirror that is in this family therapy room. She had small dabs of blue-green paint on her cheeks and her hands were dripping with paint. On the therapist entering the room Amy turned to watch him enter, then turned back to the mirror then placed her hands deliberately on the sides of her face creating the form of a full beard.

Amy glanced back at the therapist momentarily and then completed the full form of the beard on her face. Her actions were characterised by excitable aroused gestures. In the same mode Amy quickly completed the image she had been working on before 'arranging' for the therapist to be absent. Then Amy turned to the therapist and flung paint at him. This was not the art therapy room and therefore not a space safe for the libidinous splattering of paint materials. The therapist felt abused and not safely in control of what was taking place.

Milepost session reflections

Due to the therapist's own anxieties about the change of venue, the transference and countertransference in this session were poorly contained. The therapist was not initially able to 'see' the symbolic significance of the mirror – both in the context of the therapy session itself and in the context of Amy's state of bonding. The therapist's automatic response was to 'blame' himself for the changed session venue rather than to consider the session's meaning for the client. The therapist was orientated toward his own guilt as the male therapist who had changed the venue, rather than recognising the symbolic content from the client's position.

The therapist, by abandoning Amy, evoked the opportunity for Amy 'to be' the abuser by repeating the absences of Amy's biological mother. Amy had made her face into a parody of a bearded face, with blues and greens, such that she could see herself simultaneously as herself and also with a personification of the abuser. She had then performed in the mirror a series of face pullings.

The therapist, by acceding to the request for the materials by Amy, appeared to be in a mode of acting to please Amy, like a child acting to please an adult. The absence and subsequent reappearance of the therapist thus also provides the further opportunity for Amy to become the abuser in the transference, but now with the therapist in a new transference/countertransference role as the abused.

The maternal mirroring components of Amy's infant attachment processes were almost certainly missing or inadequate with a biological mother who had schizophrenia. This was hinted at with the one-way mirror of the family therapy room – to be explored further with mask making in the immediately following sessions. Amy was also inviting the therapist to be her mirror. Hence the 'milepost' session indicated the direction that the therapy was about to take, the 'sign-post' element of 'milepost'.

Amy was trying to make sense of her abusers (later known to include her biological mother) despite the inevitably damaged attachment processes to her biological mother, and simultaneously to bond with her adoptive parents. Amy's bonding with her adoptive parents was therefore also inevitably impeded by material from her previous unsatisfactory attachments and her abuse experiences. Amy had no positive model to apply to her new attachments.

However, her enactment was an explicit if unspoken acknowledgement of the existence of the abuse and indeed the existence of the perpetrator in her internal world. To be able to make this acknowledgement, Amy's mode of expression and choice of medium (the impermanence of the paint on the face), is significant. The manner of her acknowledgement contrasts with the more typical permanence of the created art object together with its capacity to 'contain', which is more usually associated with art therapy. This, is combined with the temporary change of physical therapeutic space, implicitly stated that while such an acknowledgement is necessary it is indeed a transitional moment, enabling movement to another theme or phase in the therapy.

Amy chose to end her performance by flinging paint at the therapist, bearing out that there was a simultaneous expression of the transference of 'abuser' to the therapist. Thus, in this session Amy enables herself, through a mocked persona of her abuser, to re-enact alternative childhood experiences. During the course of the session she 'was' the abuser when she painted a beard on herself. This was misunderstood during the session at the time, as the therapist had a full beard and was unaware that the abuser had also had a beard. The therapist's experience of the session didn't make sense to him. A rational analysis suggested that the beard might represent the therapist and thus Amy's staring at herself in the mirror with the beard and gurning grotesquely was interpreted by the therapist in the context of being a 'bad therapist' for the change of room. The countertransference experience did not match his incomplete information, which was therefore being misinterpreted.

So in this session a tension existed between what was 'felt' by the therapist and what the therapist 'thought' about the experience. Thus in this instance the intuitive response to the countertransference was a more reliable indicator of what was going on, rather than the incompletely informed rational analysis of the actual events unfolding, although this should not be taken as a recommendation to become reliant on countertransference as the dominant instrument of analysis.

At a later time the information that the abuser had a similar full beard became known and the therapists had an 'ahaa' (pronounced with a descending imperfect cadence on the second syllable) moment. In the transference the therapist became the biological mother and the male abuser while Amy was simultaneously her own biological mother in the mirror. Amy had to be mother to herself in the past and also to be mother to her younger sister, it later emerged.

Play in art therapy sessions with children

Over several weeks Amy constructed a cardboard house which was large enough for her to sit inside. She frequently returned to this to make additions or to play games. The therapist would sometimes be allocated specific roles within these games; the postman delivering a letter; a builder; a neighbour. Play using fantasy, myth and imagination are seen as crucial to a child's ability to distinguish between fantasy and reality. Play also provides an opportunity to resolve emotional fears and conflicts in a safe way. When play is related to a source of anxiety it can provide safe expression and a consequent reduction of anxiety.

Within the context of the art therapy session, children's images and the creative process that produces them – along with the interpersonal processes that surround them (including play), and with the therapist, create the space in which the therapy takes place. Children are naturally playful (that is, full of play) and usually much less inhibited about this aspect of themselves than adult clients. Until adults impose a more formal learning structure, children's play is their principal mode of learning, both in a practical sense and an emotional sense. Inevitably this contributes to the unique character of art therapy sessions with children, regardless of their reasons for referral to an art therapist.

The experience within the therapeutic hour was at times enabling a capacity to explore feelings that would otherwise have remained repressed e.g. the different aspects of her feelings about her adoptive parents, both as adoptive parents, but also as individuals. Amy was trying to acquire nine years of learning about them, and trying to replace missing infant experiences and shared memories.

Final individual sessions

Amy had been struggling to hold onto the ambivalence of her love for her biological mother with the knowledge that her mother had 'failed' to be a good enough mother to protect Amy. She was simultaneously forming a new attachment to her adoptive mother as her mum. Thus by being able to hold onto the contradiction between her adoptive parents' struggle to be good enough parents and her idealised view of them, Amy might begin to be able to survive other contradictions in her biological family system. When Amy was trying to process her experience of her inadequate biological mother she was also forced to process the experience of being abused. This latter contradiction threatens an annihilation, which would also simultaneously have to be fought and defended against.

Now she was also facing the more constructive contradiction in processing between her experience of adoptive parents as perfect and their struggle to be good enough new parents. Amy was aware that we were planning to move from the art therapist providing the opportunity to work individually with her past, to both therapists working with the whole family system focusing on their future. This may have given her impetus to address other unresolved aspects of her history.

Amy related accounts of several dreams during the later individual sessions, which had some of the characteristics of PTSD (post traumatic stress disorder) in their presentation. In these dreams Amy's biological mother finds out where Amy now lives with her new family, and comes there and murders them all. Note that it is Amy's mother who is the aggressor, not her stepfather/abuser. Through these dreams Amy was able to give voice to her anxieties that the adoption date would not spell the end of her trauma.

Although the dreams are useful for Amy in that they allow her to give voice to some otherwise unspoken anxieties, they are destructive in their effect on her life now. The therapists felt that these symptoms may be long-term and potentially dangerous to Amy, but they might usefully be addressed in family work. This would empower Amy's adoptive parents to be able to face the long-term effects of Amy's abuse experiences which they had found too horrible to contemplate.

Amy created images that she named as her abuser. They were chaotic, messy and paint-laden. She asked the therapist to help her to cut 'bars' on one side of a sturdy corrugated cardboard box. Although superficially a practical request – for safety reasons younger children do not use the sharper modelling knives – the therapist's help was also symbolic. The paintings that she named as her abuser were shoved into the box, which was then thoroughly shut with glue and tape. The box was painted black on the outside and the paintings could be seen through the 'bars'. Some fragments of the original painting had been left out and Amy built a second 'jail' for them. Amy asked that they would remain at the clinic when she finished attending.

During one of the last individual sessions, Amy negotiated that she could make a gift for her adoptive mother which she could take that day. Amy asked that the therapist would make a safe decorative container for the gift. The family art therapy sessions were about to begin and Amy was marking this transition symbolically.

Parallel chronologies

The individual art therapy sessions took place weekly for 14 months. During this time the adoptive mother had individual sessions and parental counselling with the clinical psychologist. The whole family received support from the adoption service. The arrangements were made for Amy's adoption, with the consent of her biological mother.

In their continuing case liaison, the art therapist and the clinical psychologist observed the affect of Amy, following the effect of the individual sessions on the family system, and the effect of the adoptive parents' own family histories on Amy and the attachment processes. So, when reviewing our practice and mapping our parallel chronologies we realised that a recommendation for future practice would be to maintain parallel chronologies, in a clear easy to read form. This allows for continuous review/supervision for all the therapists involved, because patterns emerge of which each is individually unaware. Such an overview helped to clarify what we were working with at a given time. The indicators of such themes were sufficiently subtle for each therapist not to recognise them as salient points alone. Therefore the review of parallel chronologies would have to be detailed enough to spot these themes – perhaps this is an argument for joint supervision of the therapists by a third party.

Amy was not the only one experiencing infantile states. Her adoptive parents were experiencing her as a first child, as a new child, learning to react to her like new parents learning to react to a new first baby. Their reactions would be familiar to experienced parents. Amy's adoptive parents were learning how to be 'good enough' parents, just as Amy was learning how to experience a healthy 'good enough' childhood.

Both therapists may have unconsciously processed them as a new family and their reactions may have been important in nurturing their new parenthood, as one might do for one's friends and relatives under the circumstances of a new baby. The therapists therefore may demonstrate a joint counter-transference to the adoptive family system.

Therapeutic work within systems and metasystems

Wherever psychodynamic work is undertaken in such complex circumstances, the opportunities for transference splitting multiply. An awareness of the systemic context in which psychodynamic work is taking place will help the therapist to contain the transference, and to be aware of the potential diversity of transference phenomena.

Having identified and prioritised the needs with the family, the main points to consider as part of therapeutic processes were identified:

- To empower adoptive parents in effectively containing Amy's feelings. This was achieved in part by providing them with an alternative 'container' to address their own issues. This was to ensure that these intrapsychic and interpersonal dynamics did not overwhelm the nature of their relationships and affective responses to Amy.
- Clarification of roles was an essential aspect of the overall therapeutic work, this being with the adoptive parents, between therapists and between agencies.
- The clarification of roles ensured the maintenance of effective boundaries and containment. It also ensured that processes and structures in wider systems surrounding Amy did not replicate previous abusive experiences or patterns.
- Adoptive parents went from being 'not parents' to being parents under very difficult circumstances. Amy went from being 'not parented' to being parented, with all the negative baggage that went with this.
- The family therapy with the adoptive parents worked with the transitions being experienced as a result of their new constitution as a family and their planned change from being a foster family to the permanency of being an adoptive family.
- Key therapeutic goals were to facilitate their individual scripts being 'rewritten' – to 'being a child' and 'being a parent'.
- Work with the adoptive mother was an equivalent container to that of therapy supervision.

Family art therapy sessions

As the date for the formal adoption of Amy approached, the therapists felt it would be appropriate to end the individual sessions with her, and those with her adoptive parents. These would metamorphose into family art therapy sessions to combine the modalities of art therapy within a systemic context. The change in therapeutic milieu would mirror the transition from fostered child to a member of a newly constructed family system, and therefore symbolise the forum in which they would manage many future presentations of the long-term effects of Amy's past traumas.

Amy's adoptive father expressed similar feelings to some of those that had been experienced by the art therapist in the countertransference – anger towards the abuser, bewilderment about the motives for sexually abusing a child, a disabling sense of a lack of space for an appropriate adult male role in Amy's world. Amy's adoptive father also experienced a self-perceived inability to know instinctively how to respond to Amy's needs, as a male – for example how to hug a girl who has been sexually abused.

Finally, Amy decided to change her forenames as well as her surname when she became formally adopted. She changed her name from Amy to Zandra, alphabetically symbolic of being as far as possible from her past, and also from her abuser.

SUMMARY

• Male therapists can undertake work with children who have been sexually abused by men; indeed there can sometimes be advantages.
• The male therapist's countertransference has specific dimensions that, like all countertransference, need effective supervision.
• Where more than one therapist is involved in a family system, their liaison needs to be thorough, and note making should involve parallel chronologies to facilitate the identification of patterns and subtle indicators of process.
• In the progress of a particular therapeutic episode there may be a 'milepost' session, which indicate how far the therapy has progressed and what direction it is about to take.
• Therapy, with children who have experienced sexual abuse, is concerned with righting internal models/representations/imago and attachment, in addition to the post-traumatic features.
• The family scripts may have to be rewritten.
• Working with interconnected systems within a metasystem is an essential feature, if work of this complex nature is to be effective.

Chapter 3

Nobody hears

How assessment using art as well as play therapy can help children disclose past and present sexual abuse

Lyn Douglass

INTRODUCTION

In this chapter I will explore difficulties encountered when using a therapeutic model to gain evidence for a Social Service assessment. The statutory sector predominantly uses a systematic model because in the legal framework in which the work takes place, evidence plays a crucial role in determining outcomes and whether or not an abusive act has taken place. Consequently, a heavy emphasis is on verbal disclosure and social workers have great problems securing evidence with very young or very damaged children. In these situations, other models, namely the therapeutic, are used. However, using images or the language of play within the transference can create even more difficulties, as evidence could be viewed as ambiguous. I will present two cases where art and play therapy played an important role in assessments, but questions of validity still persisted.

Assessments

It is important to look at why a family or its members could be cause for concern with regard to the Children's Act and 'Working Together' guidelines (Department of Health 1994). In both the voluntary agencies and Social Services, a referral can be made about a child through school, health, police, family member or anonymously. All referrals are investigated to ascertain the validity or non-validity and whether action is needed by the department:

> The Local Authority has a duty to investigate when there is a reasonable cause to suspect that a child is suffering, or likely to suffer significant harm. The investigation will include an objective assessment of the needs of the child, including the risk of abuse and need for protection, as well as the family's ability to meet those needs.
>
> (Devon County Council 1998: 8)

Social Services will use assessments in and out of their district to determine risk to the child(ren) and implemented by the child protection plan (see Appendix 1.1). Assessments can be required from health centres, family centres and education in order to help the social worker with a comprehensive and holistic view. Care managers endeavour to work in partnership with families and many do acknowledge their problems and willingly co-operate. But there are families where conflict is apparent and problems here are often denied.

The objectives of an assessment are:

1   to ascertain if there is a risk;
2   if there is a risk, to consider the family's potential for change;
3   to assess whether the family will work towards change.

Theoretical models

Anyone looking on the library shelves of the therapy section will see a diversity of theories, some unrelated and some working in conjunction with each other. There are a number of articles which suggest that sexual abuse might be authenticated using only pictures as evidence. Yates, Beutler and Crago (1985) compared sexually abused children's drawings with a random sample of children referred to the psychiatric clinic. Cohen and Phelps (1985) tested to see whether incest victims' pictures exposed predictive characteristics in contrast with a control group. Both findings were not significant in proving sexual abuse. Social Services are understandably anxious to get evidence that a child, especially of a young age, is being sexually abused. However the product, particularly a singular image, can easily be seen as insufficient evidence, especially in a court of law.

The triad of the child, therapist and the art process can, at the very least, provide a space to initiate a relationship of communication. This can lead to the child expressing unconscious feelings and impulses using the art object as a transitional object. Play and art are important tools, helping to explore painful issues with the child where verbal expression is not forthcoming. I strongly believe that art therapy is able to fixate fluid plastic inner experiences and in the process of actualising them, put the child in a position where he/she may contemplate these perceptions in an objective fashion. Isolating the product from the therapeutic process can be confusing and misleading in securing evidence of sexual abuse. Interpretation involves not only the image but also material within the session. What happens if the product is lost? For example in Case 1, described later, the child found his creation too painful to preserve and destroyed it. By focusing only on the product, enactment of the abuse, through the transference, is lost.

In Social Services, suspicions that a child is being sexually abused by a family member are increasing. A referral frequently demands a quick assessment, with supporting evidence, to discover why a child is so distressed. The luxury of a long-term psychotherapeutic relationship is not always an option and a more direct and structured approach is used. As an art therapist I have studied and used both psychodynamic and systemic theory. My working experience has been of a strong, almost obsessive alliance to psychoanalysis; to work in any other way can be seen as being a traitor to the cause. Personally, I see both as tools in helping and supporting a child through pain. The following two cases are examples of a systemic and a psychotherapeutic approach.

Therapeutic tools used in the sessions

1   An open-plan dolls' house, moveable furniture and dolls, some complete, some damaged.
2   A mixture of monsters – dinosaurs, snakes and teeth aggressors.
3   Two-sided soft dolls displaying happy and sad faces.
4   A play TV, remote control and telephone.
5   Puppets, including Mr Punch, crocodile and the baby.
6   A sofa bed.
7   Access to water and sand.
8   A large plastic box which has a mixture of art materials including clay and face paints. This I carry with me at all times in and out of the Centre.

The materials are needs-led, dependent on the child's wishes, the presenting problem and the level of communication. The Centre also has a toy library, which to many children is an Aladdin's cave. Older children, perhaps developmentally starved or delayed, indulge in pre-school toys or allow themselves to mess with sand and water games. This in itself can support emotional and intellectual development. We also have games helping children to explore and express their social identity and relationships with others. I have used these board games at specific times in treatment when the child has a strong enough ego to acknowledge and appreciate those other than themselves. As stated, the materials are needs-led and I often borrow items from the playroom such as dressing-up clothes, which encourage role play. These can help the therapist to gain understanding of what occurs behind 'closed doors' in the family unit.

The first referral, a short-term piece of work, was initially concerned with behavioural problems of siblings. In the second case, the request was for individual work to assess risk of sexual abuse. Both cases resulted in grave concerns over the safety of the children and illustrate the enormous difficulties where the child's evidence can be seen ambiguous and/or deemed insignificant.

CASE I

Referral

This was a referral from Social Services. The parents were having tremendous problems coping with their children's behavioural outbursts. The boys had been adopted several years earlier. The parents were unable to sort out difficulties, as the children would not communicate what was troubling them. The family was at breaking point.

Initial assessment

As part of the assessment, I met with the parents. They had adopted the boys, aged 12, 10 and 8 years, several years before. They had always experienced problems relating to the children. Lately things had reached crisis point and the parents were threatening to put the boys back into care. I decided to meet with the boys for two sessions. I was made aware that communication would be difficult, if not impossible.

In this case I used the directive and strategic approach of circular questioning from the school of family therapy. The plan, after initial sessions with the children, was to work with the family. Social Services and the parents had labelled the boys as problems. It was important to get a better understanding of each child's thoughts, feelings and views. What was their story? On meeting each boy I asked if they had experienced any problems in the family. In this way the problem became external and decreased the conflict of who was responsible. I was curious to know what was each child's perception of his family, hereditary and adoptive. How did these past experiences map his present role in the family? There was no particular sequence or timing of questions. Each boy was asked about his relations to his brothers and two sets of parents.

The art process was non-directive, either becoming a catalyst or an interpretation of the child's conscious and unconscious feelings.

The children

Paul

I met with Paul, the middle child. He was cross. The parents had not told any of the children about the referral and they were confused. The first meeting is always crucial in order to gain some form of an alliance. It was important to offer honesty, empathy and choice. I suggested Paul used art as a way of expressing upset feelings. I encountered silent anger. Retaining his sullen expression, Paul began to work with clay creating a robot figure. Paul said the image lived in a field with cows who looked after him. He, in turn, devoured them. We made a cow together to keep the robot happy. While he worked,

Paul said he had always been angry. He talked about having no friends. As he attacked the clay, Paul said his birth mother ran away because she didn't want him. Words and emotions poured from him, as he pounded the material, sharing pain around relationships. Paul printed his name on a clay plaque. This he smeared, obscuring the letters. Paul said he stole from everyone and couldn't stop. He didn't know why. He felt he was the bad child of the family.

> Abused children swill around in a mass of compressed pain, of studied avoidance and of great grief, anger and fear. Inside this emotional cauldron swirl eddies of disaffection often born out of years of mistrust of the adult world, colliding with society's indifference.
>
> (Bray 1991: 11)

In the second session, the space was used for messing. Paul poured different colours of paint on top of one another. The result was a dirty muddle. As he poured, he talked about missing his birth mother, and in some way feeling responsible for the separation. The early relationship and loss seems to have marred any present relationships. Paul dealt with pain and anger by beating up boys, including his brothers. Paul knew that this was wrong but it offered a relief to him. The paint turned into a brown sludge and Paul became anxious. He wanted to know if his brothers would see me too? The sludge dripped onto the floor. Words slipped out of Paul's mouth as he disclosed that his brothers were sexually abusing him. He shared with me how the elder brother tried to bugger him and the younger sibling was attempting to copy him. Paul had experienced abuse in his early life. But more critical was the continuous abuse now occurring.

It is no wonder that Paul was unable to control angry feelings while abuse was and is prevalent in many areas of his life. I surmised that Paul had not separated from his birth mother and the grief had not been addressed. Paul was bewildered. He was lying, stealing, and was full of rage. His capacity to love was lost.

The clay image enabled Paul to connect with these inner feelings. The robot exterior, indicative of his relationships, defensive and unreachable, illustrates Paul's cut-off feelings. This image feeds off those who care for it; an omnipotence that destroys that which is nurturing him. These are some of the issues that the adoptive family has experienced.

Simon

Simon is the youngest of the children. I suggested we play Winnicott Squiggles, a technique where one partner draws a squiggle, which is made into a recognisable image by the other. Simon presented as a charming boy, eager to talk and join in with the game.

He drew a cartoon boy who smelt and lived in dung. Simon drew a rubbish tip and house for the boy. He said the boy was alone but happy. As he worked,

Simon talked about his brothers constantly hitting him. He said that he was not with his birth mother because she didn't like him. This creation could symbolise his perception of past and present worries – unsettled, distrustful of relationships and full of unresolved conflicts. The second image was made of clay. It began as a terrifying dragon, which quickly evolved into a cuddly cat. Simon made a water bowl and a mat for this image.

In the second session, Simon was impatient to begin, eager to tell! The dung boy became a clay model, which kept falling apart. Simon said the cat was the boy's friend. The boy had no legs but a very long nose. Its shape resembled a penis. We sat and looked at it for a while. The distress had been actualised using the materials and process. I wondered with Simon what feelings had been evoked? There was silence. Then Simon disclosed that his big brother had tried to sexually abuse him. He said that his brother tried to pin him to the bed and force him to have sex. Simon was frightened and unhappy. When I told Simon that Social Services would be informed, Simon looked relieved. I wondered why he had not spoken about it with anyone else? Simon said he thought nobody would believe him. He ended the session painting a sea with landscape calling it heaven. Simon, through creativity, had found a way of making sense of the past and present muddles. I, within the transference, was a good enough mother.

'Only if there is a good-enough mother does the infant start on a process of development that is personal and real' (Winnicott 1965: 17). Simon was able to be explicit as to the abuse he was experiencing. I had yet to meet his big brother.

Peter

Unlike Paul, consumed with anger, and Simon, desperate to talk, Peter presented as amicable but lacking warmth. My presence was regarded with indifference. Unlike his brothers, he was not eager to work with the art materials and myself, showing little eye contact. For half the session, Peter attempted to solve an intricate puzzle with pieces missing. I talked about why I was seeing him and his brothers and wondered what memories he had of his birth parents? His only recollection was of hiding from them. He said he felt nothing for them. Peter gave up on the puzzle and began working with the clay. His first image was long and rigid in structure. He continued with the clay, wanting to do a duck, which he changed into a man. Neither depicted his ideas but resembled the shape of a penis. Peter stared at it and became upset. I left the session feeling sick. Within the transference, I had been left with uncomfortable and abusive feelings. Back in the Centre, I needed to regurgitate Peter out of my system.

In the second session, Peter although resistant, was more vocal, presenting as rather fragile and vulnerable. While he worked, again in clay, he commented that he had said too much in the last session although he had spoken very little. After more discussion, Peter thought I knew what he was thinking. He created a male snake and stuck a baby next to it. While he was creating, he became very demanding and controlling, telling me to shut up although I was silent. He said the snakes were going for a walk. This need to shut me up was linked to Peter shutting himself up and his desire to control himself and me. Through the clay emerged a truer representation of some of the fears Peter was experiencing, and perhaps past abuse suffered. Within the art process, males are perceived with distrust and perhaps are threatening. They also go away. There is also a lack of integration just like the puzzle. Females fail to protect by not being there or not seeing the danger.

Outcomes

As part of the initial assessment, I immediately contacted the care manager with my concerns over the children:

1   Risk of sexual abuse by one sibling to another.
2   The children had not fully separated from both birth parents, resulting in developmental and emotional delay.

Because of this information that the children could be suffering significant harm, Social Services convened a strategy meeting (see Appendix 1.2). This happened 10 days later, bringing together agencies from school, parents, police, family centre and Social Services. The meeting decided:

1   The family needed an allocated care manager.
2   I would end the sessions with the boys and hand over the case for specialist treatment.
3   I would meet with the parents to share information of the allegations of sexual abuse between the children.

It was agreed not to call a case conference, and my concerns that the children were 'suffering significant harm' as defined by the Children's Act were met by closed ears. I visited the parents and was met with a torrent of anger from the father. He had informed professionals several times about the inappropriate sexuality and abusiveness of the boys. They had inferred that boys will be boys, with the behaviour being normal. It was not surprising that this family were in the throes of despair. They were promised a complaint form.

After three months, I still had no communication with the statutory agency. The family had been allocated a new care manager who had overlooked my involvement. After many phone calls I was informally invited to a review meeting. I have to conclude that if I had been less tenacious, this would not have occurred. 'There were particular difficulties in the planning of initial protection action in cases of sibling or peer sexual abuse. In these cases the agencies were uncertain how to treat children who were both abused and abusing' (Farmer and Owen 1995: 68).

Up to this point, I felt that neither the family nor I had been taken seriously. The parents were just holding the family together. The objective of my initial assessment was to use the process of art therapy to investigate any child concerns. These were highlighted and 'Immediate Protection' (see Appendix 1.1) should have been enforced.

At the review meeting it was discovered that instead of specialist treatment, the children were placed with unqualified intervention workers. The boys had remained silent. After much discussion, the meeting concluded that a child protection conference was vital to address the needs and risks of the children.

Eventually a risk assessment was undertaken. Simon and Peter were considered a risk to others in terms of their sexualised behaviour. It was recommended that treatment should be undertaken with the whole family.

This case illustrates that although disclosures, whether verbal or using the art process, are successful, they are frequently met with resistance and denial from the statutory sector. What has been striking is the blinkered attitude of failing to acknowledge that sexual abuse between boys occurs. In some quarters, it is still viewed as sexual exploration. That women abuse children has only recently been recognised and a similar pattern of disbelief followed. In order for these children to develop 'normally', agencies need to concentrate their energies on the early identification and treatment of boy victims, who as a group have greater potential to become abusers, rather than trivialising any allegations.

Hollows states 'The overwhelming denial of the problem by managers takes two fairly distinct forms. The first is a direct denial, which minimises the behaviour or dismisses it altogether. The second is less direct, with managers paying lip services to recognition of the problem but offering no resources or support to deal with it, forcing the child or adolescent to be responded to under some other more acceptable heading' (Bentovim, Vizard and Hollows 1991: 67).

CASE 2

Referral

The initial referral was for an assessment of the parenting ability of the parents. However, it was found that the father was a convicted sex offender so a full risk assessment of the family was required. I was requested to work with a little girl, age 3 years, to explore any concerns that could be affecting her. I planned to see her for four sessions before the case conference. I used a psychotherapeutic approach.

Hannah

The child was brought to the Centre by her mother. Rather than stay with her, Hannah was very eager to go with me, a complete stranger. Once in the room she rummaged through my art box, hurriedly taking bottles of paints in her arms. Within a few minutes the table was littered with an assortment of materials. There was no eye contact. Hannah chattered but made no sense. She urged me to make the colour pink. Brushes and rollers were used frantically. Paint was showered onto all surfaces and her face was stained with red paint. The black paper resembled an intangible muddle. Hannah pushed boundaries to their limit. I was compelled to restrain her for her own safety and the upset paint became upset tears.

Once the art materials were cleared, Hannah ran randomly from one object to another, settling with the dolls' house and the baby dolls. She began piling furniture up against the doors in the house. She said that it would stop the monsters getting in. At the end of the session I took her back to mum but Hannah refused to stay, clinging to me. Her mother showed no reaction. This was to become a pattern for all four sessions.

The second session was very different. Chaos was replaced by sadness, the frenzy by an upset self. The mess continued but there was an element of structure. Hannah had brought a life-size teddy bear that acted as an important support and go-between. Her relationship with this ally was gentle and loving. She talked to me through the teddy. There was still no eye contact. Hannah wanted to paint. She made a mark, then a smudge, creating mess after mess. Each clean piece of paper was placed over the mess, creating layers of muddles. Hannah cleared up the mess and moved to the play kitchen, making a meal for teddy, Hannah and me, the nourishment replacing contamination. My role was as an observer. 'Very young traumatised children may wish to explore or to play with the materials on their own, disregarding the therapist' (Sgroi 1988: 293). Large tea parties were executed so that lots of Hannah's friends could attend. The session finished with water play and a cleansing process of dirtying and cleaning occurred, rather like a ritual. Hannah told me how much she loved her daddy.

At the start of the third session, I offered Hannah cake and a drink. She declined. The symbolic nurturing continued as she made a cake out of clay. I was now allowed to help. The cake was cut up into many pieces and seemed to represent Hannah's disconnected feelings. Within the transference, I felt isolated and cold. Hannah talked about her mummy never playing with or cuddling her. It was not easy but it was important to hold onto this emotional content until the time was right to share it with Hannah. At the end of this session, Hannah asked for some cake and wolfed it down hungrily. She cried when the session ended and she had to leave.

In the last session, Hannah began to play and talk with me. She whispered that her mother took away her clothes, forcing her to stay in her bedroom. I suggested we play 'All about me' which is a board game around feelings. One of the questions was 'What makes you frightened?' Hannah whispered that she was frightened of long things that come out at night when she is in bed. She held this card for the rest of the session.

Before and after the case conference, I shared my concerns with the care manager that this child was at risk of being sexually abused. The difficulty in working with a young child who also has a speech impediment, as Sgroi states, is that 'a child who is that young (3–5 years) frequently lacks the verbal and conceptual skills required for investigative interviewing to have validity' (Sgroi 1988: 72).

Hannah had talked about the lack of warmth and isolation from her mother but she had also spoken about her daddy playing with her at night and of long things that come out in the dark. There was also the episode with the dolls' house. There were indications that Hannah was in a vulnerable and unprotected position. I had concerns regarding her emotional as well as her physical state.

At the case conference it was concluded that there were serious issues around parenting, acknowledging there was little bonding between mother and daughter. There were also worries around safety and protection. For example Hannah would frequently run away. Punishment was harsh with physical abuse being the norm. Father minimised the several sexual offences against children he had committed, demonstrating little or no victim empathy. He presented a whole range of excuses to let himself off the hook and justify his action. For example, he said that his 9-year-old victim used her sexuality to trap him.

The decision of the case conference, although acknowledging these concerns, was that the therapeutic material was inconclusive. More sessions were sought with Hannah to secure more evidence. The child was to remain at home with her parents. Uncovering established secrets in distressed children requires great care not to fall into the trap of being pressurised to produce quick changes. I agreed to continue the work, but at the child's pace! For the next nine months, I became a container for Hannah's messes.

In the sessions some past themes continued and others were added to the repertoire. In our relationship, I experienced an overwhelming abundance of affection for Hannah. 'The children in our care, in so far as they have a need for therapy, are going through phases in which they go back (or experience for the first time with us) the early relationships which were not satisfactory in their past history' (Winnicott 1965: 16). I felt like a surrogate mother, watching and at times being allowed to share the play. Messing and cleaning were sustained and Hannah would tentatively note my response, checking to see if I was understanding the symbolism. The early sessions had been preoccupied by dirtying and obscuring drawn images of herself, possibly expressing her own nothingness. Hannah continued smearing with the paint so that the initial image was lost. She added glue to this play, attempting to stick not only paper but also herself to walls. This was followed by a process of washing, pouring water from one container to another. Alongside these processes was the theme of hoarding toys, which she gravely clutched to her person.

In the tenth session, the initial chaos reappeared and a new storyline entered the space – role play. Hannah became the 'good mummy' and I became the 'bad daddy'. She reversed these roles frequently. During these sessions, Hannah would become the aggressor and soiler, using myself as the container for these feelings. While in role, Hannah was the autocratic parent, unwilling to work with me and knowing best. There were many splits in these themes – the good and caring parent who is loving versus the aggressive tyrant who wants to abuse until it hurts. These divisions reflected not only the family but also the child. Hannah had talked about her relationship with her father as warm and affectionate. But she had also described, with terror, monsters kissing her at night.

As Sgroi states, 'sexual attention is frequently the only form of affectionate physical intimacy experienced by the child at home. Although the mother may provide the child with discipline and physical necessities, there is often an absence of affection and emotional bonding between them' (Sgroi 1988: 16).

When I tried to gather more information on these monsters from Hannah it was blocked. 'For the therapist to demand explanations too early can be to rob the client of her own process. We must have confidence in the process and wait' (Schaverien 1987: 85). In the subsequent sessions the role play altered. I was the child and Hannah the disciplinarian. She projected her negative feelings onto me. Whatever I did was wrong. Her voice became angrier and louder. With the transference, I was not good enough. I felt anxiety and exasperation. I wondered with this child whether she had also experienced this onslaught of attacks? Sadly she nodded. Further sessions became quite guarded with Hannah saying and doing little. The conversation about fathers was now absent because he was in the session. I had become Hannah and she, her father. I was ignored and rejected. In the twelfth session, Hannah said that the monster had gone. She followed me around like a puppy.

In the following session, Hannah made a white tissue baby. She placed it on white paper, stating it was full of colour. I wondered with her whether her problem might be that people, especially me, could not really see what was worrying her? This was reciprocated by Hannah painting bright colours and a red cross, which she named ambulance. Again, this child was giving lots of clues, describing her vulnerable state. At the end of this session, Hannah refused to leave. As it was the end of the day, a colleague at the Centre was pulling down the blind. Hannah ran and locked herself in the toilet. I wondered what the link was between closed blinds and abuse.

Outcomes

It was becoming increasingly clear that this child, for two possible reasons, was being put in an impossible situation:

- Her developmental stage: 'because children were small, they did not possess the intellectual maturity to process what had happened to them. A large piece of the jigsaw was missing because they had received distorted information which itself held no meaning' (Bray 1991: 44).
- Safety: Hannah lived at home. Would it have been too dangerous to unblock the energy around the secret?

As with any agency, this case was shared and discussed with all workers. The project's feelings mirrored the powerlessness and hopelessness of the child. There were further meetings with Social Services, which resulted in a strong divide between the agencies. One side believed there was insufficient evidence to take further action to protect the child. If this path was enforced but the result was unsuccessful, it could result in the child being more at risk. The family could easily move out of the district into obscurity. The opposing side voiced alarms that there was sufficient evidence, gained through the sessions, and had grave concerns about the child's safety.

Although the child had not clearly voiced whether she had been abused and/or who was abusing her, she had demonstrated that she was not being protected (see Appendix 1.1). We were all on the same side, but at times it felt like two opposing political parties, as muddled as Hannah. Finally it was decided to work with the non-abusing parent, and put safety and protection strategies in place as well as help with parenting skills. The individual sessions would end.

In our last session, I explained to Hannah that I had heard her worries, and that the care manager and I would be meeting with her mummy and daddy to try and make things better. As already stressed, we did not know who was the offending party but it was critical to instigate a protection procedure. Work continues. The relationship between mother and daughter is gradually becoming better and Hannah is clearly more contained. My colleagues and I are convinced that sexual abuse has occurred, but legally there is not enough evidence for a conviction. This little girl had experienced two Camat interviews, which are joint investigations by police and social workers using interviewing and video recordings to secure evidence of abuse. Unfortunately, both were unsuccessful in securing a disclosure. This is a common occurrence in very young children.

CONCLUSION

I have explored in detail difficulties encountered using a therapeutic tool either to convince an agency that sexual abuse is occurring or to gain relevant evidence to secure a place of safety for the victim(s). What is visible is the distress these children are experiencing.

If a child is physically or sexually abused, then they are also emotionally abused, but many children suffer neglect of their emotional needs through rejection, humiliation, lack of recognition of their right as an individual and this can impair their functioning and integration as a person.

(Cattanach 1993: 107)

Resources are seriously lacking in this field, both financial and of expertise. There is an urgent need to meet the growing demand of the large population of children who we suspect are being abused. There is probably a larger number whose secrets have not reached our ears and eyes. We know that the statutory sector has an arduous job in trying to get it right. Young children have a voice, but sometimes that voice is not heard. Professionals, inundated with high-risk cases and mountains of paperwork, seek proof, which is sometimes out of the reach of a child's vocabulary and the victim falls through the net with abuse continuing.

So what needs to be done? The legal department has to rely on sound evidence to protect and safeguard the child, as well as some adults. It is the validity of this evidence that has been debated. If we merely demand a verbal revelation, children will stay at risk, but research, using pictures as indicators of sexual abuse has not been seen as providing significant evidence.

Rubin states 'Even if it turns out that one's initial guess about meaning was correct, one should not assume that any image "always" means something specific, not even that its significance is invariant over time for any particular person' (Rubin 1984: 128). As therapists conducting research, we are reticent about using tools on which other disciplines, in their working practice, might depend. We may be cautious about the use of objective methods and statistical evidence in an area characteristically involving subjectivity and emotional material. Nevertheless, we can gather evidence with our own models such as images, pictures, photographs and video recordings of therapy sessions.

Children constantly use recurring themes to tell their story. By recording and categorising these 'clues', we can begin to corroborate evidence. Briggs and Lehmann state, 'When pictures are used in conjunction with behavioural indicators and verbal discussion they can be valuable in the early detection of sexual abuse' (Briggs and Lehmann 1989: 14) Art and play therapy are important tools in giving the young a tangible voice so that their distress and pain can be heard.

It is important to work within the system in order to educate other agencies and help re-evaluate the different insights gained from the child's internal and external world. Defences of denial and splitting by Social Services might not be eradicated, but better alliances could be negotiated, the result being a better service for the child.

REFERENCES

Adcock, M., White, R. and Hollows, A. (1991) *Significant harm*, London: Significant Publications.

Bentovim, A., Vizard, E. and Hollows, A. (1991) *Children and young people as abusers*, London: National Children's Bureau.

Bray, M. (1991) *Sexual abuse. The child's voice*, Edinburgh: Canongate Press.

Briggs, F. and Lehmann, K. (1989) Significance of children's drawings on cases of sexual abuse, *Early Child Development & Care*, 47: 131–47.

Cattanach, A. (1993) *Play therapy with abused children*, London: Jessica Kingsley.

Cohen, F.W. and Phelps, R.E. (1985) Incest markers in children's artwork, *The Arts in Psychotherapy*, 12: 265–83.

Dept. of Health (1994) *Protecting children. A guide for social workers undertaking a comprehensive assessment*, London: Author.

Devon County Council (1998) *Multi-disciplinary handbook*, Author.

Farmer, E. and Owen, M. (1985) *Child protection practice. Private risks and public remedies. Studies in child protection*, London: HMSO.

Rubin, J. (1984) *The art of art therapy*, New York: Brunner/Mazel.

Schaverien, J. (1987) 'The Scapegoat and the talisman: Transference in art therapy, in T. Dalley, C. Case, J. Schaverien, F. Weir, D. Halliday, P. Nowell Hall and D. Waller (eds) *Images of art therapy*, London: Routledge.

Sgroi, S.A. (1988) *Handbook of clinical intervention in child abuse*, Lexington, MA: Lexington Books.

Winnicott, D.W. (1965) *The family and individual development*, London: Routledge.

Yates, A., Beutler, L.E. and Crago, M. (1985) Drawings by child victims of incest, *Child Abuse and Neglect*, 9: 185–9.

APPENDIX 1.1

Working together:
Stage of child protection plan

Recognition of abuse

↓

Referral to appropriate agency

↓

Investigation

↓

Initial assessment

↓

Immediate protection

↓

Initial child protection conference

↓

Decision about registration

↓

Protection plan

↓

Implementation and further assessment

↓

Child protection review

↓

Post protection work

↓

Deregistration

APPENDIX 1.2

Assessing 'significant harm'
(from Adcock, White and Hollows)

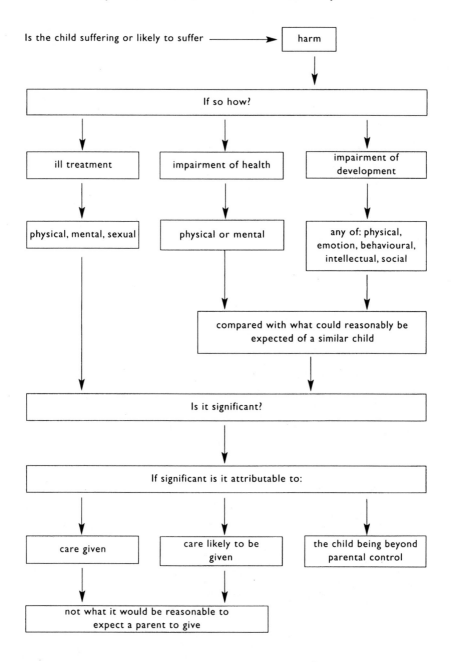

Part II

Working with individuals

Chapter 4

Using the reflective image within the mother–child relationship

Maggie Ambridge

The starting point for this chapter is the ongoing experience of working with abused children and their parents. It looks back to the valuable testimony of adult survivors and the expositions of concerned professionals, and forward with hope for a better response and outcome for children in the future. The theoretical context is illustrated by accounts from the interwoven histories of abused children and parents, some of whom were abused themselves as children.

MY MUMMY WITH A BIG MONSTER

It is the first meeting with 4-year-old Lucy; she has been referred to the Child Sexual Abuse Project because of emotional problems expressed through self-comforting sexualised behaviour. Lucy is drawing with wax crayons while her mother talks to a therapist. As she talks, Lucy's mother shifts from describing her daughter's behaviour to reflecting on her own childhood, and on finding herself listened to, perhaps for the first time, begins to disclose her own experience of trauma. Meanwhile, Lucy produces a drawing which she describes as 'Mummy with a big monster' (Figure 4.1).

In their play and art, children frequently express truths that their parents experience as inexpressible, and which may have lain dormant for many years. Time and again in work with children, themes emerge linking the child's experience with issues for the parent, and the parent's own memories of childhood experiences may be awakened by the child's current issues. Resonance between child and parent occurs frequently in parallel sessions with therapists. Six-year-old Sally had an individual art therapy session while her mother, Andrea, talked to another therapist in a different room. De-briefing afterwards revealed that while Andrea had been talking about her own very early childhood memories, linking and comparing these with her mothering of Sally, Sally herself had painted a picture of a baby in a pram pushed by her mother. In the same session, she chose to play with a set of Russian dolls, again echoing the baby–mother continuum in the doll figures, each held

Figure 4.1   My mummy with a big monster

within another from baby to adult: the mother who is able to hold and contain in her own body each stage of the growing child.

Abused children, along with their own trauma, may be holding and manifesting the burden of their mother's distress. For an increasing number of therapists this confirms the importance and significance of working not just with the child, but with the non-abusing parent or carer. The discovery that their child may have been, has been, or is in danger of being abused frequently triggers suppressed feelings or memories of abuse from the parent's own past, which need to be addressed in order to enable her to protect and heal her child.

Working in parallel with child and parent can help in understanding both and creating a wider picture. The resonance between mother and child occurs again and again – it is there if we are able to recognise it, and time for reflection on the session is essential, especially between co-workers.

Six-year-old Jenny's first drawing in an individual session was 'Mr Topsy-Turvy's house', in which, as she told me, things are opposite to normal. As she drew, Jenny said 'Sometimes I get into a muddle and put things in the wrong place.' She explained that Mr Topsy-Turvy spoke in opposites: 'He's got to say hello for goodbye and bye-bye for hello.' The inference was that Mr Topsy-Turvy had no choice – he's got to whether he wants to or not. In her own separate session, Jenny's mum, Sharon, talked of severe physical and sexual abuse to herself perpetrated by Jenny's father. At this time she was facing a dilemma of not wanting her daughter to have contact with him, but feeling she had to agree to this to comply with the court. She had to say yes, but really meant no – a situation for both of them that Jenny had already suggested in her Mr Topsy-Turvy picture. Topsy-Turvy talk is something that sexual abuse victims are well acquainted with, being thrown into a world where no means yes and yes means no, where every apparent reality has its corresponding opposite and where one can rapidly change to the other. Feelings about the abuser shift and co-exist confusingly: 'I hated him – I loved him'.

In her next picture, Jenny drew members of her family. She was reluctant to draw her dad at all, but when she did, he was separated from the others with a line excluding him – a kind of encapsulation. Cathy Malchiodi (1991) gives a definition of encapsulation as some type of graphic enclosure round something else in the picture, separating that person or object from everything else in the picture. She also quotes Cohen and Phelps (1985) who suggest that enclosure within an object or space may be an indicator of incest. Malchiodi goes further, saying, 'In some cases, the perpetrator is encapsulated by the child rather than the image of the child herself. This, too, may represent another way to separate from and protect oneself from the offender.' (Malchiodi 1991:156) Seen in conjunction, the mother's statement and the child's image alert serious concerns about the issue of contact.

THEORETICAL CONTEXT

My experience of working first with adults abused in childhood and later with mothers of abused children from the mid 1980s onwards, engendered an awareness of links between adults' and children's experience initially from the adult's focus. A trigger for a mother as a child approaches the age of her own abuse causes her to recall her own experience and make links between her inner, wounded child and her actual child. An internal struggle then ensues, between not wanting to remember, and needing to remember enough to both heal herself and be a protective mother. Group art therapy with survivors produced images and poetry that make real a communication, resonance and empathy between adult, child and inner child. Early in her therapy, a survivor who was also a mother determined to protect her child, made a powerful image of her resistance to painful memories (Figure 4.2). She went on to write a poem which both expresses the pain of the child's later knowledge, when as an adult she unlocks the memory of things she could not have understood as a child, and seems to rail at the abuser and the adult world in general for allowing such obscenities:

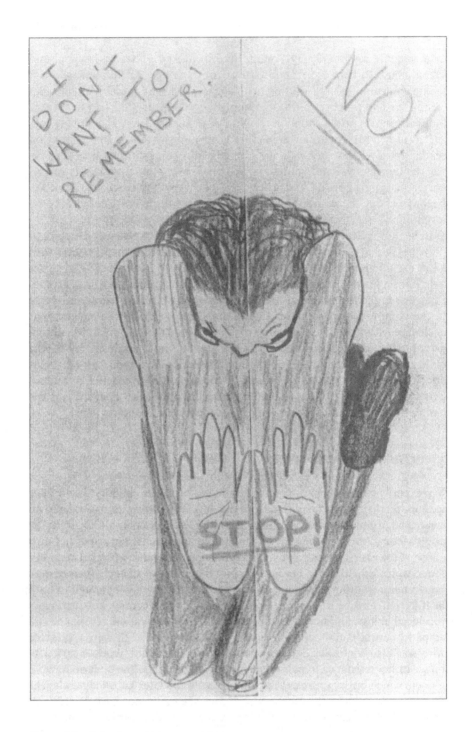

Figure 4.2 I don't want to remember

The adult knows
what the child has suffered
before she knew what words
    like

        come

           penis

              suck

                  meant

                    before she knew anything . . .

From around this time, the value of parallel or dyad work with mothers and daughters to address sexual abuse was being acknowledged and documented. Suzanne Long describes work with the child's mother as 'an integral part of treatment' saying 'she needs a great deal of support and nurturance. She generally needs a therapist for herself . . . She may be one of the many mothers who were molested themselves as children, and their own issues as a victim may have been reignited' (Long 1986: 231). Jane Silovsky and Toni Hembree-Kigin (1994: 5) citing the work and experience of other therapists say that

> enhancing the mother–daughter relationship often is a component of treatment. The daughter is frequently angry with her mother for failing to protect her, and in some cases, for not believing that the abuse occurred (Furniss 1983, 1987). The daughter's anger toward her mother is at times greater than her anger toward the offender (Furniss, 1983).

These are important observations, for, in our clinical experience of direct work with children, irrational anger towards the mother is often an indicator of hidden abuse. This leads clinicians to advocate the joint treatment of mother and daughter to focus on the issues of the loss of trust and the re-establishment of emotional bonds between them (Ribordy 1989, Timmons-Mitchell and Gardner 1991, Silovsky and Hembree-Kigin 1994). Silovsky and Hembree-Kigin also echo Long in recommending concurrent individual therapy for the mother, especially when she is a survivor of childhood sexual abuse (Silovsky & Hembree-Kigin 1994).

Addressing issues for mothers of sexually abused children, Maralynn Hagood (1991: 17) quotes Serrano regarding mothers who were themselves sexually abused during childhood:

> Her child's victimisation frequently brings up issues previously unaddressed or repressed by herself. It is of utmost importance that such mothers work through their molestation issues. (Serrano, 1989).

She goes on to talk of the defences used by mothers who flee from the knowledge of their daughter's molestation by 'blacking out', by literally leaving the household or by becoming suicidal, although reporting that in her clinical experience these women were in the minority (Hagood 1991: 18). Many family situations are, nevertheless, compounded by mothers who were abused subconsciously choosing a partner who is then abusive to their child. This can evoke sexual jealousy of the child and even dislike of the child which is very difficult to acknowledge.

Through the turmoil the mother can usually find a way of relating to a child who is herself a victim, but, when the child is male, and especially if he may also be disclosed as a perpetrator, this can evoke an even greater mass of conflicting, ambiguous feelings in the mother – how can she relate to a son whose very being mirrors the abuser? Sandra, the mother of a boy and a girl, expressed concern about her relationship with her 7-year-old son to whom she was unable to show affection because he was male, saying, 'As far as I'm concerned, if he's male he's going to grow up to be an abuser.' Not allowing herself to relate normally to her son was a form of self-protection. Sandra was aware of what she was doing but was unsure whether this was provoked by the boy's behaviour or her perception: 'I'm punishing him for what they've done to me. It's not fair, but it's easier – keep him at a distance, don't spend time on him or give him attention.'

As therapists, we continue to learn more of the complexities of relationships between child and non-abusing parent, and the effects on the therapeutic process. As is always the case, we learn most from those with whom we are engaged in direct work – the families themselves, in listening to and observing them. However, in reflecting on and responding to these observations, it is helpful to be able to refer to a theoretical framework. The present study is informed both by elements of attachment theory and current understanding of dissociative states. Bowlby brings together both theories when he describes his concept of 'defensive exclusion', a process by which external stimulus that might lead to the recall of unpleasant memories or painful emotions is excluded from consciousness' (Bowlby 1980: 45). Attachment theory addresses dyadic patterns of interaction; there is a fundamental link between the study of sexual abuse and that of disrupted attachment, with dissociation being the third side of the triangle. There is a paradox in the cases of mothers of abused children who are both unable to protect and, at the same time, determined to protect their children. This paradox is related to the phenomenon of dissociation which enables someone to both 'know' and 'not know' – a condition that produces a kind of paralysis of not seeing and not knowing which can only be shifted by the integration of experience into acknowledged reality. If something is not referred to it remains hidden. In the resonance between child and mother, in the unconscious metaphor of a child's drawing, that which is hidden sometimes becomes visible.

John Byng-Hall states that in the area of parent–child relationships, parents either 'try desperately to prevent what happened to them as children from happening to their children when they reach a similar age . . . or their memories are blunted and sensitivity to what is going on is reduced, but their behaviour is, nevertheless based on the assumption that the same thing is about to happen' (Byng-Hall 1991: 208). This describes almost exactly what we see happening in relationships between abused mothers and their children. In clinical experience the mother is often both trying desperately to prevent a repetition of her own experience, and at the same time her memory or her sensitivity to what is going on is reduced, causing her to miss the very thing about which she believes she is being vigilant.

Thus, one mother, Jan, feels she is 'doing her best' for Emily, her daughter but is, in her words, 'in the dark'. In a prolonged pre-disclosure process in which they both worked hard to enable experiences to be brought into conscious reality where they could be acknowledged, Emily on more than one occasion painted a 'big black hole' which she needed to climb out of, but sometimes fell into, corresponding to her mother's feeling of being 'in the dark'. Helping the child to reflect on her images at each stage helps to move the metaphor into reality and enable it to effect change. In one picture, Emily's black hole is surrounded by a garden, and around it and to each side of it is a path. Above is a blue-black sky and a large moon. On the path in the moonlight stands Emily. In the session I wondered aloud where Emily might be going. Emily said that she was walking away from the black hole and not looking at it. If she looks at it, it sucks her in again. When she was inside, it was very frightening, and to get out she had to hold on to something and pull herself out. The way in and out of the black hole was through a garden of flowers, grass and leaves. This image, full of sexual symbolism, as well as the darkness which engulfs and hides the truth, became a vehicle for Emily to refer to her distress and to find a way out by eventually disclosing to her mother, who even before understanding it, responded to the urgent message in the image.

At certain points in the therapeutic process a child's images may echo, in a very fundamental and primal way, her relationship with her mother with reference to their mutual but unshared secret. In another pre-disclosure painting, Emily appears to be attached to her 'black hole' by a line like an umbilical cord, while another egg-shaped black object has detached itself from the black hole and is floating into the sky. Meanwhile, her mother, also egg-shaped, and pregnant-looking, stands by. Both mother and child have expressions of consternation, but are looking away from each other (Figure 4.3). Another child, Amy, who will be referred to later, made a 'secret bag' on which she painted a face with shocked expression and hair standing on end, and wrote the words 'Do not open'. Inside the bag she placed a painting, which she made and cut out, of an incompletely formed baby in a foetal position clasping a blue, placenta-like cushion (Figure 4.4). These two images have some shared themes and references. One of these is about an unease or even fear of communication – symbolised by the averted gaze in one picture, and the instruction to keep the contents secret in the other. There are also visual references to the pre-birth state; mother and child physically (and emotionally) unseparated, the child as yet unable to function independently. There

Figure 4.3   Emily, mum and the black hole

is both the desire to remain in this state, and the inevitability of the eventual process of birth (of understanding, disclosure, individuation) however difficult and painful.

Mothers may often believe they are acting protectively while blocking out the real events that are too painfully close to their own experiences – thus the knowledge of their child's abuse comes as a genuine shock compounded by guilty feelings that they should have known. These feelings may be reinforced by relatives and even professionals who say 'How could she not know?', thereby upholding the myth of the collusive mother, but there is increasing persuasive evidence that the state of not knowing is genuine and perhaps more complex than has previously been understood.

Phil Mollon says: 'Dissociation involves an attempt to deny that an unbearable situation is happening, or that the person is present in that situation' (Mollon 1996: 4). Sometimes we seem to be looking at a situation where a mother is denying the child's unbearable position, by telling herself, for example, as in the case of Jan and Emily, that the situation is different from her own – the child is younger or older, the abuser has changed, or some other variable. But perhaps a part of her is able to conduct a different dialogue with the child, in which the unresolved pain of the survivor's inner child resonates with that of her own daughter.

Figure 4.4 Secret bag with baby inside

BALANCING THE PROCESS BETWEEN PARENT AND CHILD

If the indications are positive, and a mother is able to respond to her child's post-disclosure needs, then she can attend to her physical child and her inner child (the hurt part of herself that has not been resolved), enabling both to work towards achieving integration of traumatic experience into conscious reality and allow subsequent healing. As in the case of Jan and Emily, therapy can continue for both in parallel, with the focus on enabling mother to take on the primary role of support for the child, while receiving enough help for herself (and her inner child) until she feels fully confident to resume full adult/carer status. Emily's disclosure to her mum was especially devastating as she named a relative – the same person who had abused Jan. The fact that Jan immediately confirmed that she believed and supported her daughter was the best indicator for a good outcome. So Jan began attending therapy sessions for herself to address unmet issues from her own childhood trauma, while Emily continued with her own individual play and art therapy sessions as well as additional joint appointments for both. During this time, Emily painted a further picture which featured her recurring image of the black hole. This time it appeared as a cloud floating above the heads of herself, her sister, her mother and her therapist – the latter two Emily having insisted paint themselves in her picture, perhaps as acknowledgement of their obligation to her to stay involved in the process (Figure 4.5).

Complex issues are involved in the maternal response to the abuse of her child; these are indicated in the following extract:

> There is evidence that a substantial proportion of mothers of sexually abused girls were themselves sexually abused as children (Faller, 1989; Goodwin, McCarthy, & Divasto, 1981). Women who were abused as children often have difficulty in establishing positive relationships with their children (Cole & Woolger, 1989) and these compromised attachments may make it more difficult for those mothers to respond to the stressor of sexual abuse with a supportive focus on the child's safety and needs. Clinicians have observed that parents' own unresolved abuse issues can disrupt their ability to demonstrate an adaptive, child-centred response to the victimisation of their child. However, there has been little research on the ways in which the mother's history of sexual abuse and/or childhood attachment experiences could affect her provision of support to her sexually victimised daughter.
>
> (Leifer et al. 1993: 756)

Figure 4.5   The cloud begins to float away

Leifer et al. (1993) go on to say that from their own study, 'current maternal functioning is more strongly related to mothers' response to their daughters than is maternal childhood history' (p. 763). This is borne out in our experience that well functioning mothers, even though they had not recognised that abuse was occurring, were able to respond appropriately and supportively once the abuse was disclosed, and part of this response was the willingness to engage in concurrent therapy for their own abuse. The fact that some mothers present their children for therapy for symptom-based problems while still unaware of or denying abuse, and continue to work through and beyond disclosure, echoes Byng-Hall's theory that 'their behaviour is, nevertheless based on the assumption that the same thing is about to happen' (Byng-Hall 1991: 208).

So, where the mother is able to respond to the child's need and her disclosure, she can cope with parallel therapy and attend to both. Others, however, are unable to take on what their child is saying to them before completing their own therapy, which can in itself be an awakening to recognition. Then, mothers like Sandra who had been in therapy for several years, are better able not only to hear what their child is saying, but to bring it to the attention of professionals they already know and trust. When parents have experienced their own trauma, they need help to deal with the suffering of their own children. As Ray Wyre has said, 'Strong hands are needed to rescue children who are being abused' (Wyre 1998). It is not always possible for first and second generation abused parents to do this for their own children.

We frequently encounter, among the families referred to our child abuse project, mothers and children who are fleeing an abusive situation. Amy, 9, and her mother, Pat, moved from Scotland to escape from Amy's father who had been physically and emotionally abusive to Amy, and sexually abusive to Pat. He was also known to have previous sexually abusive behaviour. Here, the mother had succeeded in rescuing her child physically, but the trauma and stress both had experienced in this process meant that when we first met them a reflected feeling of chaos and helplessness was experienced by the therapists involved. Mother and daughter were enmeshed in their mutual need and fear, resulting in a parental child and a frustrated, angry and dependent mother.

The needs of the mother and child in this case were: to separate from enmeshment, to each have her own story, for mother to be protective, and to break out of the cycle they were in. The first task was to help Amy to play and be a child, and for Pat to be the parent. Amy's early images regularly included hearts and flowers and messages of love (and of need) to mum, indicating both her own protectiveness and her own neediness and insecurity. At this time, Amy saw herself as at least as powerful as Pat, holding a great deal of information about adult issues and therefore feeling the burden of responsibility for putting things right. She spoke of decisions being made mutually, as though she were her mother's partner. It was only after a year of therapy that Amy was able to express verbally her fear of being left to look after herself and her inability, as a child, to cope with this.

Often, the therapists working with mother and daughter experienced similar feelings in sessions – a physical sensation of extreme weariness and inability to be effective was significant at one stage. In our experience, this can often be a sign of dissociative states in the mother or child – no real feelings are expressed in the verbal account of what ought to be very distressing experiences. In this situation, non-verbal work may give clues to the more negative feelings. Pat's story indicated a parallel enmeshment in her own life, with her father. Life difficulties continued; a struggle to acquire housing and an independent way of life, to combat depression, separate emotionally from her ex-husband, and to understand the meaning of her daughter's difficult behaviour. For a while, Amy's images reflected her experience of what was going on – in heated telephone exchanges, mother's distress, helpless disembodied heads, all unable to act. Later, they began to echo the struggle to create order – shapes and patterns that could be balanced and matched, or had a possibility of this – but their resemblance to playing cards was a reminder that the outcome could still depend on chance: a game of patience that took time to reach resolution, with no guarantee of all the suits being neatly completed. Then, as if coming out of a fog, both therapists reported new contrasts and expressions of affect. Communication took on a new clarity and authenticity. Some relationship problems were acknowledged, and therefore began to be addressed. A year on from referral, Amy had regressed into a playfulness in her creativity which, paradoxically, allowed her to grow. She produced a succession of fresh, experimental and original images of which she was in control. From then on there was less urgency to use images as gifts or offerings to placate her mother, and more challenging and potentially confrontational images such as the baby in the secret bag (womb) took their place.

A different challenge is confronted in work with adolescents and teenagers, who often want to keep things quite separate from their parents and expect a good deal of confidentiality. (Apart from the life-stage of the young person the reasons for this can be complex, associated, for example, with issues of resentment over perceived failure to protect and precocious maturity associated with abuse.) Rachel, 15, maintained an ambivalent and at times antagonistic attitude towards her parents, who, over an extended period supported her treatment by making sure she attended appointments, but only having occasional involvement with the therapists in the project. Even this limited contact can bring valuable insight to the intervention. Rachel had worked creatively with image, metaphor and story, through some very complex issues, referring not only to past experiences, but also acknowledging and gradually allowing help with the resolution of a continuing abusive situation. Control was very important to Rachel, and she repeatedly reminded adults that she needed to feel as powerful as they did, but also needed them to be strong enough to help her. Images emerging in her work have included knives, walls, locked doors, barbed wire, and an allegory of a child being lost to its parents; contrasts between strength and vulnerability abound. In just one meeting with her mother several of these same images occurred as real aspects of the girl's past experience of which for a long time her parents had been unaware – for them, a long experience of locked-in feelings when they didn't know what was going on (the child lost to her parents) (Figure 4.6). The parent treads a delicate balance regarding the space to allow an older child. Push too hard and the young person withdraws. Step too far back and she feels let-down, frightened and angry.

A younger adolescent, Natalie, who found herself unable to directly back up a disclosure by a younger sister, elected to have her mother present for a number of her therapy sessions. Here she worked hard, using puzzles, questions and clues to make her position understood and to make sure the adults stayed engaged with the issues. Natalie devised games in her sessions which involved asking questions of her therapist or her mother. In some of these questions she was asking us to think about her sisters being scared and talking about sex. In another session, this time on her own, Natalie drew pictures in the form of a comic strip with images of each sister in a different situation, each one saying she was scared of something. In the follow-up family appointment, Natalie showed this to her mother who felt that this made sense and that there could be reasons why each of the girls was scared.

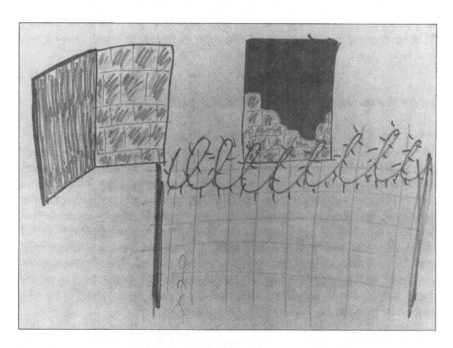

Figure 4.6 Brick walls, barbed wire and lost child

Again in this family, a to and fro process is involved. The children's distress triggered something for their mother, Lynne, who presented her children for help. Meanwhile, in her own mind, a complex struggle was ensuing – enabling her to know, yet not know (or acknowledge) what was happening. At first she disclosed a clear link with an experience of her own, then quickly set that aside in an attempt to find a more palatable explanation. (One that, however, involved self-doubt and self-blame, and made her distrust her own instincts about her ability and need to protect her children.) When Lynne found a counsellor for herself, this noticeably improved her self-confidence and enabled her to work with her children and reassure them of her belief in them and her support for them.

If a mother is able to engage in her own process – which includes becoming open to the possibility of her child's abuse, as well as acknowledging her own experience as abusive – this enables the child to engage too. This is a two way process: the child's distress pushes the mother to a position of having to act; the next stage may involve the mother's resistance to linking her own experience with that of her child. When this is gradually overcome, it is possible to move forward, working with a mother who is stronger and better able to help and validate the child. In Lynne's case, the process of disclosure by the younger daughter, Hayley, released the child's anger towards the abuser in her artwork (notably obliterating her father's face with a black handprint). She then found the courage to express her anger directly in a contact session. Her mother subsequently became empowered to express her own anger directly. Thus, in therapy, Hayley expressed the anger in metaphor which then became real behaviour.

LEARNING FROM MOTHERS AND SURVIVORS

While working with mothers of abused children, alone and in groups, significant issues for them are aired which we ignore to our cost as professionals and to the cost of the children we work with. Some mothers say that they value being asked if something has happened to them. This both validates their experience – saying it makes it more real when someone finds it hard to trust their feelings – and recognises that they may need help for themselves as well as their child. It can be easier (we hear) for a mother to deal with her child's pain than with her own, but healing is hard to achieve if a remembered experience is then ignored and the story left unfinished. At least an acknowledgement of the part played by her own experience helps the mother to talk about and deal with her own feelings of guilt, and, most importantly, may enable the integration that is vital in breaking the cycle.

Jan explains what it was like to have blocked things out for such a long time that it enabled her to discount possible dangers to her children: 'I tried to make it a separate issue – pushed it to the side. I told myself I had no choice . . . if I did feel it properly I'd sink.' Being asked directly and helped to acknowledge it came as a huge relief to her.

Something frequently mentioned by adult survivors is feelings of shame, and mothers who were themselves abused can recognise this in their children. Shame is more than embarrassment. It's related to self-blame, but there is an extra dimension. This is illustrated with shocking precision and clarity by Joyce Carol Oates in an account of a 'shaming prison visit' in New Jersey where she experienced 'the female terror of becoming an object of male sexual desire, prey.' The episode itself was forgotten for many years until triggered by a chance remark. Oates concludes 'Shame is the emotion that most effectively blocks the memory. Amnesia is the great solace, the most available form of self-protection' (Oates 1998: 199).

I refer to this because I think it is necessary to acknowledge the importance of the accuracy insisted on by these women to describe their feelings. If Joyce Carol Oates' account is used as a model, then shame can be directly and silently transmitted to a victim by a look, a posture, or any act of abusive contempt and thereby prevent disclosure as effectively as any verbal threat.

Listening to parents can give us clues about what is going on for the child at a similar stage. A mother, who as a child, had herself received treatment at the same unit returned at the time of intervention for her own daughter, a bright, charming and likeable child, but one who was disturbed and had clearly been abused; what was unclear was by whom. The girl's mother recalled her own therapy sessions and other professional intervention as a child, saying, 'I lied . . . nothing would have made me tell.' This kind of retrospective vision can help to inform our work with children and especially adolescents who go to some lengths to remove themselves from an abusive situation and make themselves safe, but are then reluctant to disclose any information.

As we gain experience of working with second and third generations of abuse, it becomes clear that we are looking at a sophisticated and complex model of abuse and family roles. Carol Sagar describes the influence of 'especially that collusive aspect which mothers can unconsciously or half-consciously adopt . . .' which, 'although passive, actively colludes with the abuse' (Sagar 1990: 97). The model of treatment, too, needs to reflect this complexity, while resisting falling into the trap of mother blaming. Clinical experience indicates that there is often not simply a lineal development by which a mother works through her own abuse and is thereby able to address her child's trauma. It may be a parallel and sometimes alternating process by which mother and child may respond to each other, and at times wait for the other to catch up. In significant ways they can unstick each other.

The process may go something like this: A mother says she is prepared to listen to, accept and believe anything her child says but if, while she is saying this, she has (albeit unconsciously) closed, or never opened her mind to the possibility, has already decided that it couldn't or didn't happen, then the child will not be able to tell or be heard. She can only say what she knows her mother will hear. At this stage there may be an escalation of acting out and attention-seeking behaviour in a desperate (and again unconscious) bid to hold mother's attention and make her listen, or see what is wrong. The exasperated mother, now at the end of her tether, concentrates on stopping the behaviour, and at worst rejects the child. This is the most difficult stage to stick with, but it is important to do so because both are now exposing the raw feelings which, if acknowledged, can be worked with rather than closing the wound and going back into denial. Again relating back to attachment theory this is, as in early bonding, the time a mother needs encouragement to hear the child's (baby's) cry and respond with confidence that she can help. Our role as therapists is to enable healing to take place between them. We are often told 'She just needs someone else to talk to – she won't tell me anything.' Therapy that involves parent and child can enable dialogue between them, putting the focus back where it belongs, so that the healing goes on in that relationship.

CONCLUSION

There are important resonances to be picked up in the process between parent and child in therapy, and these can be facilitated by the special and unique quality of art therapy that can enable a child (or parent) to express in image that which is otherwise inaccessible to either or both of them directly. These resonances can often be most usefully recognised and brought into play by the use of sensitive and reflective parallel co-working. Linked to this are the important skills of observation, listening and reflection.

We recognise the value of co-ordinating the timing of bringing experiences into consciousness, keeping the mother alongside the child, and letting her be the child's healer where possible, as well as maintaining some control for the child. This process is critical in building confidence of each in the other for the future.

Our role is principally in enabling the parent and child to hear each other, and to do this we have to continue to advance our understanding of the complex processes that are going on. We also need to remember that the healing process is theirs, not ours, so that wherever possible we neither take responsibility and ability away from the parent nor deprive the child of the mother as primary healer, carer and protector. In attachment theory terms, we allow space and time, in a safe place, for the parent to create, perhaps for the first time, a secure base for the child, to replace the insecure, ambivalent, avoidant or chaotic attachment pattern created as part of the abuse dynamic.

As this generation of mothers learn to heal and protect their children, the task for the therapist, looking towards the future, is to enable both parent and child to achieve sufficient individuation and integration to be better equipped to prevent their grandchildren and children from enduring a repetition of their pain.

REFERENCES

Bowlby, J. (1980) *Attachment and loss, Volume 3: loss: Sadness and depression*, London: Penguin.

Byng-Hall, J. (1991) 'The application of attachment theory to understanding and treatment in family therapy', in C. Murray-Parkes and J. Stevenson-Hinde (eds), *Attachment across the life cycle*, London: Tavistock Routledge.

Cohen, F.W. and Phelps, R.E. (1985). Incest markers in children's artwork, *Arts in Psychotherapy*, 12: 265–83.

Cole, P.M. and Woolger, C. (1989). Incest survivors; the relation of their perception of their parents and their own parenting attitudes, *Child Abuse and Neglect*, 13: 409–16.

Faller, K.C. (1989) Why sexual abuse? An exploration of the intergenerational hypothesis, *Child Abuse and Neglect*, 13: 543–8.

Furniss, T. (1983) Family process in the treatment of intrafamilial child sexual abuse, *Journal of Family Therapy*, 5: 263–78.

Furniss, T. (1987) An integrated treatment approach to child sexual abuse in the family, *Children and Society*, 2: 123–35.

Goodwin, J., McCarthy, T., and Divasto P. (1981) Prior incest in mother of sexually abused children, *Child Abuse and Neglect*, 5: 87–96.

Hagood, M.M. (1991) Group art therapy with mothers of sexually abused children, *The Arts in Psychotherapy*, 18: 17–27.

Leifer, M., Shapiro, J.P., and Kassem, L. (1993) The impact of maternal history and behaviour upon foster placement and adjustment in sexually abused girls, *Child Abuse and Neglect*, 17(6): 755–66, New York: Pergamon Press.

Long, S. (1986) 'Guidelines for treating young children', in K. MacFarlane and J. Waterman (eds), *Sexual abuse of young children*, London: Cassell.

Malchiodi, C. (1991) *Breaking the silence, art therapy with children from violent homes*, New York: Brunner/Mazel.

Mollon, P. (1996) *Multiple selves, multiple voices. Working with trauma, violation and dissociation*, Chichester, UK: Wiley.

Oates, J.C. (1998) After amnesia, *Granta*, 63: 188–200. [First published in full in *The Ontario Review*.]

Ribordy, S.C. (1989) Treating intrafamilial child sexual abuse from a systemic perspective, *Journal of Psychotherapy and the Family*, 6: 71–82.

Sagar, C. (1990) 'Working with cases of child sexual abuse', in C. Case and T. Dalley (eds) *Working with children in art therapy*, London: Tavistock/Routledge.

Serrano, J.S. (1989) 'The arts in therapy with survivors of incest', in H. Wadeson, J. Durkenand and D. Perach (eds) *Advantages of art therapy*, New York: Wiley.

Silovsky, J.S. and Hembree-Kigin, T.L. (1994) Family and group treatment for sexually abused children: A review, *Journal of Child Sexual Abuse*, 3(3): 1–20.

Timmons-Mitchell, J. and Gardner, S. (1991) Treating sexual victimisation: Developing trust-based relating in the mother–daughter dyad, *Journal of Psychotherapy and the Family*, 28: 333–8.

Wyre, R. (1998) [Quote from interview on BBC Radio 4 (October).]

Chapter 5

Into the body

Sand and water in art therapy with sexually abused children

Ann Gillespie

On a wide beach or in a box in a playroom, sand is greeted enthusiastically by children everywhere. They scratch designs into its surface, dig down into it, build up forms and castles, bury things underneath; it can be soft, warm and powdery, damp and firm, sometimes hard, cold and heavy. Amorphous, soft and pliable, it offers in both its visual and tactile qualities a perfect medium

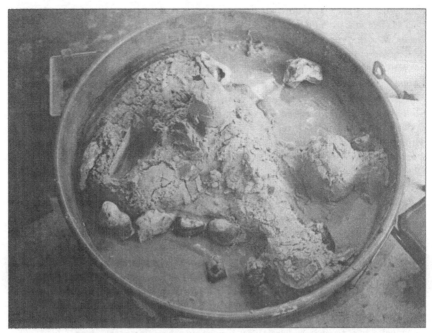

Figure 5.1 Into the body: Messing about with sand and water is an activity beloved by most children. This chapter discusses how, in an art therapy situation, the physical sensations and imaginative images offered by these substances can transform this 'ordinary' play into an opportunity for a child to explore complex body issues connected to their sexual abuse in an unthreatening and undifferentiated way

for the projection of images, dreams, fantasies and feelings. Very often water, the first play substance of an infant, is added from the sea, a puddle or a tap. With it rivers, lakes, seas, oceans can be made, the sand can be made mouldable into forms which are then dissolved – swamps and delightful soggy areas can be created. Children are drawn to play with these two universal materials naturally, wherever they find them, almost it seems with a sense of coming home. They are after all, along with fire and air, the elemental 'primary substances' of the earth, 'archaic mother symbols', with whom powerful and primitive links are made and retained throughout life (Balint 1968: 68).

In this chapter I am going to concentrate on the use of sand and its therapeutic potential in work with sexually abused children. I shall explain why, when used in the protected space of an art therapy hour, it is so important in enabling children to experiment freely and spontaneously with complex and undifferentiated body issues. The special soft quality of the sand seems to draw children to seek out skin sensations that reactivate, and are closely associated with, infantile and primitive responses and memories which would be beyond the reach of pictorial or verbal imagery. I have written elsewhere about the strong connections made with the mother body through play with the elemental substances, sand, water and fire (Gillespie 1990), and perhaps this unconscious connection to the archetypal mother image supports children as they explore their bodily abuse.

I shall draw on my 10 years' experience of working with children who had all been permanently separated from their parents due to multiple abuse and neglect, and who had endured a history of care orders, court cases, and many failed placements in institutional and foster homes. The small residential unit where they now lived was a 'last hope' placement, with the aim of breaking the cycle of abuse and rejection and preparing them to join a carefully matched family with a view to eventual adoption. Given their chaotic lives to date, with their dismal history of rejection and their difficulty in making workable relationships, this was an ambitious and often heartbreaking task.

As art therapist, I aimed to offer the children a space that was less goal-oriented, a place to explore the more unconscious, undefined and un-namable feelings and memories that surrounded their separation and abuse. For many of the children sexual abuse was already proven, but for others it was often not clear whether, amid the general abuse and deprivation, actual sexual abuse had taken place. However, all of the children had been through a great deal of probing and questioning about both painful facts and feelings, and needed some space where they could rest in the assurance that they would not be pressured into areas they were fearful of or did not understand. Certainly I felt that the non-directed art therapy hour was one of the few times where they could have the freedom to be themselves without facing evaluation or pressure to change towards being 'acceptable' to a new family, and especially without having to focus, yet again, on their sexual abuse.

There are so many complex issues involved in this specific form of abuse that one cannot know for sure what aspect is currently causing pain and confusion. It may be that the child is not even at the stage of remembering, let alone 'thinking about' what has happened to them (Alvarez 1992: 153), and that this becomes possible only by a gradual process. In my particular experience the most urgent questions often seemed to be, 'Where has my family disappeared to?' or 'Am I going crazy?' or even, 'Who am I supposed to be now?' Perhaps the major catastrophe for these separated children was the loss of the body of their birth mother, and was at least as pressing a concern for them as their sexual and other abuse. In any case, offered the open but protected space of the art therapy hour, children like these often seem to know unerringly, even though they cannot tell you about it, which areas of their damaged internal life need attention. Not of course that any area can be isolated from the rest in an overview of their situation, but they must be allowed to work through these many problems at their own pace and in the order that is right for them.

The finality of the separation from their parents and other carers removed the possibility of work being done with the whole family dynamic (Sagar 1990: 106) leaving the children carrying the whole burden of failure and blame. In addition, they currently occupied a kind of refugee status, waiting in limbo to be sent off somewhere else, and living in a very uneasy state of transition between a rejecting past and an unknown future. Without a secure and permanent background, each child was extremely vulnerable and probably too defended for direct verbal confrontation with the fundamental problems and tragedies they faced.

It seemed that very often even pictorial representation in the non-judgemental space of the art therapy room was too much of a confrontation for them, and I was initially filled with self-doubt and frustration at their refusal to engage at all with the art materials on offer. It seemed that maybe because it appeared to them that everything they had been part of had been destroyed by them, some children considered it preferable not to complete or even begin to make something rather than witness their inevitable failure to keep that object whole and good.

In order to engage therapeutically with these reluctant youngsters, I had to adapt my ways of working to minimise the sense of failure and defeat, and to avoid confronting them with a more or less explicit expectation of anything having to emerge from or survive the process, to be scrutinised by themselves or by me. I had noticed their frequent and spontaneous attraction to the sand tray and to water from the tap, and how absorbed they were when playing with these substances. I became aware of the extraordinary range of ideas, emotions and enactments that could take place simultaneously and at great speed in this kind of play, and also that there was often a 'feel' to these involvements that seemed to have to do with body issues, even if there was no visual or verbal indication that this was so. It was clearly in their bodies that the pain and confusion of their abuse was stored, rather than more explicitly in words or visual images.

Children who have been sexually abused have suffered a physical violation of their bodies in the breaching of the boundary between their insides and outsides. Such a physical challenge to the integrity of the body threatens the child, as a living organism, with annihilation. It thus constitutes severe trauma, leaving a lasting mark that is inscribed in and often on their bodies, and calling into question even the child's relation to living within a body (Young 1992: 91). The sensory perception of all deprived and abused children tends to become anaesthetised as a way of blocking out the memories and associated distress of traumatic events. In extreme cases of continual sexual abuse and or violence, complete dissociation from the body is commonplace, with the victim learning how to 'go numb' or to 'float out' of the body in order to avoid the pain (Young 1992: 92). It seemed that this problem with embodiment was central to the existence of so many of the children I worked with and explained in part their tragic lack of a sense of self.

> Perhaps one cannot achieve and maintain 'personhood' without full access to one's body, without the felt experience that 'this is *my* body', meaning both that it belongs to me, and, given my total dependence on it, that I cannot be me without it.
>
> (Young 1992: 95)

As I observed the intensity of their play with sand and water, it became clear that the special bodily qualities of these substances could become a vital means of engaging and working with these children. The many skin sensations available to them through the play would enable them to receive experiences of skin stimulation coming from the non-self (the sand and water), thus affirming the existence of that very self which is experienced in and through the body. Here, with no demands and almost no expectations, they could begin to discover for themselves a wide range of tactile experiences and to re-awaken dulled senses, even gradually to allow the existence of sensations that might trigger the memories of abuse stored in body tissues. I found that some children seemed to need the qualities of the sand desperately and used it week after week, while others used it interchangeably with enjoying and working with other materials in the room.

In my discussion of this work with sand I shall not be including the method pioneered by Margaret Lowenfeld in *The world technique* (Lowenfeld 1979), and developed with a Jungian perspective by Dora Kalff and other sandplay therapists today (Kalff 1980, Ammann 1991, Mitchell and Friedman 1994). In these methods the emphasis lies on making a picture in a shallow rectangular sand tray of specified size, using miniature objects chosen from a huge selection representing aspects of the physical, emotional and spiritual worlds. Kalff's viewpoint is that 'the sand picture which is produced by the child can be understood as a three-dimensional representation of some aspect of his psychic situation'. The arrangement of objects in the sand creates the 'ancient language of symbols' and this in turn provides the healing influence (Kalff 1980: 24–32). Relatively little has been said about the use of the sand itself.

But it is this very aspect of the physical interaction with the sand that fascinates me, and through my work I evolved a method of play in which the focus is on the therapeutic significance of the children's actions in terms of the experiential qualities of the sand and water, rather than on the symbolic meaning of the toys and sundry objects that were often incorporated. It was incidental, but maybe advantageous, that the sand tray I inherited happened to be circular. Though others will disagree, I personally found the shape without corners and four separate sides created less expectations of making a picture and was more conducive to the indication of body forms and ideas. Because it was larger and deeper than that used for sandplay techniques it held a greater quantity of sand and the child was involved physically, pushing their hands and arms into it, feeling themselves to be part of the substance, and at least as aware of the texture and temperature as of the visual effect. It is these physical properties of the sand and water that offer such important opportunities to child and therapist in terms of working with bodily abuse. I will summarise them now before introducing case material to illustrate some of the work.

First, sand is malleable and easy to manipulate, responding in a non-threatening, but not fully predictable manner. Thus it offers an opportunity to the child to play with ideas and forms with minimum physical difficulty and restrictions. It can be made into firm smooth shapes or churned up into rough textures. Holes are dug and filled in, mounds made and demolished. Divisions and separations can be made with walls or ditches, and sand can be built up and tunnelled under. Sand (with water sometimes added) offers the possibility of fast and repeated transformation and can become in a child's fantasy a landscape, a body, a cake, a bomb, and back again in the space of a few minutes. The fleeting sand forms can be left ephemeral and hazy, as there is no pressure to define them. They can be named or not, and the names changed according to the child's feeling about them, the therapist, and the internal images they may be echoing. Thus it is possible to do many things at one time, to give expression to something that does not have isolated meaning.

Play with sand and water also offers a release from expectations of skill, meaning, or art object making, and this is invaluable when trying to engage with certain children who feel threatened by anything that will in their eyes reinforce their lifelong failure. The ease and speed with which sand can be manipulated soon encourages the urge to make and build, and this helps to liberate otherwise inhibited creative activity. It offers a child the chance to experiment with the structure of their own world or objects in a fluid and completely individual way, free from the predetermined forms, meanings or expectations of other materials.

Because of their mobility, sand and water also have their limitations regarding control and manipulation, especially if too wet or too dry, and these too afford experiences of trials and errors, surprise and disappointment, which give opportunities for accepting and creatively adapting to change. Whatever attacks are carried out in the sand, however, the substance remains unchanged and recuperable, providing reassurance about the child's own fantasised powers of destruction and its effects. Its indestructibility is therefore one of its most important properties in this work.

Although in reality exterior to the child, the substances are so amorphous and infinitely changeable that they seem to become almost merged with the child. Sand goes through many changes of state, and the child receives constant feedback from the varying sensations of touch and temperature, as well as vision. As the hands touch, stroke, pound, clutch and burrow, they form a bridge between the child's own body and the body-like properties of the sand. Hands connect the inner and the outer worlds, and enable unconscious energies to take visible, touchable form (Ammann 1991: 2, 34). It seems there may be a two-way transfer of sensation and stimulation, so that not only are the emotional states of the child transmitted through the hands into the material, but they then see and feel the sand differently, are stimulated by its changing state and are able to use and modify the forms and textures that appear, which in turn will stimulate new feeling states, and so on. A multitude of skin sensations occur which are clearly fascinating to the children and which, in an unthreatening manner, lead the children to experiment with body forms, body memories and bodily sensation and feeling. This happens in a very direct, physically concrete way, but at an undifferentiated level of mental functioning.

Experimenting with the undemanding qualities of sand and water seems to encourage a more diffused state to come into being. This enables a process of withdrawal from the external world with the possibility of making an internal space in which memories, fantasies and conflicts may arise, be experimented with and reviewed over and over again. It relates to the self-absorbed quality of toddlers in play, which deprived children such as these often cannot achieve. In touching and manipulating the sand, children seem to relax at once out of the need to have a clear goal, and eagerly grab the opportunity for non-product-oriented and non-achieving activity that 'play in the sand' offers. My notes written at the time describe a little girl, aged 8, finally giving up her fruitless struggle to construct a cardboard house and,

> she goes and sits by the sand which today is very dry and powdery, puts both hands in it and spreads her fingers. Instantly all the agitation that has been in the cutting, fixing and glueing, melts away. She picks up a spadeful of the soft sand and lets it run down through the hollow handle. 'Its like a timer,' she says to me. She does it again, saying to herself, 'How many minutes've you got left . . .' Putting the spade down, she smoothes the sand with her palms round and round, 'it's a desert . . . like a

desert . . .' Dreamily, she pushes some into a heap, arms outstretched in front of her, hands buried in the little mound. She leans forward and stares into it, as one might see pictures in clouds or in the embers of a fire. Then quickly, she scoops up a double handful, brings it up against her face and gently kisses it.

This is a beautiful example of the melting away of the need to try hard, to achieve a definite goal, and also of the dreamy reverie that physical contact with the sand so often engenders. We see the girl become involved with the feel and texture of the sand, and as she brings it up to touch her face and lips, to treat the soft substance as she might a loved body.

Other children might invite me to join them at the sand tray in complex but often seemingly unintelligible stories that would involve much pouring of water in and out of pots, burying, mixing, telling me what to do, and so on. Some understanding of the content of these events might emerge, but most often I was not privy to what was going on in the child's imagination, whether formed or unformed. It is important to note that many imaginative intricacies are possible simultaneously in one piece of sand play, without the children having to commit themselves consciously to any one of them, or reveal themselves to me. At the same time they could make sure I was close by, and, by acting in unison with them to their instructions, I could become a part of themselves that would be able to hold the divergent scraps of fantasy and conflict. This part was also, I suggest, perhaps that kind of shadow or joint mother figure, supporting and strengthening the mothering part of each child as they explored these unknown and troubled waters.

Water itself is often added to the sand in various quantities, sometimes just enough to make it more mouldable, sometimes to form ponds or canals, or to create a swamp, sea or river. Mythologically, water can be either the home of sacred spirits or of terrifying monsters, but the latter are more often imagined lurking under the muddy elements in the sand tray at these times. Flooding, drowning, catastrophe, treachery, and being out of control are easily associated with the muddy water, which becomes the scene of many a bizarre and dream-like sequence, usually representing a very extreme situation. The initial excitement and gleeful addition of more and more water for its own sake easily turns to destructiveness, and while this can be useful in releasing anger, it could also cause the child to be dangerously overwhelmed in chaos and excitement. However, it seems that as the large round container of the sand tray physically holds most of the flood of water, so it concretely holds the flood of feeling released, assisted of course by the boundaries of the therapy hour and the holding presence of the therapist. In addition, the small toys often used in these scenes can form the basis of a story on which to focus, which helps to externalise such internal bodily terrors and disasters into named and therefore less overwhelming events when necessary, with opportunities also for acts of control, rescue and reparation.

Particularly noticeable is the marked change of feeling and atmosphere that accompanies the change of state of the sand substance when large quantities of water are added. There may be enormous anxiety about the crumbling forms and frantic attempts to shore them up, or the beginnings of new activity, accepting the changes and exploiting their imaginative potential. Most importantly, it seems as if the flow of water into the sand dissolves not only the shapes and forms therein, but also the boundaries of held feeling, letting it flow in a new direction.

To illustrate this, I will describe a sand sequence by a 10-year-old girl. The youngest child in a family of five, Nadia had been abandoned by her mother when she was 5 years old, and both cared for and abused by her father. The older children in their turn became chronic abusers, considered past redemption by the workers involved with the family. They hoped, however, to 'save' Nadia, and she came to the residential unit when she was 9, a large, ungainly, 'stupid' child, difficult to love. She was enthusiastic about her art therapy sessions, while I often felt as bewildered as Alice in Wonderland as we played together, led into the chaos of a child's mind that had taken refuge in not remembering, not understanding, not answering questions, in fact into being 'stupid'. It was the safest way (Sinason 1986: 152).

Nadia must have tried out every possible material available in the art room, but here I want to show how some of her work in the sand tray enabled her to experiment with body issues far too complex and multi-dimensional to understand on a conscious level. The following extract illustrates how she used the combination of sand and water in one of her many explorations:

Nadia seems depressed and quiet, resentful at having to be with me today. However, she invites me to play with her in the sand tray, and says we must each build a 'bridge'. We make two separate small mounds and begin to tunnel through them. Hers collapses and she says we will now make a big one in the centre. We spend much time making a mound and patting it down with hands and wooden spoon. She is quite rough and sand goes over me several times at which she laughs. We begin to tunnel through from opposite sides, and eventually I am invited to feel the end of the spoon coming through, then one finger, then to touch three fingers. We make the tunnel wide enough 'for the trucks to get through' [a repetition of old themes], and carefully clear away messy sand from both entrances.

But now she says, 'we are going to put it in and you will feel it'. 'It' is water, and she asks me to fill the bucket and give it to her. She pours it carefully into her side of the mound and watches the sand soften round the edges. She pours another bucket and the water runs through the tunnel. Another bucketful and the tunnel is beginning to fall in, but 'It doesn't matter because I'm going to do something else . . .' Lots more water is added and quite suddenly, she is energised, more alive, no longer depressed and flat. She is standing up and taking control. 'We must push it all down [the mound and tunnel] and cover it all up.' We do so and she says, 'You would't know it was there, would you?' With the spoon handle she digs a small hole and asks me to inspect it for water. She digs two more such holes, and having got me to admit I can see no water, says triumphantly, 'There you are, it's magic!' Now in a commanding voice she tells me I must make a bigger hole the same as hers. When this is done, she pours water into the three small holes, where it instantly soaks in, but she pours sufficient into the two big ones to make two ponds. She fetches us a boat each, and two aeroplanes; the former float, the latter sink immediately. She does not comment on this but gets two large dice and explains a 'game' in which according to the numbers on the dice, we will move the boats and planes into each other's ponds. This is completed quickly, and she 'wins'. Now with her hands she joins the two ponds together and the water flows between them. She enlarges this lake to include the three small wells. Into this she delves, scooping out the sludgy sand and placing handfuls of it on to the 'land'. I have to help her. At the end she drops some marbles into the muddy lake and debates whether to leave them there or dig them out. She decides on the latter and they are fished out with handfuls of the brownish sandy mud. She takes them to the sink and washes them all carefully so that they are clean and shiny and replaces them in their jar. She regards the muddy mess in the sand tray, makes a face and tells me that I will have to clear it up.

This example illustrates how well the sand and water can be manipulated in accordance with the child's mood and fantasy wishes, and how the substances themselves affect the child in turn, thus setting up a circular process of sensation and perception. It shows the effect of adding quantities of water to the sand, and how it appeared to change Nadia's emotional and physical state as much as it changed the state of the sand. We see the concretisation of the dissolving of resistance and anger towards me, and the making of a more intimate 'meeting' by the flowing of water through the tunnel. Nadia was then able to make the switch from downtrodden, defensively angry victim to excited controller of the action, creating a new 'game' in which I was ordered to participate. In this game, with its meetings and exchanges between us via the dice and the boats in the pools of water, I became an adjunct in her process of experimenting with several themes connected with sexual abuse. After the apparently sexual implications of 'we are going to put it in and you will feel it', we observe the covering over of evidence and the magic of making 'it' disappear. This may well refer to the covering over and denial of the sexually abusive relationship in the past which had not so far been verbally acknowledged (Sagar 1990: 105). At the time though, I was left with a bewildered feeling of 'what *is* going on?' – perhaps Nadia showing me in the

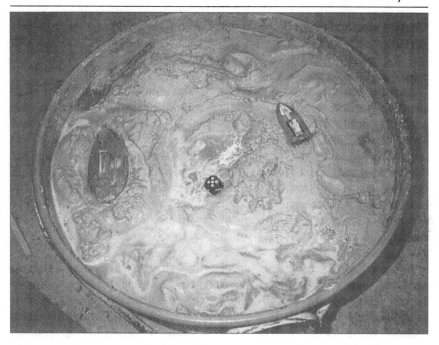

Figure 5.2 Boats and dice, sand and muddy water – the swirling confusion of one of Nadia's games in the sand, where she explores such themes as secrecy, 'dirtiness', physical damage, relationship to another body, and the possibility of healing

countertransference that very incomprehension and confusion she must have experienced in the family 'games' of her young years.

Playing with the wet sloppy sand towards the end suggests experimentation with the dirty muck that so many abused children feel fills their insides. In previous sessions there had been a lot of talk about 'bird poo' landing on my head, and being given handfuls of sloppy 'dog poo'. Characteristically, she had wanted to mess all over me in an abusive way (Sagar 1990: 96). However, in this later sequence it became important to clean up the mess round the tunnel entrances, and at the end to retrieve and clean the precious marbles from the swamp. This shows that Nadia was making some progress towards change in her process and was not just acting out the reversal of roles from victim to controller/abuser. It was also useful for her to experience having the upper hand, and in the joining with the mother who can be trusted to cope with the mess without being destroyed, we see the beginnings of healing that this kind of play offers.

It must also be remembered that Nadia was extremely deprived in her early years and had a lot of catching up to do on early play experiences around eating and shitting, which could happen at the same time in the wonderfully adaptive sand and water. For a child like her, whose verbal expressive powers were extremely limited, and whose thinking was, out of habit, choked with fear, the beauty of such a sequence lies in the fact that it was all done and experienced bodily, the only way, in fact, of reaching her.

At other times in work with Nadia in the sand I witnessed even more clearly expressed themes of sexual abuse. As the too-large trucks were pushed forcefully by both of us back and forth through tunnels, the sand above cracked and broke many times. Physically involved myself, it was impossible not to feel the penetration, the breaking of a body boundary, the damage to female form, the wounding, coercing – masculine objects through feminine spaces. Yet during all this she asked for my help in repairing the tunnels over and over again, patting the sand firm, referring to it as 'just like a mummy's tummy'. Even though the repair never held for long, she was making efforts to 'take care' of the abused (sand) body and of the mother/therapist body.

However, more important than entering into these speculations about what body issues Nadia was dealing with, was to give her the opportunity to explore open-endedly through play with these substances. Here I want to emphasise how Nadia was taking control of her own work, though it seems probable that in this enactment there was a kind of unacknowledged notion that by involving me in the sand and water with her, we became more like one body, increasing the possibility of a more direct transfer of feeling states at a concrete level. The joint play also permits the child to make a relation to 'another body', represented interchangeably as both human and substance, without the threat of having to acknowledge a relationship to a particular person, or to define what that relationship is about. Perhaps the unconscious realisation of these possibilities is one of the notions behind the quite frequent invitations to me to play with the children in the sand.

Burying things in the sand is a popular game with unlimited versions, many of which have bodily connotations. Many children like to bury something at the end of a session, perhaps to leave a part of themselves in the room until next time. At times like these, hiding and burying things in the sand becomes like lodging something in a body equivalent, which could be their own body, or a mother's body. Putting it there becomes more personal and more intimate in a way which hiding it more effectively on the shelf or in a cupboard does not.

Here the nondescript and changeable quality of the sand is important, for it can *stand in* for body, without the child having to be explicit about whose body. Objects, like a snake coiled and buried ritualistically in the dead centre of the tray, or coins, shiny marbles and little gilt cups and saucers, may impart to the sand an ominous or sacred quality, or remind one of hidden or lost treasure. The act of burying and hiding things for the therapist to find has been discussed interestingly by Caroline Case and Carol Sagar, both of whom mention particularly the theme of secrecy and revelation, a very relevant one to those children who have had to hide sexual abuse from their mother, while wanting desperately to reveal it (Case 1986, Sagar 1990).

In the case of Danny, 6 years old, burying activity in the sand was part of his efforts to control his deep anxiety and urge to sexually assault me. At the end of my first encounter with him I was physically shocked, confused and exhausted by the urgency of his explicitly sexual requests and his persistent attempts to get inside my clothes. I felt that I had been both an abuser and abused. These are not uncommon reactions to such children, and they indicated that Danny's determined sexual advances probably grew from a place of fear, and that in this new meeting alone with a strange new female he perhaps set out to abuse before he was abused himself. He was after all a child who came from a world where no adult could be trusted. His behaviour must have been as frightening for him as it was obviously stressful for both of us.

Eventually, Danny understood that not only was his physical behaviour unacceptable but that there were other ways to be with me in the art room. He soon discovered the sand tray, and remained involved with its contents for the rest of his time with me. Danny liked me to sit opposite him and watch, but not to play with him, for he had no idea of relating in this way.

There were no more sexual assaults for two months, and Danny went to the sand every week, plunging into it dozens of soldiers, horses, cars, police cars, ambulances and speed boats all mixed up. He rushed from one thing to another and back again, clumsily tripping up, dropping things, his speech stuttering and falling about in the same manner as his hands and legs. He could not even smooth the sand down, dig a hole or make a mound. It remained in a churned up state, the objects always half buried in it, and when he went to put the toys back on the shelf handfuls of sand went with them. The themes of the first weeks concerned good and bad, and which and who was which. He would ask me this question over and over again as soldiers were lined up, fought each other, were counted, rearranged and shoved into the sand. Sometimes he relished, sometimes he bemoaned, how many 'baddies' there were. As police cars endlessly chased and caught a bright red sports car, as two divers chased and overturned a black rider in a speedboat, he played out the attempt to gain control of the baddie. Perhaps this referred to the need to control his 'bad' unwanted sexual urges towards me, perhaps to the wish to control the actual past abuser. There was certainly a sense of there being some kind of controlling policeman around, along with the possibility of rescue. The intensity of the chase, the forcing of the objects deep into the sand, all showed me that here was where the sexual anxiety and excitement lay, translated now into his very chaotic and clumsy sand play, and contained in the round tray.

'But,' as Danny would say ominously each time control was gained over a baddie, 'not for long . . .'. When a holiday break approached, coinciding with a goodbye visit from a previous foster parent who he had loved and who had seemed to disappear without explanation, all his fears about being abandoned were restimulated and the sexual advances began again. He started referring to my 'boobs' again, trying to grab them and to trick me into playing games that would lead towards physical touching. He was intensely anxious not only about my going away, but also that his renewed sexual assaults would alienate him from me. It seemed he had grown to love me and his weekly sessions, and with his mounting anxiety overriding his ability to transfer his conflicts into the sand tray, he reverted to attempted possession by sexual means, and we appeared to be back where we had started.

It seemed the baddie was not buried, nor was the policeman able to control him. However, after the break he began to use the sand in a new way, suddenly becoming successful in digging a trench that did not collapse in which he lined up six cars, 'three bad and three good'. He covered them over and made a pile of sand on top. Not only did he achieve this pile of sand, but on the top of it he determined to make a little pointed piece. He patted it all down carefully. This mound now looked like a huge breast with its carefully made nipple. It seemed he had made a kind of breast/body in which he had buried all his conflicts over good and bad, his longing for the mother's breast, and his struggle with his sexualised bodily needs. He expressed his desire that the other children who came to art therapy should know what he had put in the sand mound, perhaps staking his claim to that very special territory, which maybe stood for my breast/body.

After this, Danny made the sand mound every week, carefully burying various of his play objects beneath it in the same manner. He got better and better at it, each week concentrating on making a little hole in the all-important point at the top, trying out variations until he was satisfied. To make the hole he found a way of poking a funnel down the point of the sand mound, and this had the odd effect of sending a little snake of sand up through the stem of the funnel. It was so like a little penis. There seemed to be some kind of deep connection here between a small male and a large female shape. The 'breast' seems likely to have been a composite object of breast and his own body into which objects were inserted – where what went into the hole rather than what came out was what mattered. Into the hole went various objects – sometimes it was the divers from the rescue boat, sometimes it was carefully poured water. He seemed to be creating in the sand a way of accessing both my body and his own, as well as connected processes to do with both abuse and repair between other bodies outside our current relationship. It is interesting to note that in the urgency of his need to create the breast/body with its important and meaningful details, this previously clumsy and chaotic child, who could only churn up the sand, now became able to concentrate and to control his bodily movements.

Nothing, unfortunately, could undo the early sexualising of Danny and many of the other children who came to art therapy with me. But their play in the sand within this protected environment did give them a means to experiment concretely with complex and undifferentiated issues around their abuse, offering space for the emergence of primitive and infantile memories and sensations. The soft and pliable medium of sand and water often acted as a fluid physical intermediary between myself and the child, helping partially to dissolve the boundaries between us and enabling deep unconscious connections to be made. I was often able to participate in the same physical feelings and sensations as the child, be part of the same substantial experience, without 'knowing' exactly, or sometimes even remotely, what connections if any, they were making, and without having to have it explained to me, if indeed explanation were possible.

This is not to say that facts about sexual abuse should not be brought into consciousness and verbalised. Many of the children were only too able to recount what had happened to them, as they had had to do so many times before. But even these children had almost certainly not had the opportunity to explore the feelings and sensations around their abuse in this fluid and tactile way. For those who were abused before they had words, or those who had 'forgotten' or been lied to about it, or those for whom the pain of it was unspeakable, it was important that they could play freely in this very bodily medium, only very gradually moving towards exploring fragments of their experience (Alvarez 1992: 154). Nearly always any verbal revelations or remembering would arise only after extensive experimentation in this nonspecific, non-threatening 'play', and might well be shared with their key worker, not with me. Sometimes there never were any verbal rememberings, and one could only think that this work would contribute to an ongoing internal process that might be expressed more consciously at a later date, perhaps when the child was safely in a new family with a secure base.

Finally, I would like to put in a plea for recognition that often children may be saying that they have had enough of being labelled 'sexually abused', that they want to be seen as 'normal', and to play normal boys' or girls' games. This can feel frustrating to a therapist who knows only too well how much work there is to do on the badly damaged areas of this child in the limited time available. But this 'normality' is what they have chosen for a particular session, or many sessions, and to this too they have a right. For I believe we must give space and value to the healthy child that is also there, to the reclamation of lost childhood, and to the building of a sense of self. We must work with the *whole* person and not only with the part labelled 'sexually abused', otherwise the child will never have the chance to move beyond seeing themselves as damaged goods. In this work, sand and water are ideal substances with which to offer natural, messy play which allows the explorations and reveries that are the birthright of every child.

REFERENCES

Alvarez, A. (1992) *Live company*, London and New York: Tavistock/Routledge.

Ammann, R. (1991) *Healing and transformation in sandplay*, Chicago and La Salle, Illinois: Open Court.

Balint, M. (1968) *The basic fault*, London: Tavistock/Routledge.

Case, C. (1986) Hide and seek: A struggle for meaning, *Inscape, Journal of the British Association of Art Therapists*, Winter 1986.

Gillespie, A. (1990) '*Sand, water & fire – the lost mother*', unpublished MA dissertation, Hertfordshire College of Art and Design, UK.

Kalff, D.M. (1980) *Sandplay*, California: Sigo Press.

Lowenfeld, M. (1979) *The world technique*, London: Allen & Unwin.

Mitchell, R.R. and Friedman, H.S. (1994) *Sandplay – past, present and future*, London and New York: Routledge.

Sagar, C. (1990) 'Working with cases of child sexual abuse', in C. Case and T. Dalley (eds) *Working with children in art therapy*, London and New York: Tavistock/Routledge.

Sinason, V. (1986) Secondary mental handicap and its relation to trauma, *Psychoanalytic Psychotherapy*, 2(2): 131–54.

Young, L. (1992) Sexual abuse and the problem of embodiment, *Child Abuse and Neglect*, 16: 89–100.

Chapter 6

Why can't she control herself?

A case study

Karen Lee Drucker

INTRODUCTION

I have worked as a qualified art therapist with children with emotional difficulties for many years in my art therapy career, which amounts to 20 years
and more. In my present part-time art therapy position, in a Child and Family
Psychiatry Department, I see children with emotional difficulties on an out-
patient basis. For me, in all these years, working with these children has felt
sometimes painful, sometimes helpless, sometimes de-skilled, sometimes
warm and then feelings I find difficult to name. Working with Ann over the
past two years has been an experience that has covered more feelings that I
could have imagined. I have learned more about the therapeutic relationship
from my experience with Ann than in any other previous therapeutic experience.

THE BEGINNING

Our Child and Family Psychiatry Department is a small team in the throes of
change and restructuring within the Child Health Services. When you read
this chapter we will no longer be a team of two psychiatric nurses, one occu-
pational/play therapist, one consultant, one family therapist and one art
therapist. I am the only part-time art therapist working in the department. I
first met Ann when the clinical assistant (psychiatrist), since retired, referred
her to me. Ann was 10 years old when she first attended weekly art therapy
sessions in the department. It was known that she had been physically abused
by her father for the first three years of her life, which was discovered when
Ann's older brother disclosed his abuse by his father to Social Services. After
that the children (one older brother, two older sisters and a younger sister)
were taken into care. The children were dispersed to different foster placements after two years of living in the children's home. This instability and
separation from siblings has had a major effect on Ann's own sense of security, despite having a stable foster placement since the age of 5.

Her foster family consists of two older sisters living at home and an older sister living away. The foster parents have been very supportive and caring towards Ann through difficult years of her traumatic behaviour, played out both at home and at school. At home Ann would destroy property, i.e. tear her curtains or print nail varnish on the window sills. She would often steal money and food and then deny it. At school, she would be aggressive to other children. She found working independently very difficult, could not ignore distractions within the class and was often the cause of distractions herself. Both foster parents and staff at school wanted Ann to control her behaviour. Did I want her to control her behaviour with me? No, I wanted her to be able to explore her confused boundaries in a safe environment and for myself to feel safe with a supportive team and good supervision.

Frederick has described five non-verbal signs of post-traumatic stress among younger children:

1   Sleep disturbances continuing more than several days, wherein actual dreams of the trauma may or may not appear.
2   Separation anxiety or clinging behaviour, such as reluctance to return to school.
3   Phobias about distressing stimuli (e.g. school building, TV scenes or persons) that remind the victim of the traumatic event.
4   Conduct disturbances, including problems that occur at home or at school that serve as responses to anxiety and frustration.
5   Doubts about the self, including comments about body confusion, self-worth and desire for withdrawal.

(Frederick 1985, from Cattanach 1992: 22)

Ann was showing signs of contact disturbances both at home and at school which affected her ability to form relationships as expected for her age group. Throughout our sessions she would withdraw in her imagery and play, trying to keep me at a distance, thus showing signs of lack of self-worth. The child who is abused at pre-verbal age has not been able to form a coherent sense of self; this process has been disrupted.

THE BEGINNING SESSIONS

Ann was very energetic – she wanted to draw and use clay and play with the puppets in the room all in a 45-minute session. Her pictures excluded the family – they were in the next room or they would visit the scene. One of her first pictures was of herself at the seaside (Figure 6.1).

She drew a large sand house and a small figure of herself in the waves. She said that the picnic food was for her. Ann felt isolated from her real family and saw her real mother infrequently with her social worker. Ann drew a

Figure 6.1 At the seaside

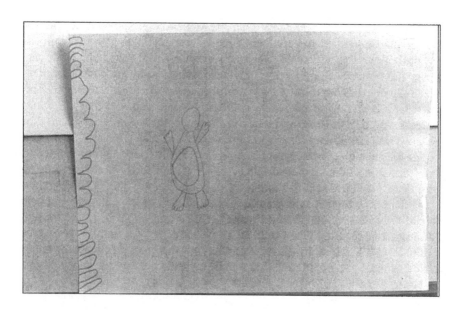

Figure 6.2 Mum

picture of her mum. She drew a round body, arms and legs, and a head without a face, but did not want to complete it. She said that her mum could not help being fat but she did lose a pound (Figure 6.2). The circle in mum's torso was the emptiness where Ann should be. Ann was not only separated from her mother but her mother was never there for her. Ann wished she was with her mother on both a conscious and unconscious level. Ann had ambivalent feelings towards her mother for finding it difficult to care for Ann but still loving her at the same time. Ann played that out with me throughout the sessions.

FEELING LOST

During the beginning of the sessions Ann tested her trust of me (as in her difficulties in trusting anyone). Carol Sagar states:

> Therefore, the sexually-abused child coming to therapy is likely to be defending him or herself against some overwhelming emotional feelings, including the experience of loss relating to the disclosure and its consequences. Although needing to share these feelings in the safe, confidential therapy situation the child may feel intimidated from doing so by anxiety, guilt feelings, and general confusion.
>
> (Sagar, 1990: 92)

I had to close my eyes and guess what she was making. She made a rainbow out of the fluorescent fun stuff (soft plasticine). She made a wish from the magical rainbow. Ann wanted to see her real mum's new house. She made clay crabs and butterflies, saying that they were magic but I had to close my eyes while she was making them. I felt vulnerable and shut out – feelings that Ann must have been feeling. She drew a Christmas tree and said that her foster parents would be putting up the tree at the weekend. She drew a present that was lost and then found. It was her present. It was Ann (Figure 6.3).

She played with the puppets. They were not really friends but pretended to be. Everything was sabotaged. Their party turned into a fight and in the middle of playing the puppet announced that his mother was in hospital and was dying. The puppet said she was 'only kidding'. Many times the puppets would fight and become friends again but then one would be tricked into a false sense of security. One would be given a present of a radio with no batteries. In role I shared my disappointment and that it was difficult for me to trust anyone. I mirrored back what was being acted out and she accepted this as her feelings.

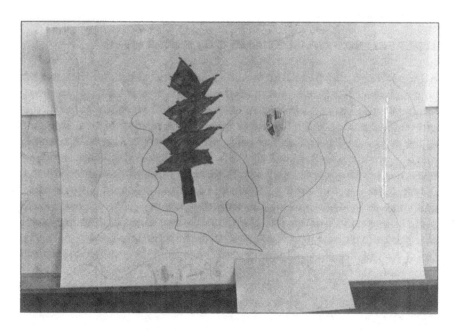

Figure 6.3 Present that was lost and then found

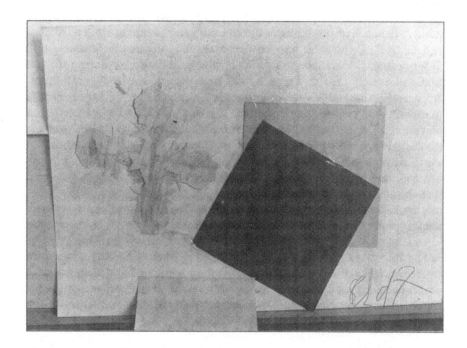

Figure 6.4 Snowflake

THE FEELINGS OF MESS AND COVERING OVER

After making a clay piece Ann would smear the wet clay and then use the gold and silver felt pens to decorate this mess. At the beginning her messy feelings would have to look acceptable. She would write my name in this acceptable mess and give it to me as a present. The relationship was changing as the mess Ann was feeling was being presented to me. Carol Sagar states, 'the overwhelming feelings of being full of mess inside which have somehow to be dealt with are expressed in art therapy through the material used' (Sagar, 1990: 97). Ann drew a snowflake on a shiny coloured piece of paper and stuck down the opposite side with the clear tape. She scribbled on it using bronze and silver crayons. She then used two sheets of coloured paper and stuck them down next to the upside-down snowflake (Figure 6.4). The messy part of herself was there next to the layers that continued to unfold throughout the sessions.

THE CHANGE OF APPROACH

After several months Ann chose a different approach to our art therapy sessions together. She decided to be the cashier in a post office and I was to be a customer waiting in the queue of people to be served. Ann directed me to stand at the back of this queue and wait for my turn, keeping me at a distance and controlling who came into her personal space. Before this session, Ann's foster mother told me about a difficulty that had happened during the last weekend which caused Ann's family and others involved great upset. Apparently Ann and her foster father used to go to football together most weekends. Ann used to stand along the side of the field and watch her father play football. After the football match she would wait for her father outside the changing rooms while he was changing. On this weekend Ann walked into the changing rooms to look for her father and saw the men changing. Ann's foster mother was angry that Ann did not listen and broke the rules. Ann said that she was afraid of standing outside. I felt that both Ann and her foster mother had their fears about boundary breaking. As it was, Ann was very unclear about her own personal boundaries and the personal boundaries of others.

The role plays became very involved and defined. Characters began to emerge and take on a life of their own. At the beginning, I had to stand in the post office queue and wait for Ann to say the word 'next' in order to move up. Carol Sagar, in her chapter of working with cases of child sexual abuse, felt that same distancing:

> I felt as if she excluded me completely from this experience, as if I could not intrude, I did not exist for her. The transference may be understood

in that her feelings towards her mother were transferred to me in the therapeutic relationship; in the counter transference I felt absent as her mother had been absent during the incidents of abuse, I felt shut out, just as her mother had been shut out from any knowledge of the incidents for several years before disclosure.

(Sagar, 1990: 99)

Ann (the manager of the post office) informed me that there was a telephone message for me (the customer) that my house was burning and that my three sons had caused the fire. I felt that I was being kept at a distance and was having pain and loss projected into my character. Ann reversed the situation and as the manager she insisted that she had three boy children and a new baby, Abbey. At the end of each session I suggested that we de-role and turn around, 'I'm Ann', 'I'm Karen'. When using role playing in sessions it is important to de-role. This showed Ann that we were playing out her feelings using characters and that after the sessions she would have to deal with her life as 'Ann'. However, she would be incorporating her knowledge and understanding of these role plays on an unconscious level in her life as Ann.

ABBEY AND CATHERINE

Ann had been 'naughty' at home. Ann hit her foster sister with an umbrella because her sister was teasing her. Ann thought that her foster sister was 'perfect' and was favoured. She felt that both foster sisters didn't like her when she came to live in their house. She admitted to talking in anger – that they 'like her now but sometimes don't'. Ann wanted to be accepted and loved but did not always find it easy when she was. Ann mentioned that she had a boyfriend called Jonathan but that he was going out with someone else. At that point we talked about wanting to feel special and have someone who was special to her. Sexuality and confused sexuality would show itself in later sessions. As we were playing shops Ann did a picture in which she wrote 'I love you Jonathan' (which was a disguise for the boy she liked) and then covered it over with silver pen – this was covered with blue (Figure 6.5).

I asked Ann if anyone said 'I love you'. Ann replied 'only Jonathan'. There were many times where Ann would need to cover up what she had made, as if it were a secret. This mirrors an abusive experience many times, where the abuser insists on the victim's secrecy concerning the abusive act and that the consequence of 'telling' would be to be punished or hurt.

Secrecy can take on monstrous proportions for a child who is often threatened and dependent on the reality defined by the offender. The burden of the secret may become an integral part of the childhood experience. These children are caught in a double bind situation. If they are to

Figure 6.5   I love you Jonathan

survive by acting out their anger in various delinquent activities, they are discredited for causing further problems. On the other hand, if they had attempted to hide their pain and shame under a serene or perfect exterior, they are equally discredited for complaining to authorities when they were not seemingly affected. Once again, pressure is frequently put on the child to assume responsibility for the situation and a fabricated 'retraction' carries more credibility than the original disclosure.

(Bagley and King 1990: 112, 113)

In the changing approach from art to play, the character of 'Abbey' would represent Ann's responsible, adult coping part of herself. The character of 'Catherine' would represent Ann's 'naughty' rejected, angry and victimised part of herself. I continued to be the customer in the post office, directed to stand at the back of the queue, or sometimes being told to change roles to become Abbey or Catherine. Ann wanted me to feel her confusion.

In Ann's next session she was particularly upset. Twice, a letter had been sent home from her school following difficult behaviour. She volunteered the reasons for this warning of bad behaviour. Once she was climbing a tree in the school grounds and the other time she slapped a girl who was teasing her about being fostered. Ann shouted back to her 'at least she had a real mum'. I said that it must have been painful to hear what the girl said to her. Ann drew a picture of a no-smoking sign with rules and consequences

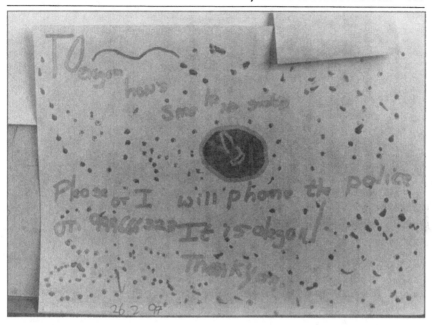

Figure 6.6   No smoking

(Figure 6.6). The no-smoking sign was a crossing out of the 'badness' and unacceptable part of herself. It was also showing her anger and her difficulty in containing it.

Ann said that when I stood in the queue I was to speak to a friend called Angela. I spoke in a raised voice so that Ann would hear me. I said 'I've done "naughty" things because I'm afraid of people liking me. It's scary if people get too close.' Ann was listening and pretended to ask the others in the shop to be quiet because it was too noisy. Abbey said that my (customer's) mum hates her and doesn't love her. I said that people could be angry and still love her. At the end of the session I was directed to be the shopkeeper and I was to feel sad. Ann said that she would tell a joke to feel better.

The sessions became a mini-series and I felt as if Ann created her 'life soap opera'. The characters became more involved and more three-dimensional. Catherine would find herself in uncontrollable, victimised situations. 'Why can't she control herself?' Ann's foster mother was to go to Australia to see relatives for three weeks. Ann said that she was going to miss her. Ann played the shop game and she drew a big purple empty space (Figure 6.7). Ann was missing her foster mother and it brought up feelings of being abandoned by her natural mother. The big purple empty space was frightening because she felt defenceless.

In the role play as Abbey, Ann said that my pretend daughter Catherine was pushed down the stairs and taken to hospital. She had to have her leg

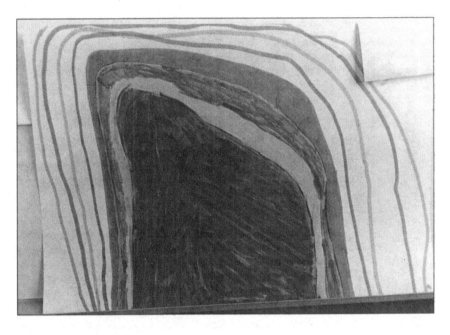

Figure 6.7 Big purple empty space

Figure 6.8 Hose pipe with water spurting out

Figure 6.9   Cave with monster

amputated. I said that she must have been hurt badly herself. Catherine turned to Abbey in the pretend hospital and asked why I was being so nice. I said that I liked her. Abbey said that it was a big joke and Catherine's leg hadn't been amputated (at the end of the role play). Ann had to hide her pain with a joke. Ann said that she had bad dreams about her real dad when he hit them (her brothers and sisters) and did 'rude' things. She did a drawing of a hose pipe going into a hole with water spurting out (Figure 6.8). It was probably her foster mother's absence that triggered bad dreams about her real Dad and the fact that her real mother was unable to protect her from her abusive father. The picture of the hose pipe was of her preverbal feelings of the abuse. I was feeling helpless, unable to mend or change the traumatic event that took place in Ann's past and in the session.

Ann did a second picture of a cave (using pastels and getting very messy in the process). She said that a monster lived in it. The monster was her and it was roaring. She felt like a monster and she was angry (Figure 6.9). Both the hose pipe picture and the cave monster picture showed me Ann's preverbal traumatic memories recorded in visual form. This seemed to me to be a turning point, as the abusive experience was very pronounced. Ann had internalised her father's projection of his own 'monster' and loss of his own control.

Generally, memories from early childhood are few; this may be due to the fact that infants are preverbal. Children encode memory through visual and sensorimotor channels rather than through cognitive processes.

(Van der Kolk 1987)

If abuse occurs during these early years, cognitive memories may not exist. Johnson (1987) suggests that there is evidence that in later years, at times of overwhelming stress and terror, the cognitive memory system may be bypassed; the event is recorded in photographic form and is not integrated with other memories through the usual cognitive processes. Because the traumatic memories were neurologically encoded through visual and sensorimotor pathways, art therapy offers a visual and sensorimotor medium that may more easily allow traumatic memories to come to conscious level (Bowers 1992).

ANGELA AND THE EVIL DAD

By this session Ann was allowing me to stand at the beginning of the queue and move around her freely. Ann wanted me to talk to the character 'Angela' who Abbey hated. Angela babysat and did horrible things – put 'stuff in her' and she felt sick, like 'cobwebs all over'. Ann playing Abbey told Angela off, but Angela said it was supposed to be a secret. Abbey said 'I don't like secrets'. After the play Ann had to go to the toilet. When she came back she

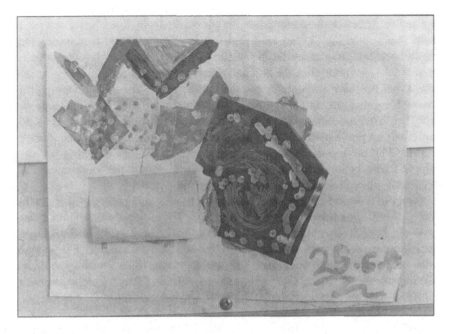

Figure 6.10   Covering over

Figure 6.11   Seeing through to the Easter egg

said with pleasure 'I had to do a poo'. I imagined all that horrible stuff that Ann was trying to get rid of inside herself. She then wrote her name in felt-tipped pens and glued paper over the top. She asked me to turn around while she uncovered her name and redrew it with a bright red felt pen (Figure 6.10).

She told me this after I was allowed to look; to see her in a different way. Ann said that she got an Easter egg from her real dad, her grandmother and her natural siblings. She started drawing a large Easter egg in different coloured felt pens (Figure 6.11). She wanted to put it on a background and cover it over with cling film so that she could see through it. I said that before this session, she had covered parts of her artwork and we couldn't see it. That week, she had taken the covering off and redrawn what was under the covering. Today, she was covering over, but it would be seen through. Could it be the obvious idea of letting me see more of her feelings? Could it be how Ann felt as a young child – vulnerable and unprotected?

Ann said that she had some good news and some bad news. The good news was that she had a friend to stay after school for the first time in a long time. The bad news was that she had a letter sent home. She owned up to the fact that she was responsible for her bad behaviour. I said that it sounded like two bits of good news. She drew yellow dots and fireworks – confusion and mess. She folded it up, asked me to close my eyes and presented it to me (Figure 6.12).

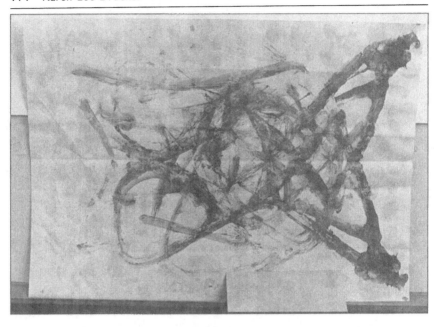

Figure 6.12 Yellow dots and fireworks

Ann was able to give me her messy feelings. She said she would want to see her real dad but just shake hands with him. She hadn't seen him for eight years.

In the next session, Evil Dad comes into the playing. Evil Dad had kidnapped Catherine played by Ann and me (mum). Mum has to meet him or he will kill Catherine. I have to protect Catherine. Abbey played by Ann speaks on the telephone to Evil Dad. She says that she hates him, but whispers that she's on his side again.

> Many young children love the person who abused them and experience conflict and confusion about loving and hating the same person, having such powerful reasons to hate. After all, to deny good in your own father is, for the young child, to deny good in themselves.
>
> (Cattanach, 1993: 128)

I talked about her confused feelings. She pretended at the end of the session that Evil Dad was waiting outside the door to scare me. Dad was trying to scare her. I felt myself getting angry inside. I was furious at Evil Dad for invading Ann's and my space that we had created together. I was feeling Ann's fury and I said that he was making me angry for being in the space with us. I could not get rid of him but it was up to Ann what to do about him. Ann was beginning to trust me and therefore we moved around the space of the room more freely.

Figure 6.13   Anniversary card

The play became more involved as Evil Dad came into the scene. He would kidnap Catherine (Ann), and it was myself and/or Abbey (Ann) who would come to the rescue. The competent part of herself was helping the not-so-competent part of herself. However, in the role play it was Catherine who was confused about her love/hate feelings towards her father. In the next sessions, Ann directed me (as mum) to get married to my new husband called David. Ann made David and myself a card for our anniversary (Figure 6.13).

It seemed at this point Ann was able to move on and make some sort of separation of her feelings. Ann regressed into being a baby and then a toddler. She used the finger paints and put together layer upon layer of these saturated pictures (Figure 6.14). Ann needed to regress back to being 3 years old again. She

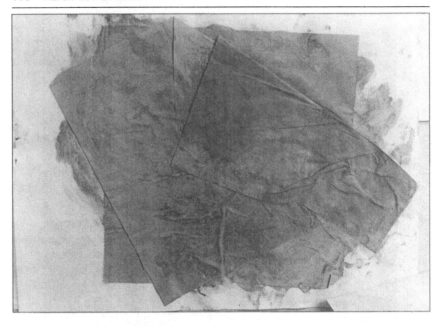

Figure 6.14   Layers of mess

retreated to a safer, happier experience of letting go and enjoying the playing. Her make-believe parents enabled her to feel safe and contained.

Our department was burgled and Ann saw the mess that was left by the people who had broken in. Our space was invaded and she was upset. She said she remembered a break-in when she was 18 months old. After that, Ann had to go into a 'home' and then moved to her present-day foster family. The abuse had changed her emotional and physical space.

ANN AND MUM

In the role play, Ann who played Abbey became a little girl of 4 and Catherine had died in a car accident. Catherine came alive again but she was a 'different' Catherine. In 'real life' Ann would be attending secondary school after the summer holiday. She was excited and scared at the same time. She wanted to do well in all aspects. She pretended that she was Abbey who had tidied the house. I had to play mum who was pleased that Abbey was being so helpful.

We had talked about the four-week summer break for many sessions before this one and now we would be saying a temporary goodbye. When Ann returned to the art therapy session after the summer break, the play reflected her feelings about her real mother. Angela, a previous character, came into the session. I was to play mum but I was kept at a distance. I was shopping,

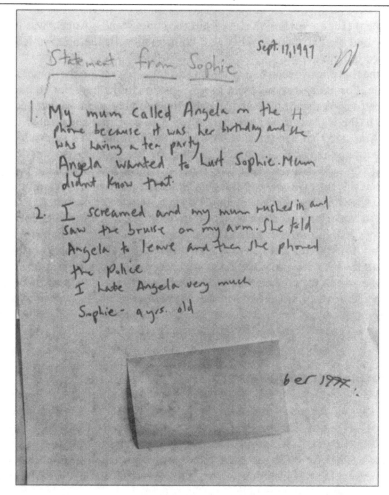

Figure 6.15 Court scene

going to visit Angela or going to make a surprise party for Angela but Ann
didn't like Angela. She came in to the party and immediately bruised Ann's
arm. (She was called Sophie in this session.) Angela apologised but was not
to be trusted. I had to tell Angela to go away. Ann was feeling angry at her
real mother for not protecting her during the abuse. Mum was not there and
still is not there emotionally for Ann. Ann does visit her natural mother
every few months and says she enjoys seeing her.

Again Ann played Sophie preparing a surprise birthday party for mum
(me). She said that she wanted Angela to attend but that we would beat her
up when she arrived. Angela attended and proceeded to squeeze Sophie's
arm. Sophie said that we had to telephone the police to come over to take a

statement (Figure 6.15). We played out the court scene – Angela was found guilty and sent to prison. This also connected with the abusive feelings aroused in Ann herself.

In the role play we then had to return and I was to prepare the dinner in the kitchen. For many sessions I was to tidy upstairs in the house or go into the kitchen to cook the meals. Ann had a meeting with her social worker and was asked if she wanted to see her real father. Ann said that she wanted to see him. Ann said that her real mother was in the hospital for a stomach complaint. In the playing she wanted me to cook her soup as she was feeling unwell. She said that she needed her potty – that she had messed her pants. I said that she must feel worried thinking about her real mother and father. She played with the playmobile hospital set and set it up for an operation. She was going to make her real mum better. In the next session, when she requested that I go away to do the pretend cooking or the cleaning, I challenged her demand. I said that I was bored with all this cooking and cleaning and was it difficult for her to be with me? I was concerned that I could be interrupting her process and my comment would set her back to the beginning of her art therapy. This was a risk I had to take. My challenge of her control allowed her to move on and find that I would not be dangerous after all. 'Why can't she control herself?' felt like 'Why is she controlling me?'

COPING AND SABOTAGING

Ann changed our play – the channels switched. Rather than a mini series, it became a chain of 'Let me see if I can achieve', 'pass the test' and 'even feel good about myself'. She decided to give me a pretend driving test and then reversed roles. We both passed. I then had to become a headteacher and reward Ann for not listening to the 'bullies' in the school and Ann even admitted to provoking the bullying (Figure 6.16).

In between feeling in control (rather than being out of control) Ann would feel frightened of this new mind set (behaviour and way of thinking) and try to revert back to the fear and tragedy that had overshadowed her in past sessions. Ann directed me to be a waitress, to serve the wrong food and poison Ann and all the customers. She and they all became well again. There was a terrible car crash in which she died but came back to life again. In play she gave birth to babies who died and came back to life again. Carol Sagar states:

> The child does not want to throw away the love but wants to purify herself from the strong, negative, impure feelings; letting go of one feels like letting go of both. To be effective, therapy needs to tease apart the mixture and give a value equally to positive and negative experiences.
>
> (Sagar, 1990: 112)

Figure 6.16 Certificate: Trying to cope

Ann was also beginning to experiment with some problem solving between her characters: a character called Caroline was bothering Chloe in the classroom. Chloe moved her seat away from Caroline which I acknowledged as a positive move. Caroline lied about Chloe doing something 'naughty'. I was to be the headteacher and I had to say that they had to work it out between them. Chloe decided to help Caroline and they became friends and thus healed the split. Perhaps this was a result of Ann finding it was safe to be with me without being in control of me.

SEEING HER NATURAL FATHER

Ann had decided to see her natural father (with social worker supervision). The social worker shared with me that Ann was 'strong and appropriate' during the meeting. Ann asked him why he hurt her when she was younger. The social worker said that her natural father had explained to Ann that he had a drinking problem and couldn't control his behaviour. Ann insisted that he apologise to her and he did. Saying sorry – in past role plays where the character was hurting other children, the word would have to be said. I fed back how it was difficult because in the past dad didn't say that to her. After the meeting Ann mentioned to the social worker that she wanted to see her natural mother more often. She missed her mother who, at the time, had moved to a flat and was living alone. When I saw Ann for her session (the for-tieth session since starting art therapy), Ann said that she had seen her father and that it went 'OK'. She said that she didn't want to talk about it because 'everyone' had been asking her what happened and 'I don't want to talk about it again'. I had never initiated a question in any of our sessions so I felt Ann's pressure and anger. I also felt left out of that important experience, as she previously said that she had told everyone else. However, Ann drew a block of flats, turning to her feelings of wanting to see her natural mum.

SEXUALITY

Ann started role playing more sexualised characters. Ann played a pop star and sang 'sexy songs'. Ann pretended to organise a party and invited her boyfriend to stay the night. However, he was to sleep downstairs and her friends and her-self were to sleep upstairs. In some of the sessions the boyfriend had 'dumped' her and in other sessions she had 'dumped' the boyfriend. Ann had not resolved her feelings about girls/boys – men/women, and this continues to be a confu-sion. Ann's foster mum was concerned that Ann might get pregnant at a young age but she spoke to Ann about her concerns.

> Inhibitions about tenderness resulting from child sexual abuse can pro-foundly and negatively influence later decisions about marriage and children. Long range effects include a variety of psychological and sexual problems, vulnerability to further victimisation, and reported unwanted pregnancies.
>
> (Bagley and King 1990: 119)

CLOSENESS

The play had changed again. Ann wanted us to play secretaries working in an office together. We would go to have lunch together and be responsible. Ann noticed that I didn't wear a wedding ring and said that someone told her that you are a lesbian if you don't wear a ring. We talked about the feelings of being close to a girl/woman, and of us being close in sharing feelings. I sug-gested that 'closeness does not always mean getting hurt, although that had happened in the past'. Ann continued to play a work colleague and we con-tinued to share experiences together. Ann would revert back to being 3 years old and messy, and other times swung to playing a much older age, testing out the limits of herself and myself (Figures 6.17 and 6.18).

The area of closeness has not been completely resolved. Ann still finds it difficult to make relationships with her peers and she continues to test the relationship with her foster parents. I feel that Ann and I have shared her con-

Figure 6.17 Reverting back to mess

fused and painful, as well as positive and happy, experiences to enable Ann to experience closeness without actual harm.

During the most recent sessions, Ann was beginning to sense that I was a person in my own right. She constantly asked about myself, my family and all aspects of me. She said 'you know everything about me but I know nothing about you'. In fact during the course of the sessions I had shared small bits of information that would not get in the way of the process of therapy. Ann wanted a real family, her natural mum and family, and this would never happen. Ann was angry and would continue to be angry.

CONCLUSION

I look over what I have written for this chapter. I know that Ann must learn to get along with other children, that she must learn to be responsible for herself and towards others, and that her anger must be channelled into a more constructive way of behaving. However, if I had been treated by adults in an irresponsible, uncontrollable way when I was small, would I respond the same as Ann has responded and behaved?

Sometimes she will like herself and sometimes it will be too difficult to allow herself to feel safe and loved. I felt her detachment of feeling in her role play as she placed me at a distance in the post office queue. I would feel her rejected feelings by the comment 'only kidding'. The expression of Ann's

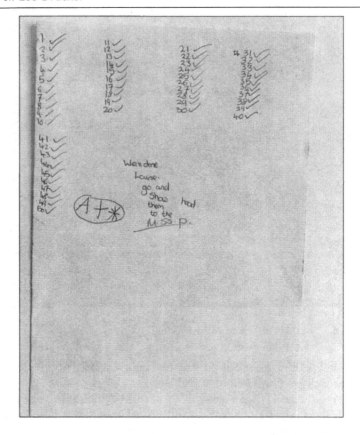

Figure 6.18   Doing well

anger, turned onto herself and towards others inappropriately, perpetuates the cycle of abusive behaviour. I have given her an area to work through some of her angry feelings safely so that she can escape this destructive cycle.

The feelings of loss and vulnerability came up in Ann's guessing games and wishing on rainbows. Ann's feelings of loss brought up my own feelings of loss. I sometimes wish for lost opportunities, things that others were able to have but which I didn't have.

Ann's feelings of being consumed by mess and uncovering this mess were an important aspect of our sessions. The preverbal images (mess) of her abuse and loss of control in the early formative years helped her to lose some of her control in our sessions and move on to some positive feelings about herself and her mother.

Ann continues to struggle with her ambivalent feelings about her natural mother. She continues to test her foster mother's love and commitment to her. I played the parts of both in our sessions.

There were certain turning points in Ann's sessions. The session in which I was allowed to come closer to Ann when playing post office was a significant show of trust within her space. The session of images of the hose pipe and the cave monster showed, on a preverbal level, her abusive experience and the internalised feelings of the 'monster inside of her'. Another turning point was the retreat back to her toddler stage of development by saturating layers of pictures with finger paints. She could feel, in her play, the experience of safety and letting go. It was encouraging to be part of the play where Ann was able to work through some problem solving and experience a sense of achievement in passing the pretend driving test and coping with pretend school conflict.

The art in Ann's sessions was used as a beginning, an introduction and uncovering to our relationship. It was used as the initial unblocking of her feelings, moving on to the acting out of some of her images. The art therapy with Ann was enriched with role play throughout her sessions. With the help of the art the role play enabled Ann to move back and forth in her development and helped to her to discover individuating and separating. She needed to use actual space to keep me away and then let me in. It helped her to make choices and experience feelings without 'real life consequences'. The play happened in a therapeutic space between Ann and myself, to define what is 'me' and 'not me' and develop a relationship that was lost or never established.

I felt I was able and willing to play as an equal participant, taking Ann's ideas and actions seriously, respecting her image-making and role play ideas and keeping the space and boundaries safe, as well as challenging when appropriate. I found it necessary to be flexible with Ann's need to change between using art materials and using role play.

The themes were of a progressive nature and had a sequence about them. Ann showed her feelings of isolation from her family and particularly ambivalent feelings about her natural mother. She showed me her lost feelings and difficulty in trusting at the beginnings of the sessions. As the trust developed, Ann was able to let out some of her messy feelings, while at the same time trying to cover them up. She was then able to explore our special relationship and the concepts of safety within it. As this became more involved, Ann was then exploring her feelings of being rejected, and looked at the 'hurt' side of herself and the more resilient, coping part of herself. Through this process, in the role play, Ann could express her angry feelings towards her abusive father and try to keep her feelings safe inside herself. This stirred up her angry feelings at her natural mother who was not able to protect her from her father. Ann then had space to explore behaviour in which she could achieve, and be rewarded with a place where she could feel good about herself. Sexuality and closeness had followed, the two areas that still needed to be worked through.

Long-term therapeutic work for children who have been abused is a necessary and important way of helping with issues of confused feelings, including those of boundaries, intimacy, anger, abandonment, control and lack of control. This was my therapeutic relationship with Ann.

Figure 6.19   Thank you

ACKNOWLEDGEMENTS

I would like to acknowledge Alison Harper for her patience and hard work in putting this chapter together. I would also like to thank Ann for her bravery and amazing amount of resourcefulness, and I thank my colleagues for their support and understanding.

REFERENCES

Bagley, C. and King, K. (1990) *Child sexual abuse. the search for healing*, London: Tavistock/Routledge.

Bowers, J. (1992) Therapy through art facilitating treatment of sexual abuse, *Journal of Psychosocial Nursing*, 30(6): 15–23.

Cattanach, A. (1993) *Play therapy with abused children*, London and Bristol, PA: Jessica Kingsley Publishers.

Frederick, C.J. (1985) 'Children traumatised by catastrophic situations', in S. Eth and R.S. Pynoos (eds) *Post-traumatic stress disorder in children*, Washington DC: American Psychiatric Press.

Johnson, D.R. (1987) The role of the creative arts therapies in the diagnosis and treatment of psychological trauma, *The Arts in Psychotherapy*, 14: 7–13.

Sagar, C. (1990) 'Working with cases of child sexual abuse, in C. Case and T. Dalley (eds) *Working with children in art therapy*, London: Tavistock/Routledge.

Van der Kolk, B.A. (1987) *Psychological trauma*, Washington DC: American Psychiatric Press, Inc.

Chapter 7

Tell me your story so far

A developmental approach to art therapy

Jo Bissonnet

There is often a natural and indeed understandable urge in therapists to 'cure' their client. At times this goal is achievable, but in other circumstances there may be factors that are not under the control of the therapist or the client, and are not resolvable at the time of therapy. It could be an ongoing family difficulty or, where the client is still a child, they may not have the cognitive ability to make sense of certain issues. In fact the word 'therapy' comes from the Greek *therapeuein* – to minister to. This in turn derives from the Greek *theraps* – an attendant. Thus it feels that attendance lies at the heart of the therapeutic relationship between child and therapist.

People come into therapy at different times in their life, and accordingly they will bring different priorities and issues into the therapy room. The content of those sessions may vary, or at least will be understood differently according to the age, developmental stage, cultural and historical background of the client. This chapter looks at the process that one child goes through during art therapy at a certain time of her life. Art therapy is unique in being able to hold unconscious material in the image until the child is ready cognitively or emotionally to deal with it. Unresolved feelings are present in the therapy room but contained.

A child's identity unfolds and develops from infancy onwards. At the beginning of life the infant is felt to be part of the mother. Slowly the infant begins to develop a separate identity from that of the mother figure, eventually moving off into the adult world. The literature on human development describes certain stages or tasks which the child uses in the process of shaping her identity. Wounding events in the child's life can distort or hamper this progression leading to regression or becoming stuck at certain stages. In this chapter the wound described is that of sexual abuse.

The effect of sexual abuse can be a global assault on the child's self. Basic trust in people is attacked, the autonomy the child is developing over herself and her life is jeopardised. She is made to feel passive, and powerless. In using a developmental approach in working with such children, a framework can be used in which to make sense of children's struggles in therapy. This chapter looks particularly, though not exclusively, at the work of Erik

Erikson. Erikson examined the psychosocial aspect of human development, taking into account an awareness of cultural heritage. This is particularly relevant to a social services setting where the sessions took place. Erikson sits within a psychodynamic perspective, but saw the ego as attempting to maintain an equilibrium between the inner world of the individual and the social setting in which the individual lives. The ego, he maintained, is strengthened by the resolution of certain conflicts which are prominent during different stages of the life cycle. Although he accepted that the resolution of these conflicts is not always possible at the time, his remains an optimistic theory, believing that there is little, given the right circumstances, that cannot be resolved later. Erikson devised a framework for these conflicts which he called his epigenetic chart. It is a helpful guide when making sense of the meaning of children's art making, although ultimately it is only a tool to think with and not a therapy manual. Three of these early conflicts relevant to the following case study are:

1   Basic trust versus mistrust. This is prominent in infanthood, the baby gaining trust over the mother figure to meet the baby's needs.
2   Autonomy versus doubt and shame. This describes the emerging independence of the child and the devastation children can feel when they have to let go of their new-found control.
3   Initiative versus guilt. As the child's contact with the outside world increases she needs to master new skills, and society requires that she take more responsibility for her actions. Failure to do this can leave a sense of guilt that the child has failed to come up to expectations.

Within the context of child abuse it is possible to see how the resolution of these conflicts can be distorted:

> We do not consider all development a series of crises. We claim only that psycho-social development proceeds by critical steps. 'Critical' being a characteristic of turning points, of moments of decision between progress and regression, integration and retardation.
>
> (Erikson 1965: 262)

This chapter sets out to describe one child's journey through art therapy accompanied by the thoughts of the art therapist within a developmental frame work. It is not the sole theory used in these observations, but provides a backdrop to the child's journey through art therapy. Also included are the theories that inform the art therapy practice itself. This chapter describes one art therapist's way of working and while it can be argued and justified, it is not intended to be an approach for all art therapists in all the diverse settings in which they work.

Art therapists are traditionally schooled in psychodynamic theory, from the work of Freud through to object relations and beyond. These too include a rich source of thoughts about child development, and insights into the possible interpretations of children's images and communication. In terms of theories for art therapy practice, the author would suggest that therapists choose a way of working that concurs with their own belief systems and sits comfortably within the work setting. 'A characteristic of contemporary art therapy practice is its eclectic nature, or rather the process of drawing upon different theoretical perspectives to suit different contexts' (Sandle 1998: 64). The centrality of the finished image versus the process of image making may vary from therapist to therapist and from client to client. The importance of verbal communication is another variable, as is the part that creativity plays in the whole process.

In order to take part in art making the individual needs to galvanise their creativity into action. The word creativity is widely used in the arts therapies. Winnicott defined it as 'The approach of the individual to external reality' (Winnicott 1971: 64), and contrasted it with compliance 'Compliance carries with it a sense of futility for the individual and is associated with the idea that nothing matters' (ibid). He uses the word creativity to describe the core of the person that remains whole in spite of life events. In beginning to contact and nurture that creativity which lives within each child and in each of us, the self-healing potential is awakened and aroused into action. In the act of creating, the child is active and not passive. In the art room the child reframes past experiences in visual terms, an opportunity to make concrete and in time work through painful experiences. Particularly in the context of working with sexual abuse, the child's core self can be made to feel valued and given the right conditions to speak. In E.M. Lyddiatt's book *Spontaneous painting and modelling* (1970), a past patient writes of her experience of art therapy:

> The therapy of painting lies in the act of painting, the application of paint on paper, rather than the analysis of the finished 'picture'. . . In the art therapy room my sick self found my whole self and the therapist by total unquestioning acceptance of me and the things that I painted, encouraged me to believe in myself as a valid person.
>
> (Lyddiatt 1970: 122)

This forms an important part of the art therapist's approach to the sessions. A strong belief that within each of us there is the potential to heal. For this healing to take place an atmosphere of acceptance and empathy is provided by the therapist. A place where even forbidden thoughts and feelings can be expressed in words and images and accepted. A space in which the client can experience their whole self.

Carl Rogers developed ideas on client-centred therapy from his own premise that the individual has a capacity for growth and self-direction. He laid down a structure for child-centred play therapy which can also provide a useful guide for the art therapist. The following formed the framework for practice within the centre where the therapy described took place:

1   The room is in order for the child.
2   A prompt start to sessions.
3   Appointments are kept and the child is told in advance if appointments need to be cancelled.
4   Confidences are kept. (Author's note: An addendum to this is the exception of unreported child protection concerns, though even in these cases there are often ways of enabling the child to still have choices within the statutory duties of the therapist.)
5   A relationship of warmth and understanding.
6   Absence of pressure. An acceptance of the child as he/she is.
7   The acceptance and permissiveness to be himself.

(Rogers 1951: 239)

CASE STUDY

Hannah was a 7-year-old girl, the youngest of three children. She was referred to the centre by her social worker. Her older brother had sexually abused her, and this abuse was witnessed by the other brother. As a result of the investigation the older brother was accommodated by the local authority and went to live with foster carers.

Our first meeting was at the family home as Hannah's mother was anxious about travelling to the centre. Physically Hannah looked extremely fragile and small for her age. Her mother too was a small and slightly built woman. Hannah seemed quite sad and down about her situation, but was able to speak out about her feelings and showed a strength of character that came through even at that first meeting. Her mother had endured an extremely difficult and painful childhood. She had been sexually abused as a child by family members, and worried that Hannah would endure the same fate. This anxiety became a strong theme throughout Hannah's therapy.

In working with women who have been sexually abused as children, it is unusual, perhaps because of the lack of recognition of abuse in the past, to come across those who have had therapy as children. Thus, feelings of worthlessness, passivity and being to blame can be internalised and played out in adult relationships, and in relationships with offspring. Abuse can affect the development of both sexual and psychosocial intimacy, so that the individual either shies away or hurls themselves into the act of intimacy (Erikson 1968: 135). Appropriate therapy, either in a safe group or with a trusted adult, can begin to unlock the burden that the parent may have carried since childhood. As with children:

> In order to work with survivors of child sexual abuse, you must have the conviction that survivors can heal. Hold a vision of your client as strong survivors, as women who can heal and thrive.
>
> (Bass and Davis 1988: 345)

At her first session Hannah's opening comment to me was that she could lift her middle brother up, and it seemed important that I should acknowledge this strength in her. I had set out a selection of art materials on the table. At first we recapped on our first meeting, confirming that the sessions were for Hannah to use as she needed and that they could give her a space to explore her feelings around her brother and the abuse. Hannah decided to draw and cut out a cartoon dog to stick on her art folder (Figure 7.1) where her work would be kept. She had been taught to draw the dog by her brother. I repeated her statement and Hannah said that although he was living away from home she would like him to come back. She continued to colour and cut out her brother's dog and stuck it very firmly to the folder. The image of her brother's dog taped securely to the front of the folder became a constant reminder of what had brought her to the centre. The first session had been planned as a gentle introduction. It is important to stay aware of the child's pace in therapy, so they remain in control and the therapy does not begin to mirror the abusive situation where the abuser is in control. This is balanced by a need for the therapist to be aware of their own reaction to sexual abuse, lest they silence the child by their own unwillingness to confront painful issues. This delicate balance forms part of the art of art therapy. If the therapist pressurises a child into naming and describing the abuse too soon, the link between thoughts and feelings can be broken, and the child simply goes through the motions of telling about the abuse. In certain circumstances, for example after a critical incident or in a post traumatic disorder, a more direct approach may need to be taken. It is sometimes argued that all sexual abuse results in post traumatic syndrome disorder, although there are ongoing debates as to the specific criteria for this diagnosis. Tillman Furniss argues that:

> All sexually abused children need some relief from their confusion and all children need prevention work. But not all sexually abused children are psychologically disturbed to a degree which needs therapy.
>
> (Furniss 1991: 140)

It feels important that each child's experience of abuse must be listened to, and the appropriate approach to therapy decided accordingly. The advantage of art therapy is that unconscious thoughts and feelings will often seep through the protective shell of language, and can be contained and kept in a safe place by the therapist until the time is right to make the link to the child's consciousness. Talking about the abuse may come during a session or with a trusted adult outside the session time. However, a child may choose not to talk

Figure 7.1   Cartoon dog

until she feels fully safe or is at the stage when she can cognitively make sense of the past. In the case of Karen, a 5-year-old child, her abuse had been non-penetrative and carried out by an uncle who had been the only person to show her love and care in the family. Although her play and images became an outlet for unconscious feelings around the abuse and a neglectful family life,

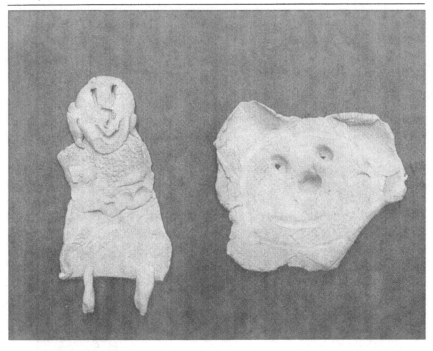

Figure 7.2   The two-dimensional girl

she retained an attachment to him and struggled to understand the difference between appropriate and inappropriate loving. Her difficulties around attachments (Bowlby 1969) formed an issue we explored both in individual sessions, and in joint sessions with her long-term foster carer.

Hannah returned the next week and chose to use clay. This material can be very cathartic and healing for children. At the start of a clay session the pounding and throwing of the clay relaxes and releases tension from the child, making her more open to unconscious expression. Clay can help to contain overwhelming feelings by its viscosity, as opposed to the sometimes uncontrollable flow of paint. However with the addition of water it also offers the opportunity to make and explore mess. In a group for adolescent boys who had been sexually abused, the use of clay in the sessions enabled them to express their anger safely, and it also became a time when they would talk about their experience of abuse.

The conflict of initiative versus guilt became evident as Hannah worked on a little two-dimensional girl made of clay (Figure 7.2). She gave it thin little arms and legs. The limbs were without hands and feet, and the piece was fragile. With the remaining piece of clay she drew a faint circle with her fingers and poked the clay to make the eyes nose and mouth (Figure 7.2). Both images appeared to be expressions of 'the self'. She began to play with the clay in an exploratory manner, pushing the clay into a scoop. She then found it difficult to dislodge the clay. After several attempts she hunted around and found a robust spoon with which she was able to gouge out the clay. Hannah seemed pleased at dislodging the clay, and I commented that she seemed to be able to find solutions for her difficulties.

Working with children in art therapy brings into question the relationship between art and play therapy. Children in therapy will, if offered, move easily between play and art materials, using both to express their thoughts and feelings. A comparison of the differences and overlap between the two disciplines is an area that would merit a chapter of its own, and so will not be expanded here. The boundaries of art itself are constantly being explored and challenged, and in time incorporated into the mainstream. Installation art, performance art, video art, are in the end accepted as valid artistic expressions. In therapy, sand tray work, dramatic role play and dressing up provide an equivalent rich source of materials with which a child can create their inner world. An individual's artistic expression surely should not be limited by another's boundaries.

Hannah operated on a baby doll in one session and removed his tonsils. He was cleaned and fed using real baby food. The food became smeared on his face and then on his body, until the doll was covered in mess. I wondered what kind of a baby this was. Hannah replied that it was a bad baby because it hit out at other people, but that it wasn't really the baby's fault. The mother made it do this. The baby was bad because the mother was bad. I reminded Hannah that the previous week she had told me the baby had been taken into foster care. Hannah told me that her brother was in foster care because he had sexually abused her. In one sense Hannah already knew that I knew this, but within the therapeutic relationship it needed to be voiced by her. Hannah began to tell me about some of the events surrounding the abuse. Hannah said she remembered these things and that she would never forget them. I was reminded of a talk given by Helen Bamber, discussing her work as Director of The Medical Foundation (a centre that offers counselling and support for victims of torture). She spoke about the role of bearing witness to her clients' personal histories. To be able to listen and to stay with them was defined as being part of the healing for those who had suffered abuse.

The doll had offered Hannah a way to describe her abuse and her thoughts around it. Her question seemed to be: was her mother aware of the abuse and in some way controlling the actions of her son?

> Another of Celia's questions regarding secrecy which was relevant to the absence of her mother at the times of the abuse, was 'Can you see what I am doing when you are in another place' . . . She seemed to have the feeling that even when she could not see her mother her mother would be able to see her.
>
> (Sagar 1990: 105)

At a certain developmental stage children may begin to question: if I can't see someone can they still see me? It also illustrates the a developing sense of separation of the self from mother and the striving to establish a separate identity. Hannah's role play also gave her the opportunity to inflict some punishment on the boy baby by messing him up and sending him away from home. The doll seemed to represent not only her brother, but also, at another level, feelings about herself – the thought that she too might be messed up, that bad internal feelings needed to be extracted from her mouth, and the fear that abuse was passed from mother to baby and maybe connected with 'badness' running in the family. Play and art offer the child a method of encapsulating all these thoughts at one moment. It gives the child a way to philosophise without the need for language.

At my next meeting with Hannah she chose to use the face paints and asked if we could paint each other. Children often ask for the art therapist to join in. Thought needs to be given on the meaning of these requests before a decision is given. The personal and tactile nature of face painting can recreate the abusive situation. It therefore needs to be set up with special care around choices and boundaries. The activity can also offer the child an opportunity to have a positive and potentially healing experience of physical closeness with another, helping to lay the ghost of past abuse. I asked Hannah to give me clear instructions of how she wanted her face painted. It was painted with a white background, gold eyes and red lips. She looked at herself in the mirror. I wondered who the person in the mirror might be. 'A princess, an ugly mean princess. She's mean because she's selfish, but when she complains nobody listens.' She continued by telling me what the princess complains about and swaying from the princess as bad, to the princess as good but misunderstood.

The struggle between good and bad is archetypal and can be found in many myths and fairy stories. This mirrors the fact that during abuse the victim often detaches herself from what is happening, and a split between mind and body can occur. Thoughts of children can centre around what is badness, and can good and bad exist together?

> It signifies a growing awareness in children that good and bad can exist in the same individual. Until children come to acknowledge this, their feelings about themselves continue to be rooted in the primitive notion that badness must be destroyed if goodness is to survive. This belief must be transcended if children and adults hope to eventually tolerate the badness that exists within themselves.
>
> (Cashdan 1988: 170–2)

This theme of bad and good coexisting was explored further in the following weeks. One time Hannah made a tree painting. Hannah chose to draw a large tree in the forest. The drawing was made on a large sheet of paper and set out on the floor so that it was bigger than Hannah herself. The shape at first was strongly phallic having hair-like grass around its base. Hannah described it as a beautiful tree by day, but at night it was scary. After the drawing was made Hannah began to pour white glue over the tree and moved it around with the glue spreader. She became engrossed in this act, the therapist simply attending to her. After a while Hannah requested some glitter to make it more magical. Glitter can be an important art material for children, enabling a re-creation of painful experiences into an image they can make their own and gain control of. Hannah had hidden the messy glue with glitter and turned her scary tree into something less overwhelming.

Her next project was a mask that was made by applying plaster bandages to a ready-made plastic mask. At first she painted a thick blue border around the face. She then painted a thick red cross over the features. I asked if the cross reminded her of anything. She began to talk about the Sunday school that she had stopped going to, because a girl had accused her of having sex with her brother. She said it had made her think again about the abuse. She developed a game where she was the teacher and I the pupil. It felt that in order to gain control and move from the position of victim she began to instruct me on how to make a picture out of scissors (Figure 7.3), drawing round them as a boundary for herself and the image. She was kind but clearly in control. I asked what she could see in the picture, Hannah said it was the face of a man but not a boy. I was to copy her picture and both were to be stuck on the wall. It was as if she wanted again to leave a sign to signify why she had come and to contain the image in a place where she could keep an eye on it.

The theme of making a sign has been used throughout history and biblical times to highlight those afflicted, or those chosen. Hannah developed this idea in the following session, and made up a mixture of sand and dark red paint. She dressed-up as a 'Roman lady', and said that it was part of the custom to paint their guests. As with the mask making I negotiated my boundaries, and her choices. She painted my hands and arms with the mixture which felt gritty and uncomfortable. She began to talk about her mother's relationships and family background. She thought that life might be the same for her, and in some way she might be marked out for abuse. We looked at the difference between her mother and herself in terms of their personal histories and their personalities. Although I offered her reassurance I recognised that it was an issue she would return to again as she reached adolescence.

During adolescence the conflict brought to the art therapy session often centres around a search for a consistent identity versus identity confusion (Erikson 1968). Issues around sexuality and sexual orientation can be particularly confusing. In one art therapy group for adolescent boys who had been sexually abused it was noticed that:

> Anxiety and excitement around sexuality was both expressed verbally and transferred on to the images. Part of the phenomenon was recognised

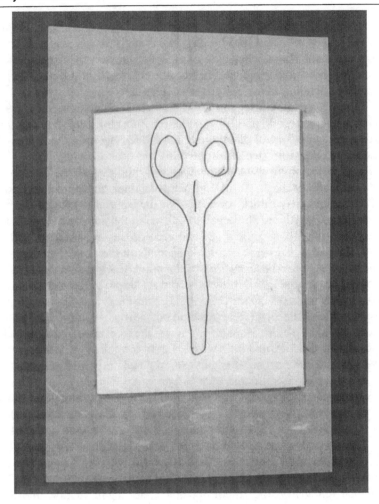

Figure 7.3   Drawing round the scissors

by the facilitators as developmental, but other aspects seemed more complex. The boys expressed through images and words their anxiety about
internal conflicts surrounding their sexuality.

(Bissonnet 1998: 127)

During her therapy Hannah was sometimes wise for her years and at other
times acted like a much younger child. Sometimes her voice was strong and
sometimes infantile. These times of regression led me to offer her a way to
explore the conflict of trust versus mistrust, an early task in human development. I had noticed that Hannah would sometimes take quick tastes of glue

or clay, as if she was in doubt as to what tasted good. I felt that Hannah needed an opportunity to trust in her senses once more. Covering our eyes we tasted different kinds of food, guessed what they were and whether we liked them or not. Slowly Hannah's opinions became more assured and she rejoiced in announcing that she definitely did or did not like what was offered. She proceeded to pour all the food she disliked into a tub, and added glue and paint and other available liquids we found such as baby lotion and washing-up liquid. Eventually a noxious and, to Hannah, poisonous liquid was created. This was left in the therapy room and regularly inspected over the coming weeks as it grew more evil looking. She labelled it 'Hannah's poison' and left it for the therapist to guard over.

In one of the ending sessions Hannah began to use clay and water, making her hands wet and slimy. She made two clay balls and wet and moulded them in a sensuous way in her hands (Figure 7.4). Hannah began to cover these in the plaster bandages, again moulding them with her hands. She began to talk about the abuse in more depth filling in previous undisclosed detail. She said she felt angry and she felt sad. She loved her brother, but wasn't able to trust him any more. She began to see the good and bad existing in him at the same time. I wondered, as she was good at thinking about how to work out her difficulties, if there was something she would like to do in the sessions to express these painful thoughts about her brother. Hannah requested to make another salt sculpture. Some weeks previously she had made one around the absence of her father. A salt sculpture is a technique where memories or feelings are linked with coloured salt or sand and poured in sections into a jar which is then securely fastened. Hannah was able to name the good things about her brother including his sense of humour and his patience when playing with her. She also included a colour for the abuse and placed this as the last section on top of the other separate feelings in the jar. At the end of the final session, this was part of the work that she chose to take home.

There is often a tension in deciding the length of therapy sessions appropriate for each child. Holding on to children in therapy can sometimes encourage a child to feel overdependent and to see themselves as different from their peers. In contrast there are the external pressures of stretched resources. In reality both may have their part to play in deciding the length of therapy. In Hannah's situation it seemed important to acknowledge the work she had done, the strength she had found in herself. The adults around her were able to feed back their confidence that she could return to an uninterrupted routine which confirmed that she was an ordinary little girl who had suffered a painful event in her life that wasn't of her making. The possibility of returning for more work at the centre if she reached a difficult stage in her life gives children the message that endings may be sad but they are not necessarily forever and do not mean abandonment.

The final session was spent going through her work and looking back over the issues that were important to her. We looked again at the artwork, which

Figure 7.4   Plaster balls

had changed in scale and in confidence. She had gained skills using the art materials, and though the images were still troubled, they were bolder and more free-flowing than her earlier images. She seemed to have a growing recognition of her own strength and that she could be strong in her mind even if her physical strength was limited. It is my belief that she had begun to separate herself from her mother and had begun to let go of the feeling that in some way Hannah herself had been responsible for the abuse.

At the final review meeting Hannah's mother voiced concerns about adolescence and the difficulties that might bring. The dilemmas she might face in adolescence were not Hannah's concern or perhaps within her understanding at the time. An assurance was given to Hannah and her mother that they could be referred again for further therapy if needed. This encouraged Hannah and seemed to empower her to get on with her life at present, knowing she has a space for herself if needed in the future.

CONCLUSION

Working with children as opposed to adults in art therapy brings new challenges for the therapist. The process of art making assumes more prominence than the finished image. Therapists not only need to have a knowledge of child development theories, but also a sufficient amount of self-knowledge. Only armed with these two aspects can they begin to meet the whole child in therapy. This chapter attempts to show one way of accompanying a child on her journey towards healing. It is not the end of the story. Hannah will need time as an adult to look back on her childhood, and hopefully armed with the insight she developed during our time together, reach a mature understanding of what happened. At the heart of the therapeutic relationship should lie a respect, admiration and trust in the child survivor as she struggles along the road to maturity.

REFERENCES

Bass, E. and Davis, L. 91988) *The courage to heal*, New York: Cedar Press.

Bissonnet, J. (1988) 'Group work with adolescent boys in a social service setting', in D. Sandle (ed.) *Development and diversity*, London, New York: Free Association Books.

Bowlby, J. (1969) *Attachment*, Harmondsworth, UK: Penguin Books.

Cashdan, S. (1988) *Object relations therapy*, London, New York, Canada: Norton & Co Ltd.

Erikson, E. (1965) *Childhood and society*, Harmondsworth, UK: Penguin Books.

Erikson, E. (1968) *Identity: Youth and crisis*, London, Boston: Faber & Faber.

Furniss, T. (1991) *The multi-professional handbook of child sexual abuse*, London & New York: Routledge.

Lyddiatt, E.M. (1970) *Spontaneous painting and modelling. A practical approach in therapy*, London: Constable & Co Ltd.

Rogers, C. (1951) *Client centred therapy*, London: Constable & Co Ltd.

Sagar, C. (1990) 'Working with cases of child sexual abuse', in C. Case and T. Dalley (eds) *Working with children in art therapy*, London, Canada, New York: Routledge.

Sandle, D. (ed.) (1988) *Development and diversity*, London, New York: Free Association Books.

Winnicott, D.W. (1971) *Playing and reality*, Harmondsworth, UK: Penguin Books.

Part III

Experiences with groups

Chapter 8

Jumping over it
Group therapy with young girls

Richard Buckland and Jenny Murphy

Young children do not have the vocabulary to describe sexual abuse and the feelings it evokes in them, but in our experience, the struggle to externalise and recognise these can be facilitated by a combination of art and play activities. When this takes place in a group, the child's sense of isolation is reduced and children who are more in touch with their feelings help those who are comparatively fearful. Indeed, group therapy is thought to be the preferred treatment for sexual abuse survivors (Knittle and Tuana 1980, Steward et al. 1986, Howard 1993).

We shall describe a group for young girls, which was part of the Specialist Child Abuse programme in a Child and Adolescent Mental Health department and has offered a programme of individual and group therapy for more than 12 years. The children, usually six in number, are grouped together by sex and by developmental stage. Groups are expected to run for 20 sessions, though occasionally extended when more time is needed to finish the work.

While the children's group takes place, a parallel group for their parents and carers is held in a different room, each group having two therapists. Parents are able to think together about the feelings that their child's sexual abuse has raised for them, appropriate ways of managing distress, setting boundaries and communicating with their child. These can be very highly charged groups, but important in underpinning the work that the children are doing and enabling parents to feel involved in their child's recovery (Howard 1993: 222). When the therapists meet to share their work following the groups, it is not uncommon to find that both children's and parents' groups have been concerned with the same issues on the same day. This coincidence of material opens our minds to the powerful mutual introjective/projective cycles in these families where the children's experience has been unwittingly determined by the thoughts that the parents have not been able to think. Bion's 'A theory of thinking' describes such processes (Bion 1967: 110–19). The presence of such unthinkable unconscious material in the minds of the parents is invariably a key element in creating the circumstances that allow the children to be abused. It is not until the parents and children encounter the intense power of the group process that these unconscious thoughts are unlocked and become thinkable for parents and children in an inter-locking way.

Sexually abused children have experienced a confusion of boundaries in their lives and are likely to be very uncertain of new social situations such as joining a group. In our reading, it seems that most therapists agree some gen-eral principles, for instance that therapists are able to create and maintain good boundaries and that the establishment of confidence in the group is helped by having a recognisable, clear and repeated pattern to each session. Also there is agreement that the carers of the children need to be involved in the overall process. Beyond this there is a great deal of variation, particularly in the tight-ness of structure, ranging from a highly controlled agenda for each session (Nelki and Watters 1989) to an open freely developing therapeutic play experi-ence within a simple 'juice time, free play, snack' structure (Steward et al. 1986). Our model, developed independently, is closest to the latter: we start with a whole-group activity, such as game playing, then a period of art, play or other creative activities, followed by sitting around the art therapy room table for drinks, biscuits and discussion. Once the group have got to know each other, the game playing is dispensed with, but substituted by an art activity for the whole group before the children make their own choice from the materials in the room. We encourage the children to make a drawing or painting on arrival in the group as a way of 'taking the temperature' of their internal world. Apart from painting and drawing materials and clay, we provide junk materials, pup-pets, dressing-up clothes and a sand tray. We take the opportunity to comment on what we see being expressed in the art and play activities, both as they happen and over drinks during the reflective ending of each group, helping the children to understand the themes arising during the session and encouraging them to share experiences.

It is our view that the intensity of the group process is a powerful tool, inspired in principle by the work of W.R. Bion (1961). For this reason, despite some cogent arguments concerning the need to cover prescribed areas as described by Nelki and Watters (1989) we hold strongly to a belief in the value of a freely developing psychotherapeutic group process within a simple overall structure.

We would agree strongly with the views of Steward et al. (1986) regarding the nature of the co-therapists required. Because the overall structure is open, the clear boundaries so necessary for these children must be provided at a psychological level by the personalities of the co-therapists, who should be a male–female pair who can create a loving, respectful, courteous and flexible relationship with an absence of aggression. This couple need to be able to share in post-session supervision their deepest countertransference feelings, to ensure one does not begin to hold onto unconscious aggressive or unpre-dictable responses.

We shall describe and discuss a group of five girls: Sally, Sonia, Cheryl, Hannah and Jackie. Sally, aged 6, lived with her single mother and had been subject to penetrative sexual abuse by a male neighbour over a long period and still lived next door to him. Sonia, aged 9, had been abused on several occasions by a teenage babysitter. Cheryl, aged 8, had been abused, along with her two brothers, by a teenage neighbour and her parents were seeking rehousing. Hannah, 7 years old, had been abused by a 15-year-old neighbour and oral sex had been involved. She was the only one of her mother's five children who still lived at home. Jackie joined the group a few weeks after it had started. Aged 8, she had suffered chronic, invasive sexual abuse perpetrated by an adult male neighbour who had been convicted and imprisoned. The mothers of Sally, Hannah and Jackie had mental health problems of their own and Jackie's mother in particular found it difficult to make a regular commitment to attending the groups.

We will present a number of sessions that are turning points, or typical of a phase in the life of the group, and then record our thoughts on the sessions in the form of a dialogue which reflects our backgrounds as child psychotherapist and art therapist, also as a male and female couple.

SESSION I

Attending: Hannah, Cheryl, Sonia, Sally.

All of the children, with their parent/s had met with the therapists for at least one introductory session prior to this meeting. Today, the four girls, their mothers and all four therapists spent the first half hour together in a carpeted room playing some games. This allowed everyone involved to meet each other in an informal way and for names to be learnt, and demonstrated that the adults and children had a common purpose. The groups then separated to their different therapy rooms. The girls left their mothers without difficulty and came with us to the art therapy room.

We had prepared materials to do a large group painting to which we would all contribute, symbolising the shared journey of children and therapists. This would be the children's first experience of a psychotherapeutic response to their material. All four joined in, although Hannah was initially rather stuck and watchful. The girls were very aware of the adults and sought links with them more than with each other. Sonia connected with RB, who had painted a representation of everyone in the group journeying through mountains. Alongside him, she painted the group travelling together in a sailing boat, with a black hole in the sky above leading to 'an unknown land'. Sally painted an empty cave and what looked like sea, but the cave grew until it engulfed the rest of her picture. Across from her, Cheryl painted brownish-red water, with two people in it. She decided one of them was RB drowning, but he would be rescued by JM and taken to the 'land of the cats'. She asked JM to help her by painting her a cat, while she painted one alongside. This led to

Hannah also asking JM to draw her a cat on a strip of green grass which she had already painted. She then sat rather helplessly, brightening again when RB offered to help her. Everyone linked the images together with blue sky and Sally added a flock of six white birds near two red ones that JM had contributed earlier (Figure 8.1).

After the painting, we sat around the table together, with drinks and biscuits, for a period of discussion before the group ended. While this was happening, Sally wrote the names of the girls on paper; Sonia did the same and included the therapists. Hannah seemed more relaxed and told the group that she did not like prayers in school and all agreed that bits of school were boring. Sally asked why it was just girls in the group and several times mentioned boy/girl relationships, such as her view that in school the boys were naughty, but the girls were all good. This gave us the opportunity to remind them of the purpose of this therapy group. Cheryl asked if JM could say a prayer for the group, which she did.

Discussion of Session 1

In this first session, we shall comment on the girls' material individually to enable familiarity with each child to develop.

Sonia

RB: *I felt that Sonia entered into a positive transferential relationship with myself right from the beginning; she was happily beside me and there were*

Figure 8.1   Group picture, first session

no hostile projections at that stage. She was able to use an idea which had occurred in discussion with me about a sailing boat and also was able to adopt another feature of my picture in that she drew each of the children individually on the boat as I had done in the picture of the mountains. The anxiety of what was hovering above her head so to speak, is a symbol of what was in her mind and clearly shown in the black hole in the sky leading to the unknown.

Sally

JM: *On the other side of you, Sally painted an empty cave which grew until it lost definition and spread out across the paper. We were aware that she had been abused by a neighbour, so her inability to maintain the boundaries of her cave in the picture seemed to pose a question about whether it would be possible to maintain boundaries in this group.*

RB: *We could perhaps also see the image as representing the mysterious environment of therapy as well as of course the abusive experiences themselves. The question in her mind at an unconscious level would be whether we would be able to contain the maelstrom of overwhelming experiences held inside her.*

Cheryl

RB: *I feel that the blood-red water in Cheryl's part of the picture expresses anxiety about damage to her own inside, and the drowning person is herself. This quality of drowning she then projects into me and being to some extent contained as a more manageable experience, she is then able to be symbolically rescued. For Cheryl clearly the strong figure is the female.*

JM: *Cheryl had considerable expectations of us throughout as people who would be helpful to her because of her brothers already having taken part in therapeutic groups at the clinic, one of them with us. I think she saw us as a lifeline.*

Hannah

JM: *Hannah was very much at a loss at the start and watchful of the other children. She had noticed Cheryl linking with me and followed her lead by asking me to draw a cat for her, too. She seemed to take a cue from Cheryl that we might be safe enough people to start to make a link with.*

RB: *Thinking about Hannah, we can see how high her defences are in this first session. This makes it extremely difficult for her to pick up any of the themes introduced by the other children. You commented on her picking up a cue from Cheryl. I would see this as fundamentally Hannah sticking on to Cheryl in an adhesive way (adhesive identification) rather than being able to pick up and use Cheryl's material to enable her to communicate her own anxieties (Segal 1978). In other words, she is copying in a mimicrous way to contain her own anxieties, and her material is asymbolic at this point.*

The session

JM: *While we had drinks and biscuits, there were more questions implicitly raised about whether the group would prove to be a safe enough environment for these girls, particularly by Sally talking about the naughty boys at school, perhaps anxious that an abusive male element could invade the room at any point. Cheryl's suggestion of a prayer for the group seemed to be asking for some protective magic for the group to ensure its safety and success. Sally and Sonia, in writing the names of everybody in the group on paper, showed a fundamental optimism about the group, that it could have meaning for them and that they would be able to invest in it themselves.*

RB: *Yes, Cheryl's use of the prayer is an interesting symbol, seeming to indicate her sense of needing help from every possible source, including an omnipotent god, but it also contains the idea of the group bringing in oppressive ideas such as she has already communicated regarding her school life. Sally already seems to be showing us her very strong imaginative life, with a great deal of healthy omnipotence. It seems that her sense of there being a largely unspoilt inner world, fundamentally the world of happy children, not needing adults, is still alive. For Sonia, who includes the names of the therapists, it seems there is a greater need to hold on to the link with parental figures to enable her to feel safe on the coming journey. For Sally, when she wonders whether we will have naughty boys in the group or not, I think this is a symbol of her anxiety about whether the therapists will be able to cope with the naughty boy parts of herself, as well as containing the idea of a split in which the bad elements are projected into the boys.*

SESSION 7

Attending: Sally, Sonia, Hannah, Cheryl arrived 20 minutes late.

The girls' engagement with the processes taking place in the art room had been leading to a slow reduction of interest in the game playing period. Today, for the first time, they elected to come straight into the art room missing out the playtime altogether.

They were immediately taken up with the idea of the drama that they had been developing over the previous few sessions. They demanded that JM moved the tables out of the way to facilitate the drama. They began with an adaptation of the Cinderella story; they had some idea of the actual fairy story, however they developed their own version in which Cinderella was a well looked after child with her own mother and father, and was a rather pretty and well dressed girl. Sonia played Cinderella, with Sally and Hannah playing the mother and father respectively. It was very significant that Hannah always represented a male, either the father or, at the end of the story, a little boy.

They began with a powerful argument scene between Sonia and her father which led to Sonia running away, hating her father. Sally, the mother, tried very hard to stop the argument between father and daughter. Mother and father were then searching for their daughter Sonia, eventually arriving at a friend's house where they had to argue insistently for the right to go in. They then did go in and brought their daughter home. Sonia was able to show and act very strong anger towards her parents, although the source of the anger was not elaborated.

Later on, Sonia was seen going off to school leaving her parents lying in bed. After she is gone, when they get up, they find the children have made a terrific mess and they are full of anger. By this time Cheryl has arrived and immediately becomes another child of the family; however, she never succeeds in becoming more than a peripheral player today, the other children had already made a strong link and it was clearly difficult for Cheryl to break in. The parents are frequently heard attempting to use a form of punishment known as 'grounding' which means confining the children to the house or to a particular room. Sonia completely ignored these attempts at punishment. Towards the end of the drama, Hannah decided suddenly that she had become a foundling, a little boy who had sprung from the earth. In a conflation of fairy stories, Sonia is then allowed by her parents to go to the woods, her mother Sally telling her that she must take a knife to protect herself. In the woods, she finds the little foundling, who briefly turns into a monster scaring Sonia, then quickly reverts to being the foundling boy again. The little foundling was then taken by Sonia to her house and invited in; however, she said 'I don't know you so I can't come in.' She was, however, persuaded to go into the house. This concluded the drama play in this session.

In terms of the children's feelings about the therapists, both Sonia and Sally were quite at ease in changing their clothes in front of them while Hannah was anxious, needing to go to the toilet to change anything. She then solved the problem in a different way, by putting clothes on, but not taking anything off. Cheryl was very pale and withdrawn and seemed to be quite unwell in both psychological and physical ways; she had of course arrived late which made it difficult for her to join in, however we felt that her vulnerability today was also a factor in preventing her integration into the group's functioning.

Discussion of Session 7

RB: *This is the first session in which the children have opted to come straight into the art room and seems to indicate an increasing sense of security and containedness by the therapists. But it could also be seen as an unconscious recognition of the idea of a 'work group' (Bion 1961) in which most children recognise that there is work going on which is significant to them and that this really begins with the symbolic play that they do in the room.*

JM: *Yes, I remember how eager they were for the tables to be put to one side to create a space to take up the play on the Cinderella theme that they had started the week before. They seemed very excited to be together again.*

RB: *The children using the story of Cinderella seems overdetermined because there are so many elements of it which would seem to be significant to this group of children. I suppose the central idea is the unfavoured Cinderella, abandoned and neglected in the fairy story and tormented; clearly this has a major resonance with the abuse which all these children have suffered. However, the children intuitively bend the story to suit their own needs and create both a mother and a father for Cinderella and her neglect is not particularly the major feature here. Most significant for the children was the way in which Sonia feels she is a bad child, that the arguments occur with her father, that she has to run away. This is a very common feature for this group of children. They feel it is their own badness which is in some way implicated in the fact that they have become abused. However, there do seem to be some quite hopeful signs in that, despite this, there is a parental couple and furthermore they do go to seek the bad Cinderella figure out and to bring her home.*

JM: *We were very struck by the fact that Cinderella was well-dressed and attractive unlike the usual character. Her uncertain place in the family seemed to be expressed differently, through the arguments between the girl and her father, the anger of the parents about the mess they found after she'd gone to school and their punishment of the children. The girls seemed to be exploring whether they were really acceptable to their families, really good enough to be loved. I think it showed how low their self-esteem was.*

RB: *Yes, I think that seems to be extremely important. Perhaps at this stage, really quite early in the work with the girls, we could see that the parental figures are ourselves in the transference, and that really the question the children have in their minds is whether we want them to be with us. Until these rather fundamental factors are established for them and internalised, the children will not be able to get into the deeper material concerning the profound nature of the abuse and the ensuing damage, which is certainly equal to any damage that occurred to Cinderella in the fairy story. We might also see this idea of mess as being the precursor of the rather more painful ideas of mess, symbolising damage, which might have occurred inside them as a result of the abuse.*

JM: *The last phase of this session had quite a different quality when Hannah stopped being the father and decided to be the little foundling boy. Suddenly, the idea of external danger emerged in the story, leading to ideas about trust and self-protection. It seems the children were starting to show us their experience of how dangerous the world could be.*

RB: *Yes, certainly the change of pace is very clear, perhaps initiated by the role of maleness, certainly adult maleness, and the terrifying element present in it, remembering that all these girls were abused by either adolescent or adult males.*

It is interesting that Hannah abandons the role of the father and becomes a magical foundling child who springs from the earth perhaps symbolising an unthreatening innocent sort of primal male child. The children then continue to struggle with the idea of maleness, in that Sally as the mother tells the daughter that she will need a knife to protect herself in the woods, and when she sees Hannah, the little boy, the monsterousness of masculinity is symbolised briefly before returning to the innocent little boy incarnation again. It did seem that for Hannah the awareness and fearfulness of sexuality was more strongly in her mind in this session, in that she alone of the children went into the toilet when she changed her clothes.

SESSION 11

Attending: Sonia, Sally, Hannah and a little later, Cheryl and Jackie.

As soon as the first three children entered the room, they became intensely involved in the drama scenario. Hannah began to paint, saying that she was at playgroup, however she quickly changed this to being a little girl at home with RB as daddy and when Cheryl arrived a few minutes later, she was willingly co-opted into being Hannah's sister at home with her. Meanwhile Sally and Sonia began enacting a scene in which one, the daughter of JM, was in hospital, and the other was her doctor. They interchanged their roles halfway through this drama scene. Sally's initial idea was to say 'Sonia has eaten mummy's money. This has made her very ill.' Sally then suddenly announced that she had had a pin stuck through her heart, left by her careless mother. She then repeatedly died and came back to life; however, she was eventually 'buried'. Sonia, as the doctor, was insistent on keeping JM as the mother away from the awful scene of the dead baby. The theme of the doctor protecting the mother from the sight of the baby being operated upon and from the blood etc. was given enormous emphasis by Sonia as the doctor.

The scene of the dead baby was then left behind. Sally changed suddenly from being the dead baby into a new version, now being JM's live baby again. Sonia joined in as another baby, both demanding mummy's attention for nappy changes and for feeding. Sonia particularly made strong use of RB as her daddy, sitting comfortably on his knee and wanting to remain very clearly as a baby.

This seemed to lead into Cheryl and Hannah wishing also to become babies; the children were very accommodating and Sally and Sonia grew up slightly to make room for the new twin babies. However, Hannah resisted the idea of becoming a twin; she was clear that she wanted to be an 'only baby'.

There was a very strong fixation on the feeding bottle. Despite the strength of the fixation the girls nevertheless took turns sharing the bottle surprisingly well. Jackie, who had joined the group slightly later than the others, remained outside all the action so far, continuing to print and paint on her own. However, when the scene moved to a ferryboat to Disneyland, she was incorporated into the scene, but still in a semi-separate way, taking on the persona of an 18-year-old girl who could stay at home on her own, so that when the four children and their parents sailed away in the ferry boat she remained at home. In the last enactment of this drama today, Cheryl fell into the sea, prompting Sally to become a mermaid who dived in and rescued her. We then cleared up and set the table and got into some discussion about today.

Clearly today's material is extremely rich and it was quite difficult for us to begin to find a way of making links that would be useful to the girls. However, the idea that occurred to us, and which we were able to conceptualise and put into words, focused around the notion of rebirth and growth without abuse taking place. Although clearly there were many vicissitudes occurring, nevertheless the vigour and liveliness of the babies and the continuity or the survival of life clearly struck both therapists as being significant. Having talked about this idea of the children symbolising the wish to be reborn and to go forward together, this time without abuse, Jackie spoke about her father, who frequently goes away for long periods of time to work abroad; this time she talked about him coming home and being changed, being fatter and having grey hair. This clearly continued the theme of transformation and seemingly damaging things occurring. We struggled hard to engage with the girls in an active way to see whether more thinking could go on about the clear representations of damage occurring in the drama as well as the more hopeful transformations and rebirths. They were quite unable to acknowledge anything to do with ideas about damage, however they responded in a very clear way to the idea of being reborn, starting life again and then going forward without being abused.

Discussion of Session 11

RB: *This group seems to set off a period in which the girls are very intensely in touch with the meaning of the abuse to them. There is a sense of great energy and intensity in their activity and at this stage they find it really quite difficult to think about the meaning of what they are doing, they are simply immersed in the material. In the beginning of the group I am struck by the very alive transference which threads through this group of there being good daddies symbolised by myself and less surprisingly, a good and loving mummy, symbolised by yourself.*

JM: *Yes, I think they wanted the good mother to clean their genital areas of the sexual abuse when they demanded their nappies be changed, but the bad mother features in the story, too. The babies were damaged by the carelessness of the mothers who allowed one to eat money, while the other was pricked through the heart by a pin. They don't seem to be openly showing their anger towards their mothers at this stage, but they are demonstrating their sense of physical and emotional damage by their uncertainty of whether the doctor can cure this or whether it will be fatal. I think this play of healing and cleaning their bodies is a good demonstration of how the effects of sexual abuse may become embodied, and how this could lead to survivors becoming involved in various kinds of self-harming behaviours or developing somatic symptoms* (Young 1992).

RB: *Yes, I am struck by the intensity of the somatic or visceral experience of this session, it was certainly a very powerful experience for us as therapists to be part of the children's expressive and repeated enactments of such terrible harm occurring to their bodies. Their images were extraordinarily vivid and painful. Nevertheless, the vividness of the continuing life also shines through and Sally perhaps typifies this by both communicating the most intensely powerful and painful feelings while simultaneously finding very important and vivid imagery to express this. The continuing nature of life is represented by the doctor who really helps the baby to keep coming back to life.*

JM: *I was interested in the way the doctor character was trying to protect the mother from seeing the suffering of the ill, or dead, baby and I wondered if, on one level, this might be a reflection of the abusive relationship where the child had been with the abusing male in private, away from the mother. It could also have been connected to the girls' memory of their mothers' distress when they had been able to make their disclosures.*

RB: *yes, it seemed to me this could be a transference manifestation of Sally's experience of the clinic; the doctor really represents the good resources of the clinic, since I think that in the children's mind the clinic is experienced not just as a psychological place, but also a medical place. Bearing in mind it is in reality part of the health service, this is perhaps quite understandable and also that for children clearly the image of the doctor is something of an archetype.*

Going on to the middle of the session, it does seem that the idea of there being healthy male figures is very much in the girls' minds, which is a hopeful sign since it is always very distressing when children make contact with the idea that maleness equals badness in an over-simple 'symbolic equation' kind of way (Segal 1978).

Another very striking feature of this session is the way in which the girls as babies really work very hard to share the resources despite the fixation on the feeding bottle which they all avidly wish to have. They do nevertheless find ways of sharing this among them in a very generous way. Perhaps this is an indication of the fundamental emotional health that exists in the girls in this group. Initially, I think there was a good deal of foreboding about the way in which being involved continuously with such a painful area of pathology could affect us as therapists. However, we have actually found ourselves moved and uplifted and not overwhelmed by the pain because of the reservoirs of creativity and loving feelings that we have found surfacing in this work.

JM: *Yes, I think this may be something that can happen in a group and would not happen in individual therapy; the children can jointly develop great resourcefulness in their attempts to come to terms with what has happened to them and show reserves of strength and a capacity for symbolic thinking which the creative environment of the group encourages them to tap into. But the more fearful the child and the more chaotic their family circumstances, the more difficult this is for them.*

RB: *Yes, it reinforces the absolutely essential nature of providing therapeutic help very near to the time of the abuse. Clearly these children are not crushed yet, but if this kind of therapeutic experience had not taken place, then we can imagine these children's lively imagination and essential hopefulness slowly sinking. It seems at the end that the ferry to Disneyland appears to be a quiet but manic flight to a never-never land where everything is always wonderful. This enabled Jackie to find a connection with the group, but Cheryl doesn't seem to be able to remain on board this fantasy escape and actually falls back into the sea from where Sally, in another creative and magical manoeuvre, rescues her.*

JM: *Remembering the group picture in the first session, Cheryl used the image of drowning and rescue then. I think drowning was an image, whether in paint or play, which showed metaphorically how much she continued to experience the lack of a solid foundation in her somewhat chaotic family.*

*Her parents' relationship was suffering partly from the stress of their hous-
ing situation at this time. I think Cheryl was often depressed and looked to
the group for a lifeline, which this time Sally provided.*

RB: *This was one of the groups where the theoretical idea of having time after
the creative activities to talk did actually take place in a fuller way than was
sometimes possible. It was here that we talked with the girls for the first
time about their wish to be reborn and then to grow again without the abuse
having taken place. The sense of the passage of time and the significance of
that was also contained in Jackie's thinking about her father and how he
might well have changed when he comes home from his work abroad. In general at this stage the girls were completely immersed in their material and
really though we talked to them about the possible meanings and connections of some of their ideas at this stage they were not really taking much
of this on board. However, the idea of rebirth and starting again was one
that they did very much understand.*

SESSION 12

Attending: Sally, Sonia, Hannah and Cheryl. Jackie was absent

They immediately set up a scene in which all four girls were babies in a family
with JM and RB as mummy and daddy. Cheryl was slightly less integrated
into the group, sometimes going off to paint on her own, however the children found a way of maintaining integration by describing this as Cheryl
being at playgroup. This interesting link enabled Cheryl to continue her connection and later again to become more fully part of the family. Hannah
was very much an inside baby, or in the process of actually being born. Sonia
was strikingly calm throughout, showing a very strong attachment to RB as
a daddy to a significantly greater degree than the other three. The bottle as in
the previous session continued to be central to the play and very much in
demand, however they continued to manage their jealousy concerning possession of the bottle extremely well.

Sally several times arrived at the door with the police explaining to us that
our neighbour was complaining about the noise. She also said right out of the
blue that the neighbour wouldn't admit he had done it; this enabled RB to
make a link with the known facts of Sally's abuse which had indeed been perpetrated by her neighbour who had steadfastly refused to admit his guilt.
Sally developed her idea of her possession of a magic ring which enabled her
to turn into 'supergirl' and in this guise we were encouraged to summon her
when the babies needed help. There was much nappy-changing, all of which
needed mummy – Sally screaming piercingly, repeatedly and intensely for
help from mummy. It seemed to us significant that the children continued to

require attention to their anal and genital areas in this session. At this time of intense infantile functioning, Cheryl continued to be rather outside the group – although being able to make some demands on the bottle, she nevertheless did not enter to anything like the same degree the regressed state of the other three girls.

Sally several times metamorphosed herself into a mermaid and also in this guise introduced the idea of finding a merman under the sea. She talked about mummy not wanting her to become a mermaid, she also talked about the merman named Jack whom she would one day marry and also spoke of her father as Triton who lived under the sea.

The intensity of the children's identification today with a deeply regressed infantile state made it extremely difficult for us to maintain the timetable of the group and it was with great difficulty that we persuaded them to dress themselves and come to the table for drinks and biscuits and the talking session. Although this is extremely rich material with multiple meanings, we were again struck with the intensity of their need to regress to infancy and to receive a very high level of loving attention as babies. We again felt the deep longing of these children to enter a state of safe and loving infancy with us as a symbolic mummy and daddy and thereby return to a pre-abuse age of existence. We spoke about this and Sally seemed to be suddenly struck with the resonance of this idea with her capacity to consciously think about it, and demonstrated her understanding by saying 'Yes, that's right, we will be babies and then we will just jump over the abuse.' This we found a really moving statement. It conveyed such an intense sense of both life and hope. Hannah in particular seemed to be finding this idea rather difficult and was blocking us out. Sally went on with her rather clearer capacity to think about the here and now, telling us about her abuser by name and describing how he had rubbed her mother's private parts and later that he had taken her to his room and done the same thing to her. She then said that she had told her mummy after she had done a poo and mummy had made it better with cream. She then said, again very movingly, 'This is a sensible group, you can really talk.' This material then led to Sonia telling us that her abuser had abused seven other girls as well. She described how on one occasion her mother had gone to a party connected to her work and her step-brother had been away. The young male babysitter had come to look after her and he 'did it', coming up to her room when she was in bed. She said that she had then heard of sexual abuse on the radio and her mother had said to her, 'If this ever happens to you, you must tell me straight away.' Sonia said she had immediately told her mother, who had believed her.

Discussion of Session 12

RB: *In this group, it seems that the children are becoming most intensely involved in their positive transference, with ourselves as the ideal mummy and daddy with whom the babies can be both completely demanding and completely provided for in a very ideal way. It was an extremely moving group to be in. It was not surprising that Sally was worried about the police complaining about the noise because the piercingness of her screams was indeed intense.*

JM: *The idea of the threatening neighbour was one that would have resonated with three of the girls present that day. I was struck by their determination that the 'family' should work as a whole, for example by sharing the bottle and by making sense of Cheryl going off to paint by herself by describing her as being at playgroup. Their sense of everybody being involved seemed important, although we ourselves were anxious about the children who seemed less involved. Sally and Sonia were very pivotal to the group and their capacity for imagination and play, for symbolising their experiences and feelings, led the others along so that they too benefited from their openness. I think this again demonstrates the value of helping sexually abused children in groups; those who are more available help the others to get in touch with painful feelings which might otherwise be avoided and at the same time they can experience the group as a 'surrogate healthy family'* (deYoung and Corbin 1994: 144).

RB: *In this respect were really were very lucky with Sally whose irrepressible imagination was so transforming that although in external reality she really has been quite severely abused over a period of at least a year, she nevertheless continued to be able to find hopefulness symbolised by men and women as we see in her wonderful fantasy of finding a new life under the sea.*

JM: *Yes, the mermaid image was one that Sally often used throughout the lifetime of the group. Female above, and fish below, the mermaid provided her with a feminine character who was safely asexual. Whereas Cheryl often has the sense of drowning, Sally finds an adaptation to her situation.*

RB: *In this session, the girls were in the depth of a very positive transference towards the therapists and it is this that led to a lot of communication about the details of the abuse which they had not been able to share with us before. Sally's delightful idea of coming forward and then 'jumping over' the abuse can be seen at a theoretical level as an imaginative symbol rather than a defensive manoeuvre. Clearly many people who have been abused simply cannot get in touch at a conscious level with the feelings that remain locked inside them and they have to find various ways of jumping over it, although not in the light-hearted way that Sally was able to use that word. It is interesting here that Hannah really demonstrated that she has not been able to face what Sally has faced and work through it. So, rather than agreeing to jump over it, she indicated that she couldn't use Sally's idea at this stage which showed us that she still had a lot of work to do on communicating the fact and the meaning of the abuse to her.*

As an interesting aside, Sonia talked about having heard about the idea of sexual abuse on radio or television and she linked her capacity to tell her mother directly to having come into contact with this. This would certainly be a powerful piece of evidence about its efficacy in helping the abused child disclose, despite the painfulness for the ordinary population who understandably find it difficult that their children should have to be exposed to the idea of sexual abuse.

SESSION 19

Attending: Sally, Sonia, Hannah and Jackie. Cheryl was absent

During the previous week's session, Sally and Sonia had started to tell the group more about their experience of sexual abuse. Hannah had so far been unable to say anything at all about her abuse and Jackie had missed the last week's session. In order to build on what had been started, we suggested that the girls might like to begin with some painting which showed how they were feeling towards their abusers.

Sally and Sonia were quick to pick up this theme, Sonia painting a picture in black of the babysitter who had abused her and writing 'dangerous, do not go near him' (Figure 8.2). Then she and Sally attacked it with black paint on large brushes, crossing it out thickly so that it was obliterated. Sonia added more words alongside the image: 'Stupid fucker, I hope your asshole gets killed from a Bitch, Dick Head, Ugly Piss Head, git'. Later, she drew a charcoal picture of '' Bum Head, Ugly Dick Head Dangerous, Do not go near him'. Also using black, Sally drew the neighbour who had abused her, including his large wig, and put a yellow diagonal line to cross him out. She then obliterated the image with thick black paint and asked JM to write for her, 'Do not go near him, he is dangerous'.

While all this was happening, Jackie quietly drew a picture of ducks and horses, but seemed well aware of what was going on. Hannah found it all very difficult and refused to join in when the other girls asked about her abuse. However, when Sally and Sonia started to use clay, she also joined in. Sonia made a model of her abuser, prone, with an erect penis. Using the wire cutter, she cut down the length of the penis and right through the body, including the brain, saying sarcastically 'Oh, he doesn't have a brain does he, I forgot.' Taking Sonia's lead, Sally made a similar model, and cut it up into quarters, then into small pieces, until she was only left with the heart which she put into the rubbish bin.

Hannah had at first used clay to make little cakes with cherries on top. She

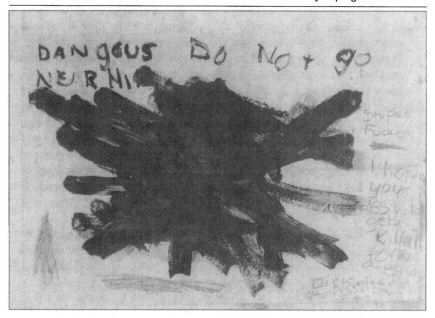

Figure 8.2   Attack on the perpetrator

moved the cherries on one to make the eyes, nose and mouth of a little face and then scratched a cross on the forehead and the words 'I hate you'. Using a pencil, she stabbed the face through the eyes, nose and mouth, then all over, finally chopping it into several sections. Towards the end of the group, we noticed she had made another cake with an upright penis in the centre. Aware of our interest, she cut it off and rolled it up in the rest of the cake. At this point, she put the pieces of the first face back together to make a little clay gravestone onto which she wrote 'I hate you and I don't like you'. She asked JM to keep this and fire it for her.

Discussion of Session 19

RB: *It is becoming clear at this stage of the group's life that the children's position in relation to the abuse is really quite far apart, Sally and Sonia being further forward than the others in both being able to face the reality of their experiences and to communicate these and work them through in the group. We decided to extend the group by four sessions to see if this would help the girls who were progressing more slowly. With their disparity of progress in mind, we suggested the girls all begin with some painting showing how they feel towards their abusers, both as a helpful procedure for the girls and also as a way of clarifying to ourselves how far they are actually able to face this situation fully.*

JM: *As we would have anticipated, Sally and Sonia were confident in expressing anger towards their abusers and the desire to punish them. I feel it is so important for these children to express symbolically the abusive feelings aroused in them, so that there is less chance of perpetuating the cycle of abuse* (Sagar 1990: 112). *We know how many sexually abused boys go on to enact their abusive feelings by becoming perpetrators and how other survivors of abuse re-abuse by harming themselves. I think it is an important part of our groups to allow a different expression of abusive feelings and in this session, Sonia and Sally did pictures that were very punishing and used strong language which would have been unacceptable elsewhere. They continued their abuse by cutting up the clay models of their abusers and disposing of them.*

RB: *Yes, in this situation, we can see how Sally and Sonia are directing their powerful and primitive rage which certainly contains exactly the same emotions as those that are expressed in abuse, in this situation clearly though expressed towards symbolic representations of their own abusers. This can be contrasted with situations in which children have become projected into, and filled up with, feelings of violence and primitive impulses which are then enacted in a generalised way against almost everything in the room, the other group members, the therapists and generally, presenting a very different picture from that which we are seeing with Sally and Sonia. Of the other two children present today, in our experience Jackie was actually able to be in touch with the material of Sally and Sonia, although she did not herself feel able to express the feelings directly. Hannah on the other hand was clearly finding it extremely difficult and painful, and our concern was the degree of her defensiveness still being maintained so far into the group process. In the last part of the group, we comment on her seeming to take up the themes introduced by Sally and Sonia in the material with the cake and the erect penis. The question of significance here is the extent to which this is Hannah complying in a passive way with the more active elements in the group process, rather than actually being fully in touch with her own feelings.*

JM: *I think Hannah had became more in touch with different feelings, those of loss in her family rather than with her abuse experience. As she was the only child left with her mother, the gravestone could be seen as representing her experience of loss, and so it was important to keep it and make it more permanent by firing it. In contrast, Sally put her model in the bin, which was an important completion of her process: creating the model of the abuser, his symbolic mutilation and punishment, and finally removing him permanently and rather concretely by putting the pieces into the rubbish bin. I see both Sally's and Hannah's images as having become a talisman, the first needing to be disposed of and the second to be preserved* (Schaverien 1987: 75). *On*

*reflection, I think we were so concerned about Hannah's difficulty in com-
municating about the abuse, that we were less aware of other issues which
may have had greater significance to her at the time.*

RB: *Yes, from this point of view, Hannah giving the little clay gravestone to you
and asking for it to be fired reveals quite a different meaning, which is that
at a deeper level she really was not imbuing this object with the qualities of
the abuser, it was actually a symbol of herself and as such she wished you
to keep it safely for her.*

SESSION 21

Attending: Sally, Jackie, Cheryl and Hannah.

The girls resisted the use of art materials that had been laid out for them and
at first focused on an illustrated 'news report' which Sally had written at
home and wanted to show everyone. The illustrations showed her abuser in
prison on his first day (he had not in fact been sent to prison, but still lived
next door) and still there looking sorry for himself 2000 years later. A third
drawing showed mermaids planning to feed him to waiting sharks. This led to
some lively discussion concerning the punishments the other girls would give
their abusers: Jackie would go to the prison and stab her abusing neighbour;
Cheryl said she would feed her neighbour to sharks and give his bones to her
dog, but Hannah was unable to think of a punishment for her perpetrator.
This discussion led Cheryl to do a painting of her abuser in prison and then
a painting of him chained up in a pitch-black cave, away from the blue sky
and green grass outside.

By this time, Sally was pretending to be a baby and Hannah linked with
her, pretending she would be a baby 'not born yet', jumping up to JM and
clinging on around her waist. When she decided to be born, Cheryl took on
the unborn baby role, with Sally allowing herself to grow up by talking in
halting sentences, pretending to have birthdays and going to playgroup. When
Cheryl decided to be born, Hannah and Jackie said they would now be
unborn twins inside JM. Cheryl asked JM to 'change' her pooey nappy again
and again, and the twins started to paint a multi-coloured image of her poos.
Hannah said there were many colours because the baby had been eating
'wrong things' which might kill her. RB reflected that being abused might
have felt like dying and like being 'filled up with wrong stuff'. Hannah seemed
to accept this. The painting of poos now developed into an even messier, but
sensual, painting of the inside of the mother's womb, with fresh, bright
orange and red added to the very wet mixture (Figure 8.3).

The unborn twins decided to be born and washed their hands. There were
now four babies and toddlers, screaming for their mother's attention, for

Figure 8.3   Inside the womb

bottles and for nappy-changing. When it was time for the play period to
close we had to de-role them by reminding them of their real ages and getting
them to sit round the table like 'big girls' and have their drinks out of cups.
In the ensuing discussion, we thought with them about their baby play both
as a way of returning to the safe time before their abuse and also as a way of
putting the clock back, knowing the group had only a few weeks left.

Discussion of Session 21

RB: *The session opens with continued expressions around the theme of the pun-*
ishment of the abuser. Sally, Jackie and Cheryl are able to continue their
guilt-free punitive attacks on symbols of their abusers while Hannah con-
tinues to be struggling with the fundamental problem of how to begin to
cope with her feelings about her perpetrator. The theme of becoming a
baby, sometimes 'a born baby', and at other times 'a baby not born yet',
recurs.

JM: *I think Hannah was helped by hearing your thoughts about how being*
abused made her feel, especially the idea that she might have felt she was
going to die. This session highlights the way we often work together in
these groups, when one of us is very much involved with the girls in their
play and the other is able to be more reflective about what is going on.
That day, I felt very caught up and moved by the painting of the mother's

womb and then their clinging on to me. I think it was important that I was fully involved in the girls' play, but equally important that you were able to process the meaning of it as it was happening, to encourage the girls to think about the meaning of it, too.

RB: *It is always so difficult to imagine the actual experience for a young girl of forcible sexual intrusiveness, in Hannah's case orally. However, when events are simply too awful to be processed then quite understandably the mind has to find a way of defending absolutely against it, and this is what we have been seeing in Hannah's case. Here we see a possible transformation in that Hannah was now able to talk about the baby having eaten 'wrong things' and it was these that might kill her. Although this was still the same idea of death, nevertheless it does seem to be the first signs of this being contained, enabling her therefore to think about it. The idea of embodiment is contained here, that is the sense of the abuse having caused actual physical damage to the inside of the body of the victim and in their painting and re-creation of the inside of the mother's womb.*

JM: *Yes, I thought the painting was evocative of the womb experience both in its final coloration of glowing reds and oranges overlaying the other colours, like when the sun shines through your eyelids, and in its undifferentiated structure, covering the page, as though nothing else existed. I found this session very emotionally intense and it reflected the degree of trust which had developed within the group. The girls were evidently secure in the transference and this enabled them to experience something equivalent to the mother/baby relationship. I especially appreciated the way they integrated art materials and play in their expression, moving fluidly between both.*

SESSIONS 24, 25 AND 26

These three last sessions continue themes from earlier groups and involved both the therapists and children trying to make more connections to reality as the end approached.

Only Sonia and Hannah were able to come for Session 24 and JM worked with them without RB. Hannah's mother was to be married in three weeks' time and Hannah wanted to make a card for her. Sonia played at being a baby, contentedly propelling herself around the room on a trolley, sucking a bottle, while Hannah made the card. They decided that Hannah was a mum, JM the auntie and the baby would go to sleep. Mum said that the baby could have a birthday when she woke up if she was 'good'. She made a clay cake and 'auntie' made a birthday card. Hannah also put out some paints for the baby to use when she woke up. Once Sonia 'woke up', Hannah decided to become a very noisy baby, too, younger than Sonia. She also wanted a

Figure 8.4   The heart

birthday card and Sonia, now the older sister, made this for her. Hannah also demanded that JM became the mother and change her nappy.

The girls found it hard to finish their story so that the ending of the group could take place. We talked about their both having a new stepfather as something they had in common. Sonia remembered meeting hers for the first time and how his overfamiliarity had made her anxious.

The penultimate group was more focused around the use of art materials symbolically than the recent regressive play, although Sally, who had missed several sessions, instantly wanted to be a baby with a bottle. RB then talked to the group about the pain and difficulty of growing up, but the need to do this, bearing in mind there would only be one more group. This was difficult for Sally, but she glumly accepted it.

Hannah finished the wedding card for her mother. Sonia and Sally made clay cakes, Sally calling hers the 'group cake' and cutting slices for everyone. Jackie made a model of a dog with a bump on his head and told the group that she calls her abuser a dog and wished he would hurt his head. She then made a clay picture of herself sticking out her tongue at him. After her clay cake, Sonia did a picture of a huge, red, healthy-looking heart and told the group she had a boyfriend.

At the start of the final group, Sonia and Sally wanted to entertain everyone with a dance and asked JM to bring them into the group on the trolley, like a carnival lorry. They included JM and Cheryl in the dance and then all the girls painted alongside one another. The heart theme was continued from the previous week, with Jackie painting a heart which she said was for the group and Hannah painting one for RB and JM. The latter heart was red, outlined in black, with a black line across it and a nought on one side, a cross on the other (Figure 8.4). Hannah then painted a big black heart and when RB connected it to the black heart of her abuser, she agreed. Sally painted a picture with everybody's initials in it. On this occasion, the girls were encouraged to sort out which artwork they wanted to take home and which they wanted to dispose of, which gave the opportunity for the whole group to look at it all, if fleetingly. When this was done, we shared a chocolate cake decorated with everybody's names and reflected on their memories of the group, including the fears of their first visit.

Discussion of the final three sessions

JM: *It is interesting to see the various ways that we all managed the closure of the final group. We the therapists encouraged reflection on the experience both verbally and through a sorting of all the art products; the sharing of a cake, in which the whole was cut into parts and eaten, both representing the individuals that had made up the whole and the nurturing which we believed they had experienced. Jackie and Sally painted images that were gifts, or represented the group. Hannah's heart for us seemed to capture her ambivalence regarding the group experience which had connected to her feelings of love (the heart) and loss (the nought and the cross). Her new stepfather had also had a heart attack earlier in the year, so perhaps again anxiety about the permanence of her own family was reflected in the image. Sally and Sonia brought a celebratory quality to the ending with their carnival float and dance.*

RB: *On re-reading the material of these last three sessions it does seem reasonable to conclude that the groups overall have been successful. By successful what I mean is that the children show themselves able to work within the context of the structure, these are the final three sessions, the girls are functioning at a symbolic level, the groups are not full of uncontained, raw emotion. With the exception of Hannah, it would seem that the children now have been able to face the internal meaning of the abuse and to work through it as far as their emotional and intellectual maturity permits. For Hannah, the situation is not as clear; it does seem likely that there are still some repressed elements in her capacity to fully cope with the meaning of her abuse. The degree of success will only be revealed by the quality of her functioning in the months following the groups. She is of course able to return to the clinic for further individual or family sessions if this is necessary. We do not delude ourselves that this is the end of the difficulties for the girls. However, it would seem reasonable to say that this has been a reasonably successful beginning to the therapeutic healing process following their abusive experiences.*

JM: *It is important to say that we arrange to meet with each child and their parent/carer after the groups have finished to see what progress has been made and whether further therapeutic work might be indicated or requested. This is likely to take the form of individual or family therapy. After this group attendance, Sonia, Cheryl and Hannah were discharged; work continued with Sally and her mother and with Jackie and her mother, both needy parents, and both these children had a second group therapy experience some time later.*

REFERENCES

Bion, W.R. (1961) *Experiences in groups*, London: Routledge.

Bion, W.R. (1967) 'A theory of thinking', in *Second thoughts*, New York: Aronson (pp. 110–19).

deYoung, M. and Corbin, B.A. (1994) Helping early adolescents tell: A guided exercise for trauma-focused sexual abuse groups, *Child Welfare*, 73(2): 141–54.

Howard, A. (1993) 'Victims and perpetrators of sexual abuse', in K.N. Dwividi (ed.) *Groupwork with children and adolescents: A handbook*, London and Bristol, Pennsylvania: Jessica Kingsley Publishers.

Knittle, B.J. and Tuana, S.J. (1980) Group therapy as primary treatment for adolescent victims of intrafamilial sexual abuse, *Clinical Social Work Journal*, 8: 236–42.

Nelki, J.S. and Watters, J. (1989) A group for sexually abused young children: unravelling the web, *Child Abuse and Neglect*, 13: 369–77.

Sagar, C. (1990) 'Working with cases of child sexual abuse', in C. Case and T. Dalley (eds) *Working with children in art therapy*, London/New York: Routledge.

Schaverien, J. (1987) 'The scapegoat and the talisman: Transference in art therapy', in Dalley et al. (eds) *Images of art therapy*, London/New York: Tavistock.

Segal, H. (1978) 'On symbolism', *International Journal of Psychoanalysis*, 55: 315–19.

Steward, M.S., Farquar, L.C., Dicharry, D.C., Glick, D.R., and Martin, P.W. (1986) Group therapy: A treatment of choice for young victims of child abuse, *International Journal of Group Psychotherapy*, 36(2): 261–75.

Young, L. (1992) Sexual abuse and the problem of embodiment, *Child Abuse and Neglect*, 16: 89–100.

Chapter 9

Is it safe to keep a secret?

A sibling group in art therapy

Felicity Aldridge and Simon Hastilow

INTRODUCTION

This chapter looks at a sibling group in art therapy. The case study is based on the themes that emerged in several sibling groups that we have run. For reasons of confidentiality we have changed all the circumstances of the case history. This chapter looks at the art therapy process with four brothers aged 5, 6, 7 and 8. We review the current literature on art therapy with sexually abused children and other work done with siblings. We discuss the various themes that came up in the course of the boys' therapy in terms of outside influences, discussion of secrets, artwork produced in the sessions and the children's behaviour, and we compare the outcomes with some of the objectives outlined in the literature review. The boys were referred to art therapy because of sexualised play between the brothers at contact sessions. The brothers were placed in separate foster homes because of sexualised contact between the siblings and also because of violence. The social workers hoped that therapy would improve their interactions at contact. We hoped it would also strengthen the sibling bonds that can easily be broken when all the children are in different foster homes.

The decision to see the brothers together was taken in consultation with the foster carers and social workers involved in the case. As art therapists we thought that this was the mode for treatment of choice because of their history of neglect, and that the children were asking for their sibling relationship to improve. It was decided that to have a male and female therapist was also important. It was felt that in having a gender mix there was the possibility of exploring the children's fantasies about family roles in terms of parental and sibling transference.

Weekly art therapy sessions were set up in an adult education pottery studio. The children had access to dustbins full of mud (clay), and pottery wheels as well as drawing and art equipment. There were games but not many toys. A contract of one year's weekly therapy was agreed to by all the professionals concerned. We found that a year of sibling therapy was about the right length of time. Sibling groups are very intense, both for the children and therapists. We agreed on the amount of organising and liaison that was required for one year, but we think any more would have been too much of a commitment for too many people. In this case the core group consisted of representatives of three schools, both teachers and Special Education Needs Co-ordinators (SENCOs), four foster families, a social worker, the family placement worker, school medical/nursing staff, numerous social services managers and us as therapists. As well as the weekly therapy we met every half term to discuss the children, which constitutes a lot of professional time for one family. Another factor in deciding to offer a contract of one year was that family finding was in place for the children, and we did not want possible adoption to be held up because of an open-ended therapy contract. A clear beginning and ending was thought to help the children with attachment as they would know about the ending before we began.

LITERATURE REVIEW

Art therapy with sexually abused children

Children who have experienced chronic sexual abuse often suffer from the symptoms of post traumatic stress disorder (PTSD). The siblings in this case had completed psychological assessments and were found to be suffering from PTSD. Several authors have explored this issue including Terr (1990), Johnson (1987) and Aldridge (1998b). Johnson suggests that trauma affects our basic attachment bonds, leaving those suffering from trauma with insecure attachments and without the basic attachment skills to re-attach to other adults. He wonders at the end of his essay if psychological trauma was the origin of the arts and if the creative therapies can offer a cure for trauma. In this case study we will see that for the siblings, working together in the art room did enable them to form better relationships with each other, their carers and children and staff at their schools. Art therapy with children who have experienced sexual abuse has a long history and there are many articles on the subject. Murphy (1998) gives a very good overview as part of her research. Other useful articles are by Stember (1980), Kelley (1984) and Clements (1996). Sagar (1990) writes about the use of mess in art therapy sessions:

> Often the way in which most satisfaction seems to be found in using art materials is by making a messy mixture which is then spread on any surface. Messy packages may be formed and given to the therapist to keep. Containers and packages of the mixture may have to be kept for a long time until the child emerges from the compulsive need to handle and examine the chaotic feelings where 'good' and 'bad' are indistinguishable. The messy package may represent the secret which the child has had to hold, often over a long time, which is now passed into the therapist's keeping.
>
> (Sagar 1990: 92)

The siblings that we worked with made as much mess as they could, possibly showing the number of secrets they had to keep. Hanes (1997) and Aldridge (1998a) also discuss the use of mess in art therapy.

Siblings in therapy

Kegerreis in *From a gang of two back to the family* (1993) describes two brothers in therapy, and shows that by seeing them together the therapist was able to see how they used their gang dynamics as a defence against difficult feelings. Seeing each other in therapy, they were able to encounter and avoid their internal and external conflicts. This was very much what we were able to observe with our larger sibling group, particularly with fighting, which was used both as a defence and as a way of expression.

In our reading to date we have not come across any art therapy literature about working with sibling groups. Most psychoanalytical literature seems to deal with sibling issues in individual therapy. *Siblings in therapy* by Kahn and Lewis (1988) is the most quoted book on the subject. It includes a chapter dealing with sibling incest where the chosen method of treatment is a family cognitive behavioural approach. The book does offer many insights into the significance of the sibling relationship throughout their lives. It seems significant to us that siblings do not occur as often as parents do in the therapeutic literature. However, incestuous sibling relationships are common in mythology, particularly in Egyptian and Greek mythology. Sibling relationships feature as a theme in fictional literature, occurring in Shakespeare (*King Lear*, *A Winter's Tale*), *Mahabharata* and in fairy tales, Cinderella being the example that is most often remembered by children. It could be concluded that sibling relationships have caused problems for many over the generations.

Siblings in care

In *Sibling relationships for children in the care system*, Marjut Kosonen (1994) looks at the importance of sibling bonds and attachment when children are in care. She gives examples of studies which show that when children are separated from their parents, sibling relationships become very significant. However, these relationships are not given significance in the care system, which is strange, considering that they are the first life-long attachments that we make. We believe therapy can help sibling relationships to become more positive so that they can last a lifetime.

Working with a sibling group that is in care, other factors need to be considered, particularly the grief of losing the parents, the loss of the normal natural family and a feeling of being different because their mother was unable to look after them. There is guilt associated with things that happened with their parents that do not happen in other families, creating family secrets. There are issues of low self-esteem because they feel different from other children. They also have to live with the pain of what has happened to them in the past, while being constantly reminded that they are different by the way our culture is centred on the birth family. Abuse disrupts our ability to form attachments, so helping the children with attachments would be one of the aims of the group. Silverstein and Kaplan (1982) go into the issues siblings face in care in more detail in their web page.

Treatment objectives

Hamlin and Timberlake in *Sibling group treatment* (1981) have eight assumptions that underlie sibling group treatment:

1   A child is the product of his or her past experiences, current life situation and biological makeup.
2   Past experience for most children begins in the family.
3   The first dynamic group the child is part of is the family. The family is composed of three interrelated groups or subsystems – the spouses, the parent/child and the sibling group. Some family therapists might say that in multi-sibling families there is no mother/child dyad, rather there are environmental and orbiting triads impacting from the earliest mother/infant symbiosis to the epigenesis of the adult neurosis.
4   The therapist is subject to sibling as well as parental transferences.
5   The child has its own unique view of the family.
6   Children are observers of the family system, and children who are disturbed affect and are affected by the sibling subsystem.
7   Prolonged sibling conflict adversely affects the overall functioning and satisfaction within the family.
8   The interpersonal relationships between siblings are amenable to observation, examination and modification.

Hamlin and Timberlake list the following treatment objectives:

1   To establish the siblings' strengths and limitations. They suggest that very often the negative aspects of the relationships are highlighted. They suggest that negative relationship roles are located within all siblings, not just the ones identified with the problems.
2   To provide a context or setting where siblings can freely express their thoughts and sentiments among themselves. Sharing thoughts and feelings among the group allows for the reworking of relationships.
3   Allowing and promoting the expression of thoughts and sentiments through various modalities to enhance the expression of spontaneous feeling.
4   To provide a space for the examination of age, sex and ordinal position issues as they relate to the sibling group and the larger family.

5   To examine and modify sibling role relationships.
6   To assist the siblings in defining themselves in relation to the spouse and parent/child subsystems.

Hamlin and Timberlake also list the advantages and disadvantages of sibling therapy:

1   The limitations are related to the parents' and therapists' reluctance to work with sibling groups, perceiving them to be problematic because of the fear that parental control will be diminished or that the therapists will ally themselves with the children.
2   Treatment is considered complicated because of the varying ages, sex and position within the family unit. Some therapists believe that a sibling group does not have enough in common and that individual problems are not interconnected.
3   Non-affected siblings can be contaminated by the identified sibling problems.
4   Therapists need to be involved with non-verbal expressions of family feelings, making it difficult to describe to parents and colleagues what is happening in the group.

So with these treatment objectives in mind we can see how our group compared to Hamlin and Timberlake's objectives.

THEMES OF THE SESSIONS

In this section we will look at several themes that came up during the year that the sibling group ran.

Outside influences

In this case the therapists were very much part of the multi-disciplinary team that looked after the children. We attended regular meetings (six weekly) with the social worker and foster parents about the children. The adult network around the children knew about the incidents that had happened in the children's past. The brothers did not seem to be aware that we knew what their foster parents knew. They assumed that all adults would not tell other people what they said about incidents because, to the boys, they were secret.

During the assessment for care, the children had been told not to talk to professionals by their parents. This was a constant problem throughout the therapy, with the children's fear of what would happen if they said anything to us. However we felt the biggest outside influence was waiting to see if adoptive parents could be found for the children and the anxiety that this waiting caused, particularly as time progressed and no family was found. The children's behaviour was a cause for concern for all the professionals involved in the case, particularly the teachers. The therapy was blamed for bad behaviour and the days when they came to therapy were identified as the days of worst behaviour. We were constantly surrounded by other professionals' anxiety about what seeing the siblings together was going to do to, and whether the behaviour of the identified worst behaved sibling would have a corruptive influence on his brothers. This was not what the therapists observed in the session, where we saw the identified good child saying and doing things that immediately wound the younger children up and caused a fight; for example, the oldest child inventing a game that he would win because he was older and more able to count, etc. The older child would be very dismissive of the younger three playing games as a way of expression, saying that him joining in was babyish or stupid. He thought that they should all be the same, and find activities that stopped talking or thinking about behaviour. The children's behaviour in the group was very difficult. We could often connect this to outside influences such as the social worker visiting and asking questions about their wishes for the future. This created much anxiety because of the fear of leaving their present placement. Our observation was that the group brought the feelings about these issues to the fore rather than the feelings being hidden.

Another outside influence was to do with other professionals' thoughts as to whether the children needed to have therapy – is the past best left in the past? Their behaviour in other situations, e.g. at school, showed that the past was indeed affecting the present; however there was a tendency to blame this on therapy. When Chris, the youngest, was found on top of a young school friend, it was the therapy that was blamed rather than the fact that he had been abused in the past. It was meeting with his brothers that was causing the problems and reminding him; rather than a behaviour that he had remembered alone. We found that much patience was required in working with these sorts of assumptions.

The boys only attended therapy during the school terms, as they were part of a holiday programme during the breaks. The break in the therapy caused the children to act out even more during the sessions leading up to and after these breaks. It seemed to intensify the feelings of loss and brokenness in their lives, the brokenness of their family. They often said that they thought we would not return after the break. This fear, that we would abandon them, was very strong, as nearly all the significant adults in their lives had done so. They had three different social workers during the course of the therapy. At these beginning and ending sessions they would try to use all the materials or make more mess than usual, partly, we wondered, so that we would remember them, but also so that they used everything before the sessions finished as they believed. Unfortunately this was also a feeling that they had about school, that they would not go back or that the children they knew would not return. The therapy seemed to emphasise these feelings and behaviours so that people could identify when there were likely to be problems. This caused the school to remove the children at times when problems were likely to occur, further emphasising the children's difference. Eventually the school problems were resolved but it took a lot of work by the foster parents and teachers. The children wanted each area of their life to be kept separate: therapy from school and school from therapy. We did not feel that it was helpful to keep this secret in the professional group. In our experience the more open we could be about the therapy, the more helpful and supportive the other professionals could be for the children. Working together with other professionals on a case takes much trust – a trust that the children also had to find in us, the therapists.

Discussion of secrets

For reasons of confidentiality we have changed all the circumstances in this case study. Ironically, in doing so we have had to keep many secrets about the cases involved to ourselves. Secrets are very powerful in helping to allow child sexual abuse to continue. Herman (1992) states:

> Chronic childhood abuse takes place in a familial climate of pervasive terror, in which ordinary caretaking relationships have been profoundly disrupted. Survivors describe a characteristic pattern of totalitarian control, enforced by means of violence and death threats, capricious enforcement of petty rules, intermittent rewards, and destruction of all competing relationships through isolation, secrecy and betrayal.
>
> (Herman 1992: 98)

These secrets are very much part of the way children relate to others and are often part of their attachments. The children expected us to have secrets and that we would want them to keep secrets, i.e. the issue of confidentiality. An example of this was bad behaviour. If we did not tell the foster carers about the behaviour in the group, we were keeping secrets, and if we did the children felt they would get into trouble for being badly behaved. So we would often find ourselves in the same trap as the children: should we tell, and will our secrets be safe to tell another?

In the first phase of therapy, secrets were the main theme. In the first session the siblings were able to discuss the fact that they had done horrible things to each other, and that the past was full of horrible memories. After the first few sessions the children disclosed to their foster parents their experiences of sexual abuse with various adults. The first sense that we had that the children were thinking of disclosing to us was when they asked us,

'What would happen if I said something to you that you didn't understand?'. The next week they said they had a secret, a real secret, and
disclosed that they had been involved in sexual behaviour in the car on the
way to therapy – holding on to each other's private parts. They seemed to be
testing us to see our reactions. The boys then went and hid under the table,
cuddling up to each under a coat used as a blanket, and discussed what they
would tell us next. They felt that talking about what happened to them in
the past was so embarrassing that it could not be spoken aloud and had to
be whispered to each of us in turn – the male therapist was told first and
after some discussion between them, the female therapist. In between
telling, they withdrew under the table to discuss what they were going to say
next, if anything. Each remark was tested to see if we really meant that anything could be said in the therapy room. There also seemed to be a scale for
the children of what they thought were the worst things that had happened
to them. Being deprived of food and drink came top of the list. We needed
to be constantly aware of this, as the children liked to eat and drink all
through the sessions. Negotiations about not eating were not possible
during the time of the group as this was too threatening a reminder of
things that had happened in the past. When things got difficult between the
brothers they would often calm down by having drinks and a share of the
sweets that they had brought to the session. Throughout the course of therapy sexual abuse was disclosed. The children disclosed to the foster parents
usually before or after the sessions. Most disclosures came when they were
being visited by their family placement worker who was looking for an
adoptive home.

At other times the children would make cards for each other saying 'I love
you', then have very violent fights with the child they had given the card to.
This seemed to be the brothers' way of telling us what had gone on between
them at home. However they were never able to tell us about the sibling abuse
that they suffered at the instruction of adults. Cards to various people saying
'I love you' were one of the commonest images that they made. Whenever
something happened they would make a card. When a foster father lost his
job they made one for him. This felt like something that the children had
learnt from professionals – sending cards when something has happened. In
their family culture, did sending a card to make up after a row replace saying
feelings aloud?

Sexual acting out

Sexual words and sayings were very much the currency of the group, with the
children being masters of innuendo. This was very difficult to deal with. How
could you show acceptable ways of behaving while not shutting the children
down so they felt unable to tell us what had happened? We remember this as
one of the things that occurred in the group that kept us from being able to

say anything. We constantly felt as though we were caught in a trap of silence. Whatever we said would be the wrong thing. We did reflect on these feelings with the children, who would often react by more sexual acting out. Sometimes this would be in the form of watering the floor with the watering can or spraying the windows with water. At other times there would be more graphic gestures, gyratory movements of the body and hands. On one notable occasion this involved the female therapist who, sitting on a chair, was talking with the oldest child. Suddenly she felt cold water running down the inside of her legs. It took several seconds to realise that one of the children was missing and that he was in fact under the table spraying water up her skirt. On another occasion the children continued spraying the therapists' hair until they were dripping with water. Nothing we could say would make them stop. We knew that they were trying to make us angry and lose our temper, which seems to be part of the therapeutic relationship with children. Much to our surprise this action didn't make us that cross, however they did succeed in flooding the room with water in the process, something that many sexually abused children seem to do. We felt that this was a representation of their feelings, the way that they have been flooded with adult feelings at times. There was no escaping from the water going everywhere uncontrollably, rather like their feelings, leaving the fantasy that their feelings were unmanageable and could not be contained by anyone. So like the water, their feelings contaminated everyone that they came into contact with, causing them to leave the brothers' lives. Although sexual acting out featured in the sessions, the boys' sexuality was not something that was explored. The boys' level of maturity prevented this from being an issue.

Dramas

On calmer days when things were quieter, the children would put on plays together. The themes of the plays would be about ghosts and dying. The theme of death and ghosts did not change during the course of the group. Usually one child would play a corpse lying on the table, while the others danced over him. Young (1992) puts forward an argument that survivors of childhood sexual abuse can become fixated with the death of their physical bodies. A wish to be rid of one's body is seen as a desire to expunge all the horrible feelings and emotions evoked by the abuse. In practice this takes the form of deliberate self-harm, including the development of eating disorders. Disassociating oneself from one's body also functions as a means of escaping from the things that are being done to it. In the case of the boys, death was experienced as a fear of what might happen to them, rather than as an ideation. This fear always seemed to be present. Herman (1992) states:

Sometimes the child is silenced by violence or by a distant threat of murder; more often survivors report threats that resistance or disclosure will result in the death of someone else in the family.

(Herman 1992: 98)

This was particularly so at the end of sessions when the children would worry if they were going to be collected. What would happen if no one came? We found it interesting that the children didn't seem to give us the power to 'fix' the transport if it went wrong. They also worried about what would happen if their birth parents turned up in the building, would we be able to protect ourselves from their violence and protect the children? The children seemed to think that us merely talking to their parents would leave them very vulnerable, and they seemed to want reassurance that we were prepared to physically fight their parents to keep them safe. Being safe in the building was a constant issue. The children were in need of constant reassurance that the other people using the building were safe and that we knew who they were. This led us to wonder if threats of abduction had been made.

Fantasies about the therapists

At times the children would articulate their fantasy that we were going to kill them. After these sorts of disclosures the children wanted to make a mess. This involved playing with the wet clay in a bowl, adding and subtracting water. Sometimes they would add hot water which would make the clay soft and warm to the touch, then pour it out and add cold, making the clay cold and clammy. As you can imagine, playing with bowls of mud created lots of mess. The brothers never used the mud to its full potential by throwing it around the room, but they smeared it over each other and our hands and arms, as part of the sensual exploration of the touch of the mud. The tactile sensation of the clay seemed to help resolve the primitive anxiety that had been raised in the therapeutic discussion of their fantasy about being killed. Another fantasy that the children often voiced was whether we were married to each other. Would we get married and when? Did we have a sexual relationship? On one occasion they speculated that we had got married secretly and had not told them. We felt that this was connected to the search for a permanent family for them, and them wondering if we were going to be their parents. This is a fantasy that is often present when working with children awaiting permanent placement.

Fighting

During many of the sessions the brothers would have physical fights. Sometimes these would be short-lived, at other times they would continue for the whole session. Knowing whether to intervene or not was difficult. The children seemed to deliberately wind each other up into a fight. It seemed better for them to make someone else angry rather than saying that they were angry themselves. The children also seemed to be making an excuse to physically touch each other. The fighting would make them very hot. They also sweated a lot which seemed to have some sort of reminder of the family scent. If we intervened in the fights we would become the baddies, holding them or allowing another to get a kick in. We were often accused of not looking after them by allowing them to hit each other. Yet when we asked if they wanted our intervention, the winning one would say 'no', while the other wanted our help to get him into a winning position. We were accused of not stopping fights when we both intervened. It seemed that we were often caught in the children's transference to the parents, who hadn't stopped the fighting or sexual acting out before. Understanding this was vital for our work with the foster parents who wanted to know why we were not stopping them from getting hurt in the room.

Some of the fighting seemed to have another function – of being able to stop us from thinking. When we intervened in the fights we were not able to make any suggestions as to what was happening. In time we were able to do both. Sometimes the fighting was so bad that the sessions had to be stopped. This didn't seem to affect the therapy other than the children feeling deprived because they had not had their allotted time. After any session when there had been a lot of fighting, we often wondered if therapy was the right thing. However we continued because reports of sibling contact sessions recorded that their behaviour was improving, and that they were able to discuss some of the previous week's behaviour. At these sessions we tried to reinforce the rules and safety issues. This would result in them ganging up against us, something that seemed to happen often. It reinforced the idea that we, as therapists, were outsiders of the family, but it also seemed to help establish family bonding and attachments. It was a technique they used to dis-empower us, particularly when they thought we were working together as a couple. The children perceived us as more powerful in this light, giving rise to the possibility, in their fantasy, of us abusing them. At this point they would usually leave the room. When they returned we would often see them play at washing the windows and, if they thought they could get away with it, their hair and ours. We understood this to be the washing away of bad feelings. At other times we tried to control the fighting by holding fighting tournaments using paper swords as weapons. Often this worked well and at times the children came up with elaborate ways of scoring these games. During the early phase of therapy, when the fighting and misbehaviour were very bad, the children said they were doing it on purpose so that they wouldn't have to come back to therapy.

Susan Kegerreis in *From a gang of two back to the family* (1993) talks of being referred siblings that constantly fight. Her sibling groups invented games and battles which were similar to the competitions that were going on with the boys. She describes them as fighting because they wanted that intensity of relationship, but also because they wanted to be the best. She wondered if, by having an exciting fight, they could exclude the adult. The siblings that she described worked together to defend themselves against the anxiety and sadness of their situation. Their ganging up stopped them getting into a close relationship with an adult. Adults are rendered stupid, useless and excluded. Kegerreis suggests that the fights are an external representation of their internal world; their destructive impulses conflicting with life/love-giving impulses. The child has an internal gang fighting in their head which they act out when they are with other children. In therapy we need to establish separate entities for the gang. Artwork helps this by enabling each child to make their own separate image.

The children also expressed their rivalry over us. If one sibling had a good feeling about one of us, that would cause rivalry for the therapists'/parents' attention among the other siblings. This also caused rivalry between the siblings for each other's attention. Good feelings were usually destroyed immediately by another sibling. This would create a situation where all the children were competing for our attention. Being unable to respond to all the demands for attention at once creates anxiety in the children that they are too much for anyone. It can then become the therapists' fault that bad feelings are remembered, and not the parents'. The family can then be remembered as good.

Houses and homes

During one phase of therapy the children each made himself a house and decorated it. They painted the houses red with decorations. The houses had roofs and chimneys as well as windows and doors. We were requested to help with the construction of the houses but under no circumstances were allowed in. However the children soon destroyed the houses. We felt that some boundaries had been established, like them having their own space within the room. However, sibling jealousy about the other houses was soon in play. This brought up issues of the family hierarchy and who could tell whom what to do. The idea that only grown-ups could tell children what to do was obviously new to them.

The houses also brought on fights which made us wonder about whether they were thinking of the frightening things that had happened when they lived at home, and how scary houses can be. The children liked this concept and were able to produce pictures for each other during the remainder of the session. Having established the boundaries of the houses, they all made cups and bowls for themselves from clay. This felt like the establishment of their individual boundaries. It also enabled us to look at differences, all their cups being unique, without the boys getting into rivalry. They also made clay houses and castles.

Hide and seek

Many sessions started and ended with games of hide and seek which we felt were about attachment and feelings of loss. Were they wondering if their mother would come back to get them? We also wondered if it was a way for them to deal with their anxiety about the beginning and ending of sessions. The children would also express this ambivalence by saying they were bored and there was nothing to do. This seemed to reflect their fear of connecting with any feelings, in case they were unable to control them. When we discussed being safe they no longer said they were bored. At times the boys did express a fear about talking and so we spent a lot of time trying to make the sessions safe. However the fear of being taken by someone against their will was always present. We acknowledged this feeling, but it was a reality that the children could be moved suddenly for any reason. (When working with children in foster care sudden moves are common.) We could only reinforce the boundaries of therapy by helping them with when, where and how often it was going to happen.

When the children were feeling particularly anxious together, we found playing games a good way to calm things down. They particularly liked playing cards and seemed to get others to teach them games that we could play in the sessions. With one child this progressed to being taught card tricks which he would play with us. They did try to make up games but their appeal was not as great as the universal games which they could play with others outside of the sessions.

Artwork

At first when we worked with this group we expected the amount of artwork produced to be similar to other groups that we had run. However the sibling group seemed to produce less work, the artwork being the beginning of an interaction that the children then carried on by playing or acting out. At times it felt like the artwork brought out feelings which they then experimented with and experienced through interactions with their brothers. On one occasion the discussion of the holiday break during painting led to the brothers putting on their own strip show, inspired by a film on at the cinema at the time. Fortunately this only involved taking off their coats and jumpers. As we came nearer to the end of the therapy images did start to feature more strongly. We often made group squiggle-like images, each person taking turns to make a mark on the paper. The children liked these images but they usually cut them up to make into cards for their foster parents. Making a mess was always part of every session. Working in a pottery studio and having a dustbin full of mud was a wonderful experience. We worked there because it was a large room and gave the children plenty of space. We found our fears about the mud being too messy were short-lived. It was much easier to clean up than paint, being easier to wash off clothes etc. All the children seemed to find the texture of wet clay fascinating and it always seemed to get smeared over the tables. We wondered about what the mess in these sessions might mean. Many children that we have worked with who have been sexually abused have spent a long time working with mess. It seems to provide a substance with a texture that reflects how they are feeling. In the group the children left their mud mixtures in their bowls. They enjoyed the fact that during the week the mud transformed back into hard clay and then with the addition of water, went back to a liquid state.

HOW DID THE GROUP COMPARE TO HAMLIN AND TIMBERLAKE'S OBJECTIVES?

1 The negative aspects of seeing the children together were experienced in the professional group who thought that the youngest was learning behaviours from his older siblings, however in the group we did not see this behaviour. The brothers needed lots of encouragement to try new modes of expression. When they did make an object it had to be taken home for fear of its destruction or loss while they were away from the room.

2 The siblings could freely express how they felt about each other. The group was able to contain a lot of expressed emotion often in a very contained way. We were able to make the group safe enough for the children to say how they felt.

3 The expression of feelings was often represented in various creative expressions, e.g. artwork and plays.

4 As the group progressed, a clear hierarchy was established, with the oldest clearly at the top. We think that this was why this group worked so well. In another sibling group we ran, this hierarchy was not established and the children became unable to find their place in the family.

5 The children became able to play with each other at contact sessions and on other occasions when they met.

6 The group helped the children to be able to make attachments to their foster carers and express how they felt about the losses of these attachments.

We felt that our group did meet the objectives set out by Hamlin and Timberlake. Although simple in their aims, these objectives did help us identify where the group had been successful. When working with these levels of neglect and abuse, we found it very helpful to concentrate on what we had achieved, as what could ideally be different was too much, and if thought about too often made us want to give up.

CONCLUSION

Group therapy with siblings is hard work. The therapist is constantly an out-sider to the group, the person who has to take on all roles. However for many children this is the only way to repair the bonds broken by abuse. Games seem to be very much part of sibling groups and help to establish universal rules for the family. Artwork helped to bring up issues, which were then explored by play and acting. Working with children in foster care, loss issues are always present and special attention needs to be paid to beginnings, breaks and end-ings of sessions. Clear aims in the therapy are needed, to which the children as well as the carers agree.

We felt that as the group progressed, the children came to feel that sharing secrets was better than keeping them. During the course of the group secrets were disclosed on a regular basis to foster parents and ourselves. At the beginning of the group it was unsafe to discuss the children's secrets, but as the safety of the group was able to be maintained by the children and the therapists, disclosures were made. We think the group was helpful in resolv-ing the issues of their past because of what Yalom calls universality, i.e. being in a group with others who have experienced similar events:

> Some specialist groups composed of individuals for whom secrecy has been an especially important and isolating factor place a particularly great emphasis on universality. For example, short-term structured groups for bulimic patients build into their protocol a strong requirement for self-disclosure, especially disclosure about attitudes towards body image and detailed accounts of each patient's eating and purging prac-tices. With rare exceptions, patients express great relief at discovering that they are not alone and that others share the same dilemmas and life experiences.
>
> (Yalom 1985: 9)

Being together they could be stronger than when they were apart.

The main benefit of working with sibling groups is the improvement in the children's behaviour. For children this is particularly important, as foster placements can break down when a child is constantly badly behaved. The reduction of sexual acting out by siblings is also important for professionals working with the children and for their chances of being adopted. Our group seemed to allow the children to express some of their feelings collectively about what had happened to them. It gave them the chance to reprocess some of the feelings that they had about the past and to think about what sort of future they would like. During the group the children chose to be adopted separately.

No adoptive placements were found during the time we were working with the children. It seems likely that only the youngest will be adopted. The waiting seems to cause behaviour problems as more and more meetings are held, with no permanent place being found for them.

We see working with siblings as being part of the therapeutic package that children in care need. It helps them to know each other better, so that hopefully their relationship will last for the rest of their lives. Groups do seem to help children with other relationships generally. These siblings did start to make their own friends for the first time while in the group. Individual therapy would not have been possible to start with, because of the children's past experiences with other adults. We now think that because of the experiences that they have had in the group the children could go on to individual therapy if they chose. As a group the siblings did get some positive therapeutic thinking time together, something that often gets forgotten when we look to individual needs first.

REFERENCES

Aldridge, F. (1998a) Chocolate or shit: Aesthetics and cultural poverty in art therapy with children, *Inscape*, 3(1): 2–9.

Aldridge, F. (1998b) 'Images of trauma in brief family art therapy', in D. Sandle (ed.) *Development and diversity: New applications in art therapy*, London: Free Association Books.

Clements, K. (1996) The use of art therapy with abused children, *Clinical Child Psychology and Psychiatry*, 1(2: 181–98.

Hamlin, E. and Timberlake, E. (1981) Sibling group treatment, *Clinical Social Work Journal*, 9(2): 101–10.

Hanes, M. (1997) Producing messy mixtures in art therapy, *American Journal of Art Therapy*, 35(February).

Herman, J. (1992) *Trauma and recovery*, New York: Basic Books.

Johnson, D. (1987) The role of the creative arts therapies in the diagnosis and treatment of psychological trauma, *The Arts in Psychotherapy*, 14: 7–13.

Kahn, M. and Lewis, K. (1988) *Siblings in therapy: Life span and clinical issues*, London: W.W. Norton.

Kegerreis, S. (1993) From a gang of two back to the family, *Psychoanalytic Psychotherapy*, 7(1): 69–83.

Kelley, S. (1984) The use of art therapy with sexually abused children, *Journal of Psychosocial Nursing and Mental Health Services*, 22(12): 12–18.

Kivowitz, A. (1995) Attending to sibling issues and transferences in psychodynamic psychotherapy, *Clinical Social Work Journal*, 23(1).

Kosonen, M. (1994) Sibling relationships for children in the care system, *Adoption and Fostering*, 18(3).

Murphy, J. (1998) Art therapy with sexually abused children and young people, *Inscape*, 3(1): 10–16.

Sagar, C. (1990) Working with cases of child sexual abuse, in C. Case and T. Dalley (eds) *Working with children in art therapy*, London/New York: Routledge.

Silverstein, D. and Kaplan, S. (1982) '*Lifelong issues in adoption*', From website: www.adopting.org/silveroze/html/lifelong_issues_in_adoption.html

Stember, C. (1980) 'Art therapy: A new use in the diagnosis and treatment of sexually abused children', in *Sexual abuse of children: Selected readings*, Washington DC: US Dept of Health and Human Services.

Terr, L. (1990) *Too scared to cry*, New York: Basic Books.

Yalom, I.D. (1985) *The theory and practice of group psychotherapy*, New York: Basic Books.

Young, L. (1992) Sexual abuse and the problem of embodiment, *Child Abuse and Neglect*, 16: 89–100.

Chapter 10

Between images and thoughts

An art psychotherapy group for sexually abused adolescent girls

Ani M. Brown and Marianne Latimir

In this chapter we present our group art psychotherapeutic approach with sexually abused adolescent girls, drawing from art therapy and cognitive therapy. An overview of the literature pertaining to the patient group and the treatment approaches of art therapy and cognitive therapy is presented. We combined these approaches to treat the emotional and cognitive disturbances characteristic of victims of sexual abuse. This chapter presents case material of the group in order to illustrate our approach in resolving themes that emerged from the group process.

LITERATURE REVIEW

The adolescent victim

The literature shows that adolescent victims of sexual abuse manifest a variety of symptoms of psychological trauma, i.e. psychosomatic illness, depression, flashbacks, nightmares, sleep disturbance, agoraphobia, anxiety, suicidal gestures, and in particular, fear of men, self-harm, drug-taking or promiscuity (Blick and Porter 1982). Additionally, they manifest extremely low self-esteem, poor self-image, social isolation, stigmatism, impaired trust and decreased perceived credibility (Mannarino, Cohen and Berman, 1994: 204–11).

The effects of the sexual abuse are to arrest ordinary development and alienate the adolescent victim from her peers. Secondary problems may occur such as drug and alcohol addiction and prostitution, to which these girls are particularly vulnerable.

The adolescent's sexuality becomes confused and damaged by the abuse for a number of reasons. The victim has been coerced into satisfying the abuser's rather than her own needs. The abuse may have been part of a relationship where she received attention, and she is consequently overwhelmed by feelings of guilt, fear and shame. Many sexual abuse victims become sexually provocative and seductive from an early age – this emerges from the distorted belief that sexual behaviour is the only way that they will receive attention (Jehu 1989). Price (1993) suggests that the victim may perceive herself as having powers that contributed to the abuse and may develop unconscious fantasies to overcome these feelings of power. These fantasies may be manifested in seductive or promiscuous behaviour.

Price summarises the long-term effects of sexual abuse, proving that in regard to character formation 'incest is noted to cause impairments in ego functioning, sense of self, internal and external boundaries, and interpersonal relationships' (Price 1993: 215). She emphasises that the defence structure that develops may involve a multitude of defences including dissociation, repression, denial, idealisation and splitting. The mechanism of splitting is a way of the victim denying and repressing the abusive aspect of the perpetrator in order to maintain the attachment.

Treatment approaches

Group therapy

Group psychotherapy has been particularly indicated for the treatment of adolescents, as it draws on the normal developmental needs of the young person to participate and belong to a group (Blos 1962, Copley 1993).

The following literature supports a group treatment approach for sexual abuse victims identifying a variety of psychodynamic factors: Pines 1978, Herman 1981, Hall 1992, Welldon 1993. Welldon (1993) explains that the secrecy and isolation of victims of abuse are replaced by disclosure and belonging within the containing atmosphere of the group. The fantasised threats of intimacy and risks of seduction are reduced for both patients and therapists. Furthermore, Welldon maintains that the group functions as both an auxiliary ego in supporting members as they face past pain and abuse, and the super-ego in modifying the sadistic need for revenge which may result in their own perpetration of abuse.

The group's processes of dysfunction will relate to their familial dysfunction which colluded to allow the abuse to occur. It is thus essential that the therapists identify and confront abusiveness in the group and be protective. Some victims have learned to deny their own needs and become helpers within their family to keep the family together. This may emerge in the group when members become 'assistants' to the therapists, and others become competitive and bewildered by this (Welldon, 1993).

In contrast, Pines (1978) explains that group members perceive authority figures as threatening and intrusive, but could identify with peers. According to her, the group gradually becomes a good transitional object which is internalised at a deep unconscious level, symbolically becoming a mother for the group members.

Hall (1992) points out the cognitive and emotional value of the group process through group members experiencing the anger and distress on behalf of other group members. This enables them to begin to more objectively understand their own experiences, shift blame and responsibility to their abusers and feel less guilty and ashamed. Herman (1981) seems to echo this view when explaining that the group members will be able to exonerate each other in a way that is not possible for therapists.

For the therapists, group therapy reduces the intensity of the transference and countertransference dilemmas inherent in individual therapy with victims of sexual abuse, i.e. the therapist's feelings of collusion with being either a seductive parent or a consenting child (Welldon 1993).

Art therapy

There is agreement among art therapists that the efficacy of art therapy for survivors of sexual abuse is in its capacity to evoke emotional rather than intellectual responses (Johnson 1987, Spring 1988, Howard 1990, Anderson 1991, Peacock 1991).

Johnson (1987) explains that the psychological defence of dissociation is an attempt to maintain a positive sense of self, and suppress aspects of the trauma from consciousness. When situations trigger a memory of abuse into consciousness, further repression ensues. A 'psychic' numbing occurs which can be characterised by both an inability to attach words to feelings, and a suppression of memories. Anderson (1995) explains that the victim often dissociates from herself as a means of coping during abuse incidents. Feeling and thinking are therefore purposely disconnected and this mechanism continues into adulthood. Several art therapists assert that by itself, verbal psychotherapy may permit the survivor to maintain and reinforce the defence of dissociation, and the split between feeling and thinking, and is therefore less effective than the expressive therapies (Blake-White and Kline 1985, Johnson 1987, Craighill-Moran 1990, Anderson 1991, Waller 1992).

Art therapists working with adult groups of sexual abuse survivors emphasise that art therapy facilitates group processes and enables survivors to process and integrate their thoughts (Garrett and Ireland 1979, Spring 1985, Serrano 1989, Simonds 1992, Waller 1992, Anderson 1995). Art therapists working with groups of sexually abused children have stressed the central therapeutic value of art-making processes (Carozza, Heirsteiner and Young 1983, Malchiodi 1990, Murphy 1996). The art therapy literature regarding work with sexually abused adolescent girls is limited to individual rather than group therapy.

Anderson (1995), in particular, makes the link between the emotional and cognitive needs of the sexual abuse victim. She is in agreement with other art therapists that the process of working with the art materials is the treatment. It contains the client emotionally when abusive experiences are invoked, and leads to a re-integration of affect and intellect within the personality.

However, she views catharsis as not only a physical expression of feelings but a means towards a different mental state, which leads to a re-organisation of perceptions, view of the self and the world. The process of art-making itself, in her view, is a means of challenging entrenched beliefs and assumptions about the self, inferring that cognitive factors need to be addressed.

Cognitive therapy

Cognitive therapy has become increasingly used in treating the behavioural and emotional problems in sexual abuse victims, although more commonly this is largely conducted in individual therapy rather than a group setting.

It is postulated that young people's mood disturbances and related emotional difficulties are in large part a result of various distorted beliefs about the victim's experience of sexual abuse. These beliefs are therefore seen as leading to distressing feelings and inappropriate behaviour, while their therapeutic correction will alleviate the disturbances. This cognitive model and the cognitive restructuring intervention originate from the work of Aaron Beck and his co-workers (Beck 1976, Beck, Rash, Shaw and Emery 1979, Beck and Emery 1985).

Jehu (1989) provided empirical evidence as to the efficacy of cognitive approaches, in which the victim's faulty cognition, i.e. that she is to blame for the abuse, is examined and challenged. Workers in the field of cognitive therapy, such as Janoff-Bulman (1985) suggest that the experience of sexual abuse challenges and undermines the cognitive beliefs the victim has held. These can include assumptions regarding personal invulnerability, the perception of the world as meaningful, and the view of self as positive. Self-blame and an extreme sense of vulnerability result from the destruction of these beliefs (Janoff-Bulman 1985).

Briere (1989) identifies the cognitive changes that victims of child sexual abuse may experience, such as negative self-evaluation, guilt, perceived helplessness and hopelessness, and lack of trust in others. Therefore, for treatment to be effective, these distorted and damaged beliefs must be addressed and changed to become more accurate, flexible and functional, which in turn will result in changes in behaviour.

Cognitive restructuring therefore constitutes a crucial part of treatment with abuse victims. In addition, research has revealed that a large percentage of victims manifest difficulties in social skills, in areas such as communication, problem solving, assertiveness and with stressful encounters (Jehu 1988). Cognitive techniques such as communication training, problem solving, conflict resolution, decision making and anger control have been shown to be effective in tackling these difficulties.

BETWEEN IMAGES AND THOUGHTS

Our approach

We developed our integrated approach, drawing on our individual practices of art therapy, group psychotherapy and cognitive therapy, through 10 years of working as co-therapists with adolescent sexual abuse victims. We view art-making processes as central to the group's functioning and to victims' capacity to become aware of unconscious thoughts and feelings. Furthermore, we incorporate a cognitive therapy approach in order to address the cognitive distortions that are characteristic of sexual abuse victims. This involves us helping the girls to examine and explore the feelings, thoughts and beliefs evoked through the art processes as they emerged. A 'free-flowing' interplay between image making, thinking and talking occurs within the group. This promotes the group's capacity to explore negative feelings through the materials more intensely and deeply, as well as beginning to challenge distorted beliefs.

Our foremost aim for the group is to enable the adolescents to move from acting out their distress to expressing it symbolically. Second, we aim to help the group address cognitive distortions relating to feelings of guilt and shame, as well as understand the impact of the abuse on themselves and significant relationships. Third, we work towards the group symbolically experiencing a non-abusive 'family'.

The treatment setting

The group met weekly, for one and a half hours, in an art therapy room located in an NHS adolescent mental health clinic, for approximately one year. This was followed by monthly group sessions for six months. A range of art materials, freely accessible, were provided for modelling, painting or drawing, to maximise the potential for the girls to discover a means to express themselves. The girls were given folders and cupboard space to contain and secure their work confidentially. The girls were encouraged to make their own choices about how and when materials were used, and could decide whether to keep, store or destroy their artwork. These practices conveyed the significance and confidential nature of their work, as well as offering a concrete symbol of emotional containment.

The group

The group began with eight adolescent girls, between the ages of 15 and 18. They were referred by general practitioners and social services, and had undergone family and individual work in preparation for commencing the group. Each had recently disclosed long-term (i.e. four years or more) sexual abuse by a male family member, i.e. grandfathers, fathers, stepfathers and brother. The girls were at different stages with regard to the prosecution and resolution of criminal charges against their abusers. Each girl presented a profound degree of psychological disturbance, manifesting many, if not all, of the symptoms described in the literature. In the following descriptions of sessions the group members have been arbitrarily assigned fictitious initials for reasons of confidentiality.

The beginning of the group

We will begin by presenting the first three sessions in some detail, as they demonstrate our approach, the 'feel' of the adolescent group and the emerging themes that were repeatedly revisited throughout the life of the group.

In Session 1 the central issue for the group was that of control. This was expressed through adolescent 'ganging' against us, with intense competition and hierarchical positioning within the group. The session began with six girls, and two others joined 30 minutes late due to transport delays. We started by offering refreshments and the girls spoke about their journeys to the clinic. We then spoke briefly about the structure and purpose of the group. The girls seemed tense and apprehensive, and started giggling when AB (art therapist) spoke about the purpose of the art materials. They looked away from the therapists and towards each other, as if grouping together. We then asked them to say something about themselves and what they thought about coming to the session. Five out of six introduced themselves, while one declined.

One member, AJ, then spoke about how she had used a diary as a way of coping with her feelings. This led to others revealing that they too had diaries, some of which were being used as evidence in their court cases. There were expressions of anxiety and vulnerability, and feelings about being exposed. The two late-comers arrived and were briefly informed about what had transpired up until then. EN spoke about how she expressed her anger at work, and although her fellow-workers were supportive, she was seeking other ways to express her feelings.

DM was the last to say something about herself, asking who the youngest member of the group was, and was relieved that there were others her age. They then talked about their birthdays, with AJ's occurring the next weekend. EN was the eldest and joked about needing a zimmer frame. Suddenly CL, who had arrived late, asked whether she had missed out on hearing about what had 'happened' to people. ML (psychologist) replied that she hadn't, and CL asked whether anybody had been to court. This developed into a discussion between those members of the group who had been to court and those who had not or wished they were going to court. The group began to talk openly about their abuse experiences, becoming distressed and tearful. EN dominated in describing details of her abuse, ignoring and interrupting others. The rest of the group seemed unable to challenge or interrupt her, and we became anxious about the high level of emotional expression the group was experiencing at such an early stage. We intervened and acknowledged the powerful feelings being expressed, voicing concern that the group was soon to finish. We commented on how the group had not used any of the art materials, and EN, rather triumphantly said, 'Yes, we never did get to the doodling today.' BK, who had been very distressed and had said she was frightened while talking about her abuse, aligned herself with EN by joining in the derision of the art materials. Others spoke of their relief about no longer feeling alone as a result of the abuse, and were eager to meet the following week.

Commentary

We were struck by the swiftness and power of the group's process, and the intensity with which the girls joined with each other, after our introduction. The group seemed to become an adolescent gang, defending against adult female 'mother figures'. Their rejection of any use of art materials seemed significant and we felt that this resistance reflected a fear of exposure, already experienced within the legal system, and an overriding need to be in control. We were concerned about EN's rivalry and domination of the group, and her misuse of disclosure which escalated the group's distress.

Additionally, the group needed to know whether we could contain and survive their feelings. The art materials may have represented bribery or seduction to the girls, and it therefore seemed crucial to accept their rejection while commenting on it. It was essential that we could bear and contain their distress and disclosures, as this contrasted with their mothers' difficulties in hearing and coping with the girls' experiences. However, we were concerned by the fragility of personal boundaries being threatened by the compulsive nature of the disclosures.

Paradoxically, our countertransference following the group was our anxiety that the group members, by precipitously revealing their abusive experiences, would feel exposed and distressed, and consequently not attend the next group. We thought that this was related to the group's anxiety about whether we could survive their distress.

In Session 2, all eight girls arrived together. A tension developed between the group's manic defences versus their need for self-expression. A loosening of defences occurred through the art making, which marked the beginning of a therapeutic alliance. In striking contrast to the distress of the first session, this session began with manic laughter and conversation, and the girls' retreat into pairs and subgroups. Once we had commented on the group's need to reject the use of art materials and to be in control, each member began experimenting with art making, becoming increasingly free and spontaneous. They spoke about their different experiences of fathers – one had committed suicide, several were absent, one natural father was abusive, and another idealised. We explored this idealisation with the group member and the group then attempted to question her reality. Several girls became involved in drawings and doodles, with some disposing of their work at the end of the session. When we commented on the disposal, the girls said that it was rubbish and unwanted.

Commentary

Although several girls did not keep their artwork, it seemed that the art making served to contain the group emotionally. We thought that the group's handling of materials put them in touch with their sensory and emotional experiences of abuse. The 'rubbishing' of their work highlighted the girls' low self-esteem and shame, as well as their need to 'dispose' of unwanted feelings. The conversation about fathers within the group served as a focus for the girls' feelings of loss, abandonment and their longing for nurturing and protection. The defence of idealisation revealed a distorted hope of being rescued, and provided an opportunity to explore such distortions within the group.

In Session 3 the girls' destructive coping mechanisms of self-harm, their abusive interaction towards others and their feelings of blame emerged. AJ, who in the previous session had revealed her need for her absent natural father, disclosed having taken an overdose the previous week. She explained that she had expected her father to come and see her because of the overdose, which she hoped would bring them closer. While one member responded with accounts of her past overdoses, two other girls distracted themselves by eating biscuits. A discussion then developed regarding their mothers' reactions to their disclosures, including not being believed and accusations about being responsible for the abuse. For example, DM said that her mother had accused her of flaunting herself and inviting the abuse. The group expressed their outrage regarding this, and in addition, spoke about their mothers using the fact that they had a boyfriend in order to minimise the effects of the sexual abuse. BK remained hopeful that her mother would eventually believe her, although she had not been believed since her disclosure. The group explored ideas about how to defend themselves against their mothers' accusations, identifying the distortions in these, and noticing each others' incorrect assumptions, e.g. blaming themselves for the abuse.

The atmosphere of the group became intense and competitive, with members' urgent accounts of their experiences and feelings. An enactment of intrusion across personal boundaries occurred when EN drew a sun on DM's stormy, cloudy picture. DM responded by saying, 'I did not want a sun in this picture', and painted it out. We encouraged DM to express how she felt, which she did. Later on in the group, she still seemed to be angry when she remonstrated with FR about her lack of feeling when speaking about her abuse.

Commentary

Throughout the session we found that we had to persistently comment on and manage the rivalry of the girls' interactions, helping them to think and support each other. It was important to recognise and contain any unhelpful and abusive responses. There was a tension between the need to be in control of feelings and the need for our attention, which was reflected in adolescent rivalry and hierarchical positioning. Experiences were discussed regarding the use of self-harm and abuse towards others in response to coping with painful feelings. Additionally, the group began to explore their relationships with their mothers. Alongside the interplay of the group and art-making processes, in this session we were able to incorporate cognitive restructuring to examine the underlying issues of responsibility and blame. The group members were able to challenge each others' distortions, which constituted a first step towards internalising this process for themselves.

Co-therapy and countertransference

In our experience a co-therapy model may increase the levels of containment, provide support for therapists and ensure the continuity of the group should one therapist be absent. After each group we discussed our experiences of being in the group, including our countertransference feelings. We used the latter to reflect on the group's process and to formulate interpretations. In addition to this, we arranged external supervision which further helped to contain our experience and increase our awareness. In the first few sessions we were often left feeling anxious about whether group members would return (see Session 1). A further issue that arose during the group was our sense of being intrusive in relation to the girls' artwork. It seemed that whenever we took notice of their artwork, the group grew suspicious and made defensive and dismissive comments about their work, i.e. 'it's nothing, just a few marks', or 'it's just rubbish, just scribbles'. This seemed to convey the girls' sense of worthlessness, and communicated to us that our interest was regarded with suspicion. We felt at times that we were witnesses to something horrifying and disgusting, i.e. abusive. This voyeuristic feeling was acutely uncomfortable and yet necessary to withstand in order to provide containment and counteract the taboo of secrecy. Furthermore, this indicated to us the group's intense need for privacy and control over their artwork. When we commented on this to the group, they then spoke at length about their feelings of mistrust and related this to their experiences of abuse. We felt this also signified a reduction in feelings of shame. The development of the group's cohesiveness in this session facilitated the growing experience of the symbolic 'safe family', one of our primary aims for this client group.

Our continued interest in the meaning of their art making was gradually met with acceptance. Group members began to show interest in each other's work; i.e. HS protested when BK announced she would dispose of her picture; GW helped BK with some messy plaster-casting of her arm; FR invited others to join her in marbling paper, and the girls devised ways of sharing the use of the potter's wheel from week to week. Images began to resonate or reappear from week to week as they were discovered by one and taken up to be explored by others.

Victim or perpetrator: Shifting boundaries

The internal tension between victim and perpetrator was evident to a greater or lesser extent in all the group members, and manifested itself either covertly or overtly in self-harm or abusiveness towards others.

For example, in Session 10, AJ drew frightening-looking faces – blank eyed, with pointy noses and jeering expressions, with no external line or boundary. She spoke at length about her worries regarding her younger brother, and disclosed that she had sexually abused him when he was 5 and she was 9 years old. We supported AJ in her disclosure and acknowledged the risk she was taking in the group. We asked the group how they were feeling as they had become withdrawn. While two members sought to condemn AJ for her actions, others supported her in her distress. We reminded the group of FR's earlier disclosure of abusive impulses towards her foster mother's grandson while she was babysitting. FR then explained how informing her foster mother and social worker had enabled her to feel more in control and prevent her from acting out these impulses. HS, painting a page black, verbally supported AJ in spite of group pressure to be angry with and judge her. Because of the group's struggle in supporting AJ, we pointed out that she was a confused child acting out a response to her own abuse. We encouraged the group to think about the different ways in which they had responded to their abusive experiences. BK admitted that she had begun abusing drugs and GW said that she hit other people. The group then began to explore their angry and destructive feelings, which developed into exploring the impact of the sexual abuse on their relationships with other people.

We felt this was a particularly significant session in that the members were faced with considering how the victim part of themselves could become abusive. A split ensued in the group, which held either the angry, judgemental feelings or the sympathetic, loving ones. The artwork functioned in both expressing and containing these painful and complex feelings, freeing the group's capacity to think, discuss and address the cognitive confusions and distortions that arose.

Ambivalence

One of the central issues that emerged in the group was that of ambivalence towards their abusers, and how this often became generalised in current relationships. This began, in the middle phase of the group's life, to be reflected in the imagery in various ways. For example, HS and BK each made clay representations of their abusers, evoking both feelings of attachment and revulsion. Others used paints in a free and experimental way, creating vertical and horizontal splits in their depiction of landscapes and seascapes. These seemed to convey a struggle to manage and integrate ambivalent feelings. A series of gravestone images emerged in the group, initiated by HS, who grieved for her absent father, but said she wished he was dead. This imagery seemed to express both mournful and murderous feelings. It opened the way to exploring the girls' mixed feelings regarding their abusers, the consequent cognitive distortions about responsibility and blame, and the underlying feelings of guilt.

As the group proceeded, it was apparent that some resolution regarding the group's ambivalent feelings occurred. AJ painted a dramatic black and red sunset, DM, a red triangle surrounded by black, HS, a totally black page and FR, a tree against a dark background. These images appeared to reflect a shift from ambivalence to a more resolute negative expression about their abusers. BK spoke about her brother and said 'Abusers never change'. AJ pointed out that it was how one coped differently with the feelings that mattered. Some members then discussed how they had changed their ways of coping, for example GW and AJ said they had stopped taking overdoses and BK said that she no longer took drugs.

The working through of ambivalent feelings played a crucial role in facilitating the deeper exploration and disclosure work that followed. Intense anger with mother figures emerged, and further disclosures of sexual abuse occurred. Parallel to this, there was a mixture of very messy and expressive work, and more integrated and contained work. Symbolic imagery depicting groups emerged, which conveyed a sense of holding and reflected the group's cohesiveness.

Sexuality

The sensory experience of using the art materials, particularly clay, facilitated the group's exploration regarding feelings about their bodies, self-image and sexuality. Discussions developed about the impact of the abuse regarding their sexuality. For example, GW used the group to explore feelings around why she felt worse about being abused by her aunt than by her father. It emerged that she feared that others would view her as being homosexual, and spoke of her confusion about her own sexuality. BK said that she found it difficult to talk about sexual feelings because it made her feel 'dirty'. Some group members felt that sexual relationships were motivated by a need to replace the bad feelings of abuse with affection. HS and FR, who resisted using clay, revealed that they were too frightened to become involved with boys. Over the course of the group, AJ's clay work included the creation and destruction of phallic shapes and bowls; she eventually created several shapes that she kept. Other group members began using the potter's wheel and were freely messy in and destructive of their creations. Their ability to enjoy being messy seemed a significant step in discarding their feelings of 'dirtiness', shame and contamination due to their sexual abuse. Alongside these processes, AJ made a further disclosure of current sexual abuse by her mother.

The impact of the abuse on their self-image was manifested in their physical appearance in different ways, e.g. an overtly sexualised, provocative appearance, a childlike look or more masculine, boyish appearance. Some spoke of their inability to wear swimsuits or more revealing clothes, feeling ashamed and uncomfortable in their bodies. The group themselves began to question and confront these feelings, gradually disentangling their distorted and confused thoughts.

External systemic factors: Social and political

A particular difficulty in the treatment of sexually abused adolescents is the degree of support they receive between sessions, which directly impinges on their ability to make use of the group. While five girls lived with their mothers, three others were forced into other circumstances, i.e. two lived in foster care and another lived independently. These differing life circumstances impinged on the use of the art materials, the attendance to the sessions, and at times evoked envy and destructiveness within the group process.

For example, in one session, three girls began to noisily use clay when a member spoke about an abuse experience. When we commented that it seemed difficult for people to listen to that member, DM admitted that she did not want to hear as she became so upset after the session, thinking of her own abusive experiences of which she could not speak to her mother. HS echoed this experience, and said that she coped by 'shutting down'. BK (who lived independently) became withdrawn and unresponsive. However, with the group's encouragement, she spoke of the loss of her family and her struggle with living on her own.

We had noticed a pattern in BK's attendance, i.e. she would become withdrawn in the group and then absent from the following session, before returning again. We felt it necessary to arrange more support for her, through providing transport to and from the session and organising a social worker for her. As a consequence, she then attended regularly and used the materials more expressively. However, her feelings of rejection and the inadequate support from her family continued to affect her use of the group and her relationships within it. We had to continually address her feelings of rivalry and envious attacks upon the group. A turning point in this process occurred when other group members urged BK to keep her work, commenting on it with interest and appreciation. One member poignantly advised, 'Keep your pictures, they are your feelings.'

A further major political influence on the group dynamic was the different responses from 'society' which the girls experienced following their disclosures of sexual abuse. While BK, CL, and DM's cases never reached the stage of prosecution due to insufficient evidence, in GW and HS's cases, their abusers' prosecutions occurred during the life of the group and both were unsuccessful. In contrast, the perpetrators in the cases of FR, EN and AJ were all found guilty and were currently serving prison sentences.

Furthermore, some group members had been awarded criminal injury compensation, while others were still in the process of making applications. We found that these different outcomes profoundly influenced the individual's feelings of power and self-worth. Additionally, feelings of rivalry and the alliances that developed in the group required frequent processing. This occurred through the interplay of self-expression and cognitive restructuring. Our main focus here was to enable the girls to develop empathy with one another, whatever their experiences or the responses from 'society'. Through the group's outrage at the injustices of the legal system, group members were gradually able to reapportion blame and responsibility. For example, after several weeks of BK being withdrawn, and at times very angry and abusive, she finally spoke openly of her rage regarding her family and the legal system, both of which had failed her. She then painted a picture of devils in prison and spoke poignantly about her sense of her, rather than her abuser, being imprisoned and punished. This marked a significant point in BK's and the group's capacity to identify and process these feelings of injustice, which had previously led to underlying conflict and maintained the group's distorted beliefs and poor coping mechanisms.

CONCLUSIONS

In conclusion, we wish to consider our work in reference to the literature and discuss the group in relation to our treatment aims.

Between them, the group members manifested all of the symptoms of psychological trauma as described in the literature. Additionally, we found that their academic functioning and school attendance were severely disrupted or attenuated due to these problems. While several group members had participated in promiscuous behaviour, we found, in contrast to the literature, that others denied their sexuality, avoided intimate relationships and had regressed to an earlier stage of development before the abuse occurred. Through the group's interactive processes and artwork, the long-term effects of abuse summarised by Price (1993) were evident, i.e. those related to impaired ego functioning, managing internal and external boundaries in relationships, sense of self, and the defences of dissociation, repression, denial, idealisation and splitting.

We found that our approach was to some extent similar to those presented in the literature with, however, some significant differences. In regard to group therapy practice, we agree with Welldon's (1993) viewpoint regarding the capacity of the group to counteract secrecy and isolation, promote disclosure, provide containment and act as an auxiliary ego. Furthermore, we found Welldon's formulation of group dysfunction and abuse fundamental to our approach in identifying and understanding abusive processes in the 'here and now' and thereby resisting becoming collusive mothers. While some group members sometimes acted as 'assistants' (Welldon 1993), we found that the group tended to cohere as adolescent peers in opposition to our authority, as well as perceiving us, at times, as threatening or intrusive (Pines 1978). While we would agree that the group could reapportion blame and responsibility (Hall 1992) and offer exoneration (Herman 1981), when confronted with disclosures of their own abusiveness, splitting occurred, evoking both condemnation and support. Our communication as co-therapists, both within and following the group sessions, was central in processing and resolving this conflict.

With regard to art therapy practice, we would concur with Johnson (1987), Malchiodi (1990) and Anderson (1995) who maintain that art therapy is effective in enabling those thoughts and feelings that have become disconnected through dissociation to be reintegrated.

In contrast to approaches such as that of Anderson (1995), in which art therapy groups with sexual abuse victims are structured, focused and brief, our approach permitted a longer-term, psychotherapeutic approach. As it was unstructured and allowed issues to emerge gradually from the group art therapy process, fragile psychological defences were supported. This, as well as the range of materials and freedom of choice, facilitated the group gaining a sense of control, and shifting from a passive to a more assertive position within their relationships. We used reflection upon and interpretation of processes in the here and now of the group. Furthermore, we developed the use of cognitive therapy within our art therapy group, which has not been mentioned in the literature found to date. As cognitive distortions are a fundamental part of the aetiology and maintenance of the emotional disturbances found in sexual abuse victims, it seemed imperative to us that we incorporate cognitive restructuring as an integral part of our therapeutic approach, while retaining the freedom of the experiential nature of the art psychotherapy process. We found that distorted beliefs emerged both in the art processes and imagery, in the girls' relationships to their artwork and in what they said. It appeared that group members' most frequently held distortions were related to their confusion regarding their responsibility for the abuse, and their self-denigratory beliefs resulting in low self-esteem, shame, depression and feelings of guilt. As the group progressed they began to use these cognitive explorations with one another which seemed to reinforce its effectiveness. Thus a group member would frequently be able to provide more accurate beliefs as alternatives to the distorted beliefs of one or more group member, which proved far more effective than arriving at such a conclusion on her own behalf. This process then enabled her to distance herself from her own strongly held ideas and eventually shift to a more objective view regarding these. In this way we were able to work with the group members' feelings of guilt and shame, and increase their awareness of the impact of abuse on their lives, one of our primary aims for the group.

Furthermore, we believe that our aims were facilitated or undermined by two main influences i.e. the internal psychological state of each group member and the external factors. We found that there was a reduction in self-harm and other destructive behaviour within the first six months. The group's capacity to use the art materials expressively and symbolically was a gradual but turbulent progression which reflected their feelings of ambivalence and abusive relationships with adult figures. The art processes and work were used by the group to express, explore, integrate and contain feelings and thoughts relating to the abuse. The group members who found this most difficult were those who had the least support systemically, either from their families or the court system.

We discovered that creating a symbolically non-abusive 'family' was one of the most challenging aims of the group to fulfil. Any acknowledgement of abusiveness within the group evoked past familial abusive experiences and resulted in splitting, aggressive behaviour and rejection of some group members. Addressing and confronting these processes often evoked hostility towards us. However, we found that by identifying this as an issue of trust, and examining the group's unconscious fantasies and projections about each other, a sense of safety within the group developed.

By the end of the group, we felt that some members had made dramatic shifts in their emotional development and were ready to terminate treatment, while others were still in need of further help. The group served different functions for its members. For some it represented the beginning of a process of identifying issues and exploring feelings, which they continued either in the monthly follow-up group or in individual therapy. Other members seemed to integrate their experiences and were free to resume their adolescent development, previously so profoundly arrested, e.g. establishing intimate relationships, continuing their education, initiating career options, and living independently.

At the end of the last group session, each group member took their artwork home. This seemed to indicate a discarding of shame, an internal capacity to integrate and 'live with' their experiences, and a symbolic internalisation of the group.

REFERENCES

Anderson, F.E. (1991) *Courage! Together we heal. A report on the development and implementation of an art therapy short-term ceramics group for incest survivors*, Normal, IL: Illinois State University.

Anderson, F.E. (1995) *The Arts in Psychotherapy*, 22(5): 413–27.

Beck, A.T. (1976) *Cognitive therapy and the emotional disorders*, New York: International Universities Press.

Beck, A.T., Rush, A.J., Shaw, B.F. and Emery, G. (1979) *Cognitive therapy of depression*, New York: Guilford Press.

Beck, A.T. and Emery, G. (1985) *Anxiety disorders and phobias: A cognitive perspective*, New York: Basic Books.

Blake-White, J. and Kline C. (1985) Treating the dissociative process in adult victims of childhood incest, *Journal of Social Casework*, 66(7): 394–402.

Blick, L.C. and Porter, F.S. (1982) 'Group therapy with female adolescent survivors', in S. Sgroi (ed.) *Handbook of clinical intervention in child sexual abuse*, Lexington, MA: D.C. Heath.

Blos, P. (1962) *On adolescence*, New York and London: The Free Press.

Briere, J. (1989) *Therapy for adults molested as children: Beyond survival*, New York: Springer Publishing Company.

Carrozza, P.M., Heirsteiner, C.L. and Young, J. (1983) Young female incest victims in treatment: Stages of growth seen with a group art therapy model, *Clinical Social Work Journal*, 10(3): 165–75.

Copley, B. (1993) *The world of adolescence: Literature, society and psychoanalytical psychotherapy*, London: Free Association Books.

Craighill-Moran, M. (1990, January) [Personal correspondence with F.E. Anderson].

Garrett, C. and Ireland, M.S. (1979) A therapeutic art session with rape victims, *American Journal of Art Therapy*, 18(4): 103–6.

Hall, Z.M. (1992) Women survivors of childhood sexual abuse Group analysis, *The Journal of Analytical Psychotherapy*, 25(4).

Herman, J.L. (1981) *Father–daughter incest*, Cambridge, MA and London: Harvard University Press.

Howard, R. (1990) Art therapy as an isomorphic intervention in the treatment of a client with post-traumatic stress disorder, *American Journal of Art Therapy*, 28(3): 79–86.

Janoff-Bulman, R. (1985) 'The aftermath of victimization: Rebuilding sheltered assumptions', in C.R. Higley (ed.) *Trauma and its wake: The study and treatment of post-traumatic stress disorder*, New York: Brunner-Mazel (pp. 15–35).

Jehu, D. (1988) *Beyond sexual abuse: Therapy with women who were childhood victims*, Chichester, UK: John Wiley & Sons.

Jehu, D. (1989) Mood disturbances among women clients sexually abused in childhood, *Journal of Interpersonal Violence*, 4(2): 164–84.

Johnson, D.R. (1987) The role of the creative arts therapies in the diagnosis and treatment of psychological trauma, *The Arts in Psychotherapy*, 14(1): 7–13.

Malchiodi, C.A. (1990) *Breaking the silence: Art therapy with children from violent homes*. New York: Brunner/Mazel.

Mannarino, A.P., Cohen, J.A. and Berman, S.R. (1994). The children's attributions and perceptions scale: A new measure of sexual abuse-related factors, *Journal of Clinical Child Psychology*, 23: 204–11.

Murphy, J. (1996) *Group art therapy with sexually abused girls*, Unpublished essay, Goldsmiths College, University of London.

Peacock, M.E. (1991). A personal construct approach to art therapy in the treatment of post sexual abuse trauma, *The American Journal of Art Therapy*, 29(3): 100–9.

Pines, M. (1978) Group analytic psychotherapy of the borderline patient, *Group Analysis*, XI(2): 115.

Powell, L. and Faherty, S.L. (1990) 'Treating sexually abused latency girls', *The Arts in Psychotherapy*, 17: 35–47.

Price, M. (1993) The impact of incest on identity formation in women, *The Journal of American Academy of Psychoanalysis*, 21(2): 213–28.

Serrano, J.S. (1989) 'The arts in therapy with survivors of incest', in H. Wadeson (ed.) *Advances in art therapy*, New York: Harper and Row (pp. 114–26).

Simonds, S.L. (1992) Brief report; Sexual abuse and body image; Approaches and implications for treatment, *The Arts in Psychotherapy*, 19(4): 289–93.

Spring, D. (1985) Symbolic language of sexually abused, chemically dependent women, *American Journal of Art Therapy*, 24(1): 13–21.

Spring, D. (1988) *A perspective: Art therapy treatment model for the effects of rape and incest*, Unpublished manual, Ventura, CA.

Waller, C.S. (1992) Art therapy with adult female incest survivors, *Art Therapy: Journal of the American Art Therapy Association*, 9(3): 135–8.

Welldon, E.V. (1993) *Group analysis*, London, Thousand Oaks, CA, and New Delhi: Sage.

Index